Guide to First-Year Composition

Department of English

Edited by Leslie Harper Worthington, Anita Turlington,
Kristin Kelly, Patricia Worrall, and Brad Strickland

GAINESVILLE STATE COLLEGE

As a textbook publisher, we are faced with enormous environmental issues due to the large amount of paper contained in our print products. Since our inception in 2002, we have worked diligently to be as eco-friendly as possible.

Our "green" initiatives include:

Electronic Products
We deliver products in non-paper form whenever possible. This includes pdf downloadables, flash drives, & CD's.

Electronic Samples
We use a new electronic sampling system, called Xample. Instructor samples are sent via a personalized web page that links to pdf downloads.

FSC Certified Printers
All of our printers are certified by the Forest Service Council, which promotes environmentally and socially responsible management of the world's forests. This program allows consumer groups, individual consumers and businesses to work together hand in hand to promote responsible use of the world's forests as a renewable and sustainable resource.

Recycled Paper
Almost all of our products are printed on a minimum of 10-30% post-consumer waste recycled paper.

Support of Green Causes
When we do print, we donate a portion of our revenue to green causes. Listed below are a few of the organizations that have received donations from Fountainhead Press. We welcome your feedback and suggestions for contributions, as we are always searching for worthy initiatives.

Rainforest 2 Reef
Environmental Working Group

Books may be purchased for educational purpose.

For information, please call or write:

1-800-586-0030

Fountainhead Press
Southlake, TX 76092

Web site: www.fountainheadpress.com
Email: customerservice@fountainheadpress.com

ISBN: 978-1-59871-535-4

Printed in the United States of America

CONTENTS

Acknowledgments

The editors express sincere appreciation to the following people for their valuable assistance in creating this guide: Amanda Adams, Jeannie Nash, Stacy Turner, Deborah Prosser, Frank Sherwood, Nicola Dovey, Karen Dodson, Shannon Shockley, and Shannon Gilstrap.

CHAPTER ONE

Introduction to the English Department

Welcome to Gainesville State College and the First-Year Composition Program.

All students must take both ENGL 1101 and ENGL 1102 (or their equivalents) in order to satisfy Area A requirements of the Core Curriculum.

These are foundation courses that provide students with the reading, writing, research, and critical thinking skills necessary to be successful in their college and professional careers. GSC's highly dedicated and qualified faculty offer dynamic courses in composition that reflect up-to-date writing theory and pedagogy as well as best practices methodology. Students take these classes in computer labs with state-of-the-art technology and software programming.

This guide will introduce students to the English Department faculty, Department and College policies, academic and extracurricular opportunities, and available academic support. It also contains basic information about rhetoric and writing and excellent sample student essays.

Benjamin Franklin once wrote, "If you would not be forgotten as soon as you are dead, either write something worth reading or do something worth the writing."

Leslie Worthington, PhD
Chair, Department of English

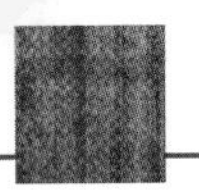

GAINESVILLE STATE COLLEGE ENGLISH FACULTY

Christopher Van Barnes, Associate Professor of English. Dr. Barnes received his BA in English from Shorter College, an MA from the University of Georgia in Modernist British and American Fiction, another MA from the State University of New York at Buffalo with a concentration in literary theory, and a PhD also from the State University of New York at Buffalo. For the PhD at SUNY Buffalo, his major concentration was the English novel and his minors were British Victorian literature and literary theory. He has taught learning support, composition, world literature, and British literature courses. His research interests include composition pedagogy, Charles Dickens, Elizabeth Gaskell, and the Victorian novel.

Christopher B. Bell, Associate Professor of English. Dr. Bell received his BA in English from Piedmont College, his MA in English at Western Carolina University, and his PhD in English from Georgia State University. For the PhD, his major area of concentration was American drama and his minor was modern British and continental drama. He has taught learning support English and reading, composition, American, world, and multicultural literature. His research interests include post-World War II and contemporary American and British literature, particularly August Wilson, Tennessee Williams, and Martin McDonagh.

Gloria Bennett, Assistant Professor of English. Ms. Bennett received her BA in English from North Georgia College and State University and her MA in English with a concentration in creative writing from Kennesaw State University. She has taught learning support, composition, American Literature, and creative writing courses. Her creative work has appeared in various literary journals and reviews, and she is a Pushcart Prize nominee. She is also the lead advisor for *The Chestatee Review.*

Ezekiel Black, Lecturer of English. Mr. Black earned a BA in English and a BA in Philosophy at The University of Georgia as well as an MFA in Creative Writing at The University of Massachusetts Amherst. He teaches learning support and composition courses. His areas of interest include modern poetry, the literature of World War I, and contemporary poetry. He is the faculty advisor and coach of the GSC Fencing Club and edits the online poetry journal *Pismire.* He is also currently pursuing his PhD at Georgia State University.

Leverett Butts, Assistant Professor of English. Dr. Butts received his BA in Philosophy and MA in English from the University of West Georgia and his PhD in English from Georgia State University. For his MA, his major concentration was American fiction of the late twentieth century. For his PhD, his major concentration was Southern literature and his minor was American fiction of the early twentieth century. He has taught learning support, composition, world literature, American literature, and creative writing courses. His research interests include Southern literature,

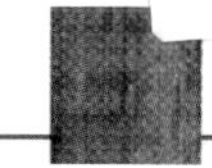

particularly Robert Penn Warren, contemporary literature, especially Joseph Heller, and popular fiction such as science fiction/fantasy, magical realism, and graphic novels. He is a member of the Pop Culture Association of America and the South Atlantic Modern Language Association as well as the President of the Robert Penn Warren Circle, which seeks to advance scholarship of Warren's work and to expand his presence in secondary and post-secondary schools.

Dan Cabaniss, Associate Professor of English and Journalism. Professor Cabaniss holds a BA degree in English from Harvard University and an MA in English from the University of Georgia in addition to professional experience as a newspaper reporter and editor. His main areas of interest include colonial and nineteenth-century American literature, Korean

Department of English Faculty

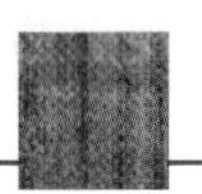

and Vietnam War narratives, Old and New Testament typology, film history, the war film, news reporting and writing, New Journalism, composition pedagogy, ESL, public speaking, and technical writing.

Mary Carney, Associate Professor of English. Dr. Carney currently serves as Director of the Honors Program and Director of the Center for Teaching, Learning, and Leadership. She has taught courses in American literature, technical and professional communication, composition, learning support, Introduction to English Studies, and special topics, such as Americans Abroad and Studies in Culture: War, Technology, and Media. She has also directed senior capstone projects. Her published work includes essays on Emily Dickinson, Lewis Nordan, Edith Wharton, and the intersection of gender and information technology. Her current research focuses on how the aesthetic choices in Wharton's war literature convey complex ideological stances. She holds a PhD and MA in English from The University of Georgia and a BA in English from Louisiana State University. Her concentrations include American literature to 1865, American literature after 1865, women's war literature, and poetry. She earned a Certificate in Electronic Pedagogy and a Certificate in Web Design and Production from the Georgia Institute of Technology.

Macklin Cowart, Assistant Professor of English. Mr. Cowart received his BA in English from the University of Georgia, his MA in English from Georgia State University, and is currently working on his PhD in English at Georgia State University. His major concentration is Medieval literature and his minor concentration is language history. He has taught learning support, composition, early British literature, late British literature, and late world literature. His research interests include Robin Hood, Medieval outlaw literature, Chaucer, monsters and the marvelous, Irish folklore, and English language history.

Jessica L. Cooke, Lecturer of English. Ms. Cooke received her BA in English from the University of Florida and her MA in British Literature from Florida Atlantic University. Her primary concentration for the MA was British Renaissance literature and drama with secondary concentrations in rhetoric and composition as well as writing center theory and administration. She teaches learning support, composition, and British literature. Her research and publication interests include creative nonfiction, rhetoric and composition, writing center theory, and British literature, particularly deployments of spatial theory in Shakespearean drama.

Robert W. Croft, Professor of English. Dr. Croft received his BA from the University of Florida, MA and EdS from Valdosta State College, and PhD from the University of Georgia. For the Ph.D, his concentration was American literature. He has taught learning support, composition, American literature, world literature, and cinema. He has written books on novelists Anne Tyler and Zora Neale Hurston. His research interests include American literature and the scholarship of teaching.

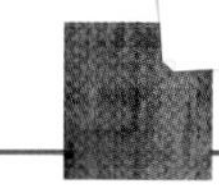

Christopher Scott Davis, Adjunct Instructor of English. Mr. Davis received his AA from Young Harris College, BA from Piedmont College with a minor in religion, MA from East Tennessee State University, and is currently working on his PhD at Georgia State University. For the MA, his major focus was on gender criticism and queer theory as it pertains to Victorian poetry. He teaches composition and literature. His research interests include an application of gender criticism as it applies to both Victorian and late eighteenth-century poetry.

Karen Dodson, Lecturer of English. Ms. Dodson received her BA in English from Piedmont College, her MA in English from Western Carolina University, and is currently working on her PhD at Georgia State University. For the PhD, her major concentration is Early Modern British literature, with a specific emphasis on Milton studies, and her minor concentration is eighteenth-century literature. She has taught learning support, composition, world literature, and British literature. Her research interests include virtue/chastity issues in Early Modern and Restoration-era women characters.

Terry Easton, Assistant Professor of English. Dr. Easton received a BA in Literature at the University of California, Santa Cruz. He received his MA in English from the State University of New York, Binghamton. He earned a PhD in American Studies from Emory University's Graduate Institute of Liberal Arts. His graduate work focused on American literature, documentary studies, and popular culture. He has taught learning support, composition, technical writing, American literature, American identities, and consumer culture courses. His research interests include representations of work, immigration narratives, oral history, and documentary studies.

Ann Marie Francis, Adjunct Instructor of English. Ms. Francis received her BA in Technical Writing and her MA in English from Louisiana Tech University. She teaches composition and technical writing.

Shannon N. Gilstrap, Associate Professor of English. Dr. Gilstrap received his BA from Piedmont College, MA from Clemson University, and PhD from Georgia State University. For the PhD, his major concentration was the English prose tradition (Renaissance to Victorian) and his minor area of concentration was Victorian literature. He has taught learning support, composition, world literature, American literature, British literature, ethics, orientation, and creative writing courses. His research areas include Victorian literature (particularly Matthew Arnold and Arthur Conan Doyle) and Renaissance literature (Christopher Marlowe).

Jürgen E. Grandt, Assistant Professor of English. Dr. Grandt holds an MA from Universitat Zurich and a PhD from University of Georgia. He has taught composition as well as the full range of American literature courses on the undergraduate level in the United States, and graduate courses in American, African-American, and Southern Studies in Europe. For his PhD, his major

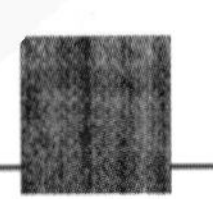

concentration was on African-American literature and critical theory. His most current research projects all focus on the intersection of music, particularly jazz, and literature.

Beverly Hall, Instructor of English and Reading. Ms. Hall received her B.A. in French, with minors in Art and English, from Murray State University, her MED. in English from the University of Georgia, and her Ed Specialist in Leadership from Lincoln Memorial University. She teaches learning support English as well as composition. She also supervises student teachers for the Education Department. Her interests focus on Flannery O'Connor, F. Scott Fitzgerald, Emily Dickinson, 20th century women writers, and children's literature.

Matthew Rush Horton, Assistant Professor of English. Dr. Horton received his BA, MA and PhD in English from the University of Georgia. For the PhD, his major focus was twentieth-century American literature with minor concentrations in critical theory and the ethics of reading. He has taught learning support, composition, world literature, American literature, British literature, and film. His research interests include modern fiction, T.S. Eliot, Cormac McCarthy, literary theory, the intersection between ethics and reading, and humanities computing.

Alexander B. Johns, Associate Professor of English. Mr. Johns is currently working on his doctorate in English Education at the University of Georgia where he received his MA and his BA, both in English. His dissertation focuses on the reading practices and aesthetic reading experiences of combat veterans newly enrolled in college English. He has taught learning support, composition, world literature, American literature, film and culture, and creative writing courses. His research interests include postsecondary English pedagogy and contemporary poetry, and he also writes and occasionally publishes poetry.

Kristin Gaiser Kelly, Assistant Professor of English. Dr. Kelly received her BA and MA in English from the University of Georgia and her PhD from Georgia State University. For the MA, her concentration was modern American poetry, especially the poetry of William Carlos Williams. For the PhD, her major concentration was modern American fiction and poetry and modern British fiction. She has taught learning support, composition, and world literature courses. Her research interests include the literature of the Vietnam War, especially the fiction of Tim O'Brien, and the novels of British author Barbara Pym. Her work has been published in the *South Atlantic Review* and *Green Leaves: The Journal of the Barbara Pym Society*.

Monique Kluczykowski, Assistant Professor of English. Professor Kluczykowski received her BS and MA from Murray State University. For the MA, her major concentrations were nineteenth- and twentieth-century British and American literature and the teaching of rhetoric. She has taught learning support, Regents' Essay remediation, composition, world and American lit-

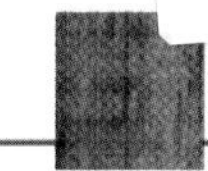

erature, and creative writing courses. Her poetry, short fiction, and non-fiction have appeared in national and international literary and popular journals.

Jeff Marker, Associate Professor of Film and English. Dr. Marker received his BA from Ball State University and his MA in English and PhD in Comparative Literature from the University of Georgia. He teaches composition, literature, and film courses.

Mary Katherine Mason, Adjunct Instructor of English. Ms. Mason received her BS in English Education from Kennesaw State University. After teaching at the secondary level, she earned her MA in Literary Studies from Georgia State University. Her thesis concentrated on exploring Samuel Johnson's *Rasselas* as a humorous eighteenth-century imitation of Ecclesiastes. She is currently working on a PhD at Georgia State with a primary concentration in eighteenth-century British literature. Her secondary concentration centers on fin de siècle romances in British fiction. While her primary focus is British literature, she also enjoys exploring genre theory, literary and film adaptations, and visual rhetoric. She currently teaches composition and film and culture classes.

Laura Ng, Assistant Professor of English. Dr. Ng received her BA and MA from Morehead State University. She received her PhD from Louisiana State University at Baton Rouge. Her major focus for her doctoral studies was American literature. Her minor fields included gender theory and Renaissance literature. Her dissertation, *Feminist Hard-Boiled Detective Fiction as Political Protest in the Tradition of Women Proletarian Writers of the 1930s*, brought together her major field of American literature and her minor field of gender performance theory. She has taught composition, learning support, world literature, American literature, and Renaissance literature survey courses. Her current research interests include gender performance, politics, culture and violence.

Samuel Prestridge, Associate Professor of English. Dr. Prestridge received his BA in English from Mississippi College, his MA in creative writing from the University of Southern Mississippi, and his PhD from the University of Georgia. Additionally, he worked toward an MFA in creative writing from Goddard College in Plainfield, Vermont. His PhD concentrated on twentieth-century Southern literature, Southern culture, modernist and postmodernist American poetry, and applied rhetoric. Coursework taught includes the complete cycles of American, British, and world literature, Southern literature, film and culture, and creative writing. His research interest includes nineteenth- and twentieth-century Southern literature, modernist poetics, contemporary Southern fiction (Barry Hannah, Mary Hood, Cormac McCarthy), and Southern culture, specifically Agrarian assumptions and the resurgence of the radical right in politics.

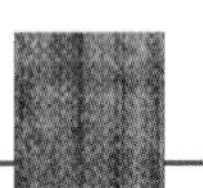

Karen Place Redding, Assistant Professor of English and Reading. Professor Redding received her BA, in English from James Madison University and her MA in English from the University of Georgia. Her Master's thesis, *The Grand Inquisitor: Seeking the Sublime in Alastair Reynold's Revelation Space*, focused on the significance and the scope of both modern and historical science fiction. She has taught learning support reading, composition, world literature, service learning, and college experience courses. Her research interests include science fiction, popular culture, film, and Shakespeare, and she co-authored the article "Fresh Perspectives on New Literacies and Technology Integration" in the education journal *Voices from the Middle* in March 2010.

Kya Reaves, Assistant Professor of English. Dr. Reaves received her BA in English with a minor in women's studies from Austin Peay State University, MA in English with a concentration in African-American literature from the University of Memphis, MFA in Creative Writing with a concentration in poetry from the University of Memphis, and PhD in English with a concentration in textual studies from the University of Memphis. She has taught learning support, composition, world literature, critical theory, introduction to literature, and African-American literature courses. Her research interests include African-American literature, particularly how marginalization affects both the American and African-American canons.

Darren Rhym, Assistant Professor of English. Professor Rhym earned his BA in English at Bucknell University, in Lewisburg, Pennsylvania. He focused on the African-American novel when he earned his MA in English from Pennsylvania State University. Currently, he is working on his doctorate in Language and Literacy Education at the University of Georgia. He has taught learning support, composition, and world literature courses. His research interests include the African-American novel, nineteenth-century American literature, the Harlem Renaissance, and the Black Arts Movement. In 2001, Mr. Rhym wrote a historical text entitled *NAACP*, which was part of Chelsea House's African-American Achievement series.

Kristen Simmons Roney, Assistant Professor of English, Assistant Vice President for Academic Affairs, and Interim Assistant Vice President for Academic Enrichment. Dr. Roney received her BA in English from Norfolk State University and her MA and PhD in Comparative Literature from the University of Georgia. For the PhD, her major concentration was nineteenth-century and anglophonic literatures and her minor concentrations were European and British medieval literatures and literary theory. Her dissertation investigated the redemption narrative in Faustian texts from multiple cultures and was grounded, in part, in Walter Benjamin's theories of art and redemption. In addition to her academic degrees, she received certification in Leadership from Phi Theta Kappa. She has taught learning support, composition, world literature, British literature, multicultural American literature, black diaspora literature, Asian-American literature, and film courses. Her research interests include punk music and culture, literature and music, translation theory, redemption studies, and addiction.

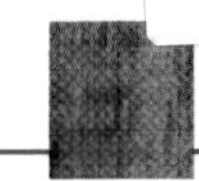

William Bradley Strickland, Professor of English. Dr. Strickland received his BA, MA, and PhD in English from the University of Georgia. For his PhD his main concentration was American literature and his minors were British Renaissance literature and the novel. He has taught learning support, composition, world literature, American literature, British literature, Southern American literature, creative writing, and science fiction and fantasy courses. In addition to his education, he is a widely published author, with sixty-six published novels ranging from mainstream to historical, science fiction, and fantasy, many of them for a young adult audience.

Peggy Reed Strickland, Professor of English and Reading. Dr. Strickland obtained her BA in English at Furman University; spent a year in the English Master's Program at the University of Georgia; received her MA and MEd in English Education at Teachers College, Columbia University; and achieved her EdD in English Education at the University of Georgia. For her dissertation, she focused on audience and reader response to Shakespeare's *Taming of the Shrew*. She has taught learning support reading and English, freshman literature and composition, world literature, and American literature courses. She also has extensive experience as an actor and director in various colligate, community, and professional theatre venues.

Anita Turlington, Associate Professor of English. Professor Turlington received her BA and MA in English from the University of Tennessee and is currently a PhD candidate in Literary Studies at Georgia State University. Her major concentration in the PhD program is Victorian fiction, specifically the transitional fin de siècle period beginning in 1880, and her scholarly interests include the New Women writers and late nineteenth-century dystopian novels. Her secondary area is early twentieth-century British fiction of the transitional Edwardian period, particularly the work of E.M. Forster and Virginia Woolf.

Anastasia Turner, Assistant Professor of English. Dr. Turner received a BA in English and a BS in Chemistry from Wofford College and a PhD in English from the University of Georgia. Her doctoral work focused on multiethnic literature and linkages between modern American poetry and Chinese language and literature. Dr. Turner tested in three areas: early American literature, American poetry after 1865, and Asian American literature. She has taught composition, ESOL, world literature, and American literature. She is also a former Fulbright scholar to Taiwan and a speaker of Mandarin Chinese. Her current research focuses on contemporary Asian-American poetry and improving multiethnic pedagogy.

Patricia Worrall, Professor of English. Dr. Worrall received her BA and MA from Jacksonville State University in Jacksonville, Alabama and her PhD from the University of Georgia. Her major areas of concentration are Medieval and Renaissance Literature, with a minor concentration in eighteenth-century and Victorian literature. Dr. Worrall has taught learning support, freshman and advanced composition, British and world literature, Arthurian literature, and technical communication courses. Her interests include performance theory and multi-modal communication. She has published performance and book reviews for the journal *Shakespeare Bulletin* and also co-authored a chapter in *Approaches to Teaching Henry James' Daisy Miller and Turn of the Screw* (MLA).

Leslie Harper Worthington, Associate Professor of English and Department Chair. Dr. Worthington received her BA, MA and PhD in English from Auburn University and her EdS in Education Administration from Troy University. For the PhD her major concentration was Southern literature and her minors were British Romantic poetry and modern American fiction. In addition to her academic degrees, she received certifications in Electronic Pedagogy and New Media Theory from the Georgia Institute of Technology. She has taught learning support reading and English, freshman and advanced composition, world literature, American literature, American novel, modern short fiction, modern drama, Southern literature, film, communications, and creative writing courses. Her research interests include Appalachian literature, particularly Cormac McCarthy and Lee Smith, and Mark Twain. She is chair of the Appalachian Studies panel for the Popular Culture/American Culture Association and a Quarry Farm Fellowship recipient. Her book on intertextual connections between Mark Twain and Cormac McCarthy, *Cormac McCarthy and the Ghost of Huck Finn*, was released in January of 2012. Additionally, she has published scholarly articles and creative pieces.

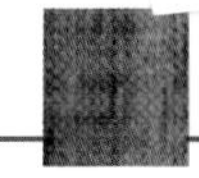

THE MAJOR IN ENGLISH

Studying literature offers access to ideas, cultures, social mores, and political concepts of any given time or setting. You can explore British, American, and world literature, spanning centuries, cultures, and genres. If you are interested in creative writing, you can pursue your interests in the English program at GSC. We offer classes for students interested in writing fiction, drama, poetry, or creative nonfiction. You can study with our many gifted faculty authors, poets, and playwrights, all recognized for excellence in their chosen fields. You could also have the opportunity to work on GSC's award-winning literary magazine, *The Chestatee Review*.

An Associate's degree in English at Gainesville State College will prepare you to transfer into a Bachelor of Arts degree program at any of the institutions in the University System of Georgia or any outside the state of Georgia. Many employers are increasingly recognizing the value of the skills a graduate with a degree in English can bring to an organization. From management consulting firms to foundations supporting the arts, employers find valuable the strong analytical skills, clear and persuasive written and oral forms of communication, and generally flexible, expansive thinking that a major in English fosters.

In addition, a major in English can serve as an excellent background for law school and graduate school in a variety of disciplines. In fact, an English major, when combined with other areas of study, can support careers in medicine, business, and public or educational policy studies.

ENGLISH COURSES OFFERED AT GSC

- **ENGL 0099**—Learning Support English
- **ENGL 1101**—Composition I
- **ENGL 1101H**—Honors Composition I
- **ENGL 1102**—Composition II
- **ENGL 1102H**—Honors Composition II
- **ENGL 1502**—Film and Culture
- **ENGL 2010**—Technical Writing
- **ENGL 2111**—World Literature I
- **ENGL 2111H**—Honors World Literature I
- **ENGL 2112**—World Literature II
- **ENGL 2112H**—Honors World Literature II
- **ENGL 2121**—English Literature I
- **ENGL 2121H**—Honors English Literature I
- **ENGL 2122**—English Literature II
- **ENGL 2122H**—Honors English Literature II
- **ENGL 2131**—American Literature I
- **ENGL 2131H—**Honors American literature I
- **ENGL 2132**—American Literature II
- **ENGL 2132H—**Honors American Literature II
- **ENGL 2135**—Mythology
- **ENGL 2170**—Fantastic Literature
- **ENGL 2180**—Introduction to Creative Writing
- **ENGL 2181**—Creative Writing: Poetry
- **ENGL 2182**—Playwriting
- **ENGL 2183**—Creative Writing: Fiction
- **ENGL 2185**—Creative Nonfiction Writing
- **ENGL 2302**—Literature and Film
- **ENGL 2401**—Multicultural Literature

- **ENGL 2525**—Contemporary Literature
- **ENGL 2801**—Magazine Production I
- **ENGL 2802**—Magazine Production II
- **ENGL 2901**—Special Topics in Literature and Composition
- **ENGL 2902**—Special Topics in Literature and Composition
- **ENGL 2903**—Special Topics in Literature and Composition

The Martha T. Nesbitt Academic Building (Academic IV)

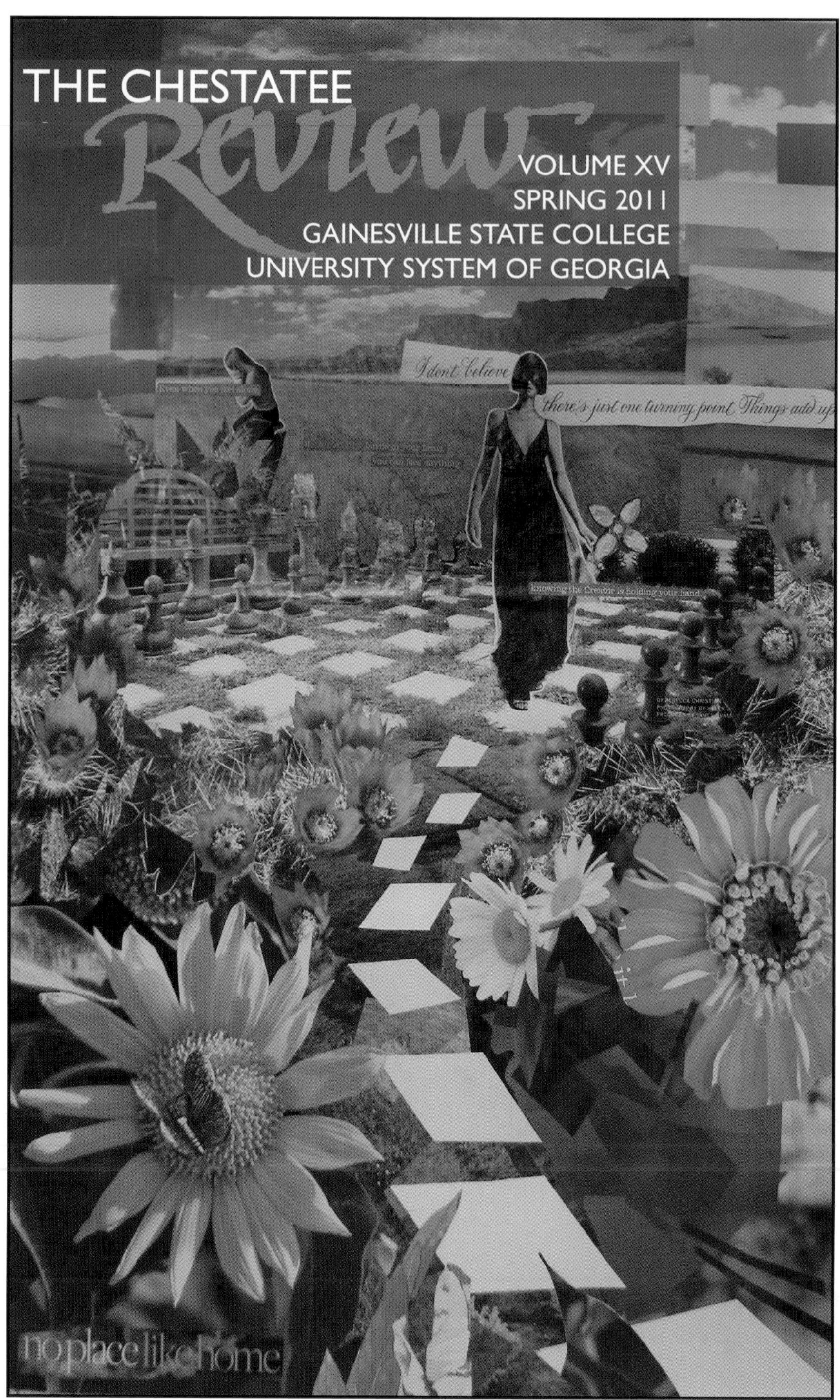

The Gainesville State College Literary Magazine

CHAPTER TWO

Student Opportunities

Gainesville State College and the Department of English provide many opportunities for students to get involved in college life, in and out of the classroom. This chapter discusses some available academic and extracurricular activities.

THE CHESTATEE REVIEW

The Chestatee Review is Gainesville State College's prestigious literary and art magazine. Published annually in the spring, the award-winning *Chestatee Review* features myriad superb student work, including poetry, short stories, plays, essays, and art. In addition to the publication of student work, several literary events and workshops are organized, funded, and hosted by *The Chestatee Review*. Students who participate as staff members not only receive course credit, they also learn valuable skills in marketing, event planning, editing, graphic design, writing, collaboration, and communication. For more information about upcoming events, visit http://itec.gc.peachnet.edu/clubs/chestateereview.

The Chestatee Review Contest Submissions: Submit your original, unpublished works to the annual GSC writing contest. The deadline is December 1 of each year. The contest categories include poetry, short fiction, one-act plays, formal essays, and informal essays. Cash prizes include $100 for first place, $50 for second, and $25 for third in each category. Winners will be announced in January of each year. First and second place winners, as long as they meet contest guidelines, will automatically be entered into the Southern Literary Festival Writing Contest. The 2011 issue of *The Chestatee Review* won third place in the literary magazine category of the Southern Literary Festival for 2012.

Send submissions via GSC e-mail to chestatee@gsc.edu.

Rules for Submission:

- You may submit works in more than one category.
- Stories, plays, and essays may not exceed 5,000 words; poetry may not exceed 100 lines for either one poem or a group of related poems.
- Entries must be submitted as Microsoft Word documents.

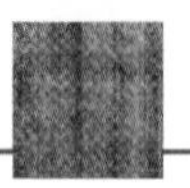

- Documents must be double-spaced (poems should be single-spaced) in Times New Roman size 12 font.
- Prepare a cover page for each submitted work that contains the following information: title of the work, author's name, GSC student number, mailing address and telephone number(s), and a fifty word bio (written in third person).
- Paginate your stories, plays, essays, and long poems but do not include your name anywhere in the body of the work.
- Send your entry as an attachment; do not copy the entry into the body of your e-mail. Put the category in the e-mail subject line: poetry, fiction, etc.
- Works submitted cannot have been published except in GSC campus newspapers or publications.

WE BELIEVE IN THEM

We Believe in Them is both a philosophy and an evening gathering of student writers and readers. As a philosophy, We Believe in Them is a statement of support by the English Department for our talented student writers. The We Believe in Them evenings are celebrations that occur each fall and spring semester at which composition students read their This I Believe essays to faculty, staff, family, and friends. These brief, incisive essays cut to the core of their authors' beliefs and values. Audiences have been enjoying these evenings of essay reading since Fall semester 2008, and several GSC students have had essays published on the national This I Believe Web site at <www.thisibelieve.org>.

WRITERS' GUILD

The Writers' Guild welcomes all writers to join. This participation can include writers of fiction, non-fiction, poetry, plays, and essays. The Guild offers an opportunity for students to perfect their craft by presenting their works to a supportive and active audience who serve as a sounding board for ideas and methodologies. Meetings are also a wonderful opportunity to learn the ins and outs of editing effectively, reading one's own writing critically, and adhering to personal deadlines. The club also hosts a number of events, ranging from talks with published authors to graduate school Q&As. Guild meetings alternate Mondays and Wednesdays each semester. For more information contact Leslie Worthington at lworthington@gsc.edu.

"Writing is an exploration. You start from nothing and learn as you go."
—E.L. Doctorow (American author and editor)

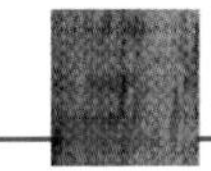

CHAUTAUQUA SERIES

Chautauqua is an adult education movement in the United States, which was highly popular in the late nineteenth and early twentieth centuries. Chautauqua assemblies expanded and spread throughout rural America until the mid-1920s. The Chautauqua brought entertainment and culture for the whole community, with speakers, teachers, musicians, entertainers, preachers, and specialists of the day. The Chautauqua Series at GSC has featured author Danny Duncan Collum, Athens musician and producer Dan Wentworth, short story author Mary Hood, and poet Thomas Lux.

CIRCA: CONFERENCE FOR INNOVATION, RESEARCH, AND THE CREATIVE ARTS

Gainesville State College holds an annual interdisciplinary conference to showcase students' scholarly, creative, and innovative research. Entitled CIRCA: Conference for Innovation, Research, and the Creative Arts, the event is a celebration of academic excellence in all disciplines and provides students with the opportunity to share their work with fellow students, staff, faculty, and the public. Founded by the Honors Program in fall 2010, CIRCA has showcased the work of approximately 60 students, and nearly 200 individuals have participated. Attendees listen to the students' explanations of their work, ask questions about artistic techniques, examine geospatial data, and discuss the research conclusions. This conference extends classroom learning and promotes cross-disciplinary dialogue.

Participation in CIRCA appears on students' co-curricular transcripts. Students can apply to present their work in one of five formats:

Posters should be printed and laminated.

Visual Arts should be portable and able to be displayed on its own easel or other stand. Painting, sculpture, digital media (providing your own computer), and other forms of expression are welcome.

Performances Several short performances will be offered at each campus, but decisions regarding these will be based, in part, on the availability of proper venue.

Oral Presentations are ten minutes each.

Oral Presentation Panels should have three or four students presenting ten minutes each.

On each campus, a committee reviews all abstracts submitted. These committees, along with the current and former Honors Program Directors, read and choose the abstracts to be accepted for presentation. The abstract must be written well and in language understandable to the general public. Discipline-specific jargon should be avoided, or if necessary, should be clearly defined.

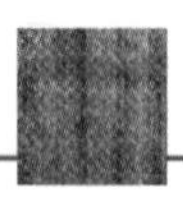

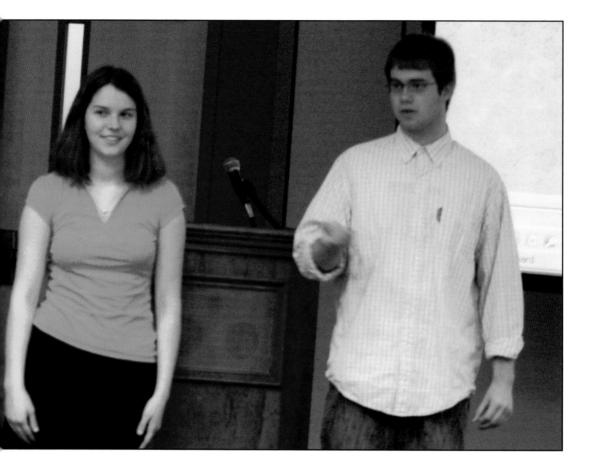

Further information and the application can be found on the Honors/CIRCA Web site at <www.gsc.edu/academics/honors/Pages/CIRCA.aspx>.

GUEST SPEAKERS AND WRITING WORKSHOPS

The GSC English Department offers a variety of opportunities to attend workshops and lectures presented by acclaimed authors. GSC professor and author Brad Strickland presented a workshop in September 2011 entitled "Writing for Young Adults" in which he read selections from his children's novels in the Wishbone series and his versions of classic books. Winton Porter, 2010 Georgia Author of the Year for *Just Passin' Thru*, read and signed books in March 2011. Funded by the Literary Grant of Georgia, which is sponsored by the Georgia Council for the Arts, the poet and novelist Anthony Grooms read his work and conducted a workshop in June of 2011. He was the winner of the Lillian Smith Book Award in both 1996 (for his collection of stories *Trouble No More*) and in 2002 (for his 2001 novel *Bombingham*).

SCHOLARSHIPS

The Chestatee Review Scholarship

Awarded annually to the editor of *The Chestatee Review,* the college creative arts magazine.

Outstanding English Student Scholarship

The Outstanding English Student Award is presented each April to an applicant who demonstrates both high achievement and dedicated service to the Department of English. The 2012-2013 winner of the Outstanding English Student Award is Amanda M. Adams.

STUDY ABROAD

GSC offers several study abroad opportunities. The following steps will help you decide if you would be a good candidate for a study abroad program:

I. Identify your program of choice
- A. Ask yourself some basic questions:
  - Have I always dreamed of going to one particular place?
  - Do I want to do something special related to my major, or am I interested in a broader cultural experience?
  - How long do I want to study abroad... several weeks, a semester, a year?
- B. That should help you narrow the choices. Now see if you meet the requirements of the program.
  - Is there a language proficiency requirement?
  - Do I have to have a certain major or other academic prerequisites?
  - Do I have to be in a certain year (freshman, sophomore, junior)?

Now, schedule an appointment with a study abroad advisor to go over the application process.

Apply for any financial aid, scholarships, or STARS work study that you may need.

Apply for a passport if you do not have one.

Schedule any immunizations, medications, or other pre-departure medical procedures that are necessary based on your destination and your personal medical history.

Keep up with payment dates for your program. Be sure to meet program deadlines.

If registering for classes at GSC as part of your study abroad program, be sure to pre-register for those summer courses and pay any tuition you may owe.

Attend orientation meetings, complete any pre-trip assignments.

Bon Voyage!!

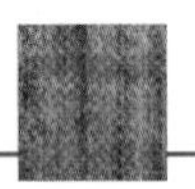

LEARNING COMMUNITIES

Learning communities consist of two or more courses from different disciplines that are linked around an overarching theme. To enroll in a learning community, students must co-register in all of the courses together. Because the professors collaborate on course content and the syllabus, students are able to see the shared knowledge that exists between these different courses and are able to apply their knowledge in different arenas. The positive effects of learning communities include increased student engagement, strong relationships, more one-on-one attention from professors, and increased student and professor engagement.

Sample GSC English Department Learning Community Offerings:

One example of an active GSC English Department learning community is ENGL 2401 and EDUC 2120, "Educating Otherwise: Exploring Our Diverse American Identities." This project supports a learning community combining EDUC 2120: Exploring Socio-Cultural Diversity and ENGL 2401: Multicultural Literature. Both classes fulfill requirements for education majors. This community seeks not only to deepen student awareness and understanding of multiculturalism, but also to encourage student engagement and support of diverse communities and schools in the area. Over the course of the project, in-class student learning will be enhanced through team teaching and field trips to locales that bring students face to face with an array of cultures and environments. Students will also take what they've learned and apply it in meaningful ways through the creation of lesson plans, participation with local schools serving diverse populations, presentation of films that explore multiethnic issues to the GSC community, and presentation of a capstone project. Ultimately, the project aims to enhance student learning through a focus on application; because each student in the learning community aspires to become an educator, the instruction and activities of the course have been developed to suggest models so that students may later deploy their knowledge in their own classrooms. Results from the learning community will be shared through presentations at conferences and workshops.

THEMED COURSES

Themed composition courses at GSC allow students to read about and research an important theme in great depth. Themed composition course offerings have included concentrations on American myths, American identities, detective fiction, monsters, and the war in Afghanistan.

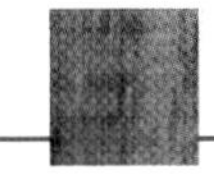

HONORS PROGRAM

The GSC Honors Program offers an opportunity for talented and motivated students to take enriched versions of selected courses. Honors classes offer a more in-depth study of the course topic. Students excel because they are a part of a group of highly motivated peers and have more personal attention from their professors. Class size is usually limited to 12-17 students. They develop intellectually and creatively in a supportive environment. Classes focus on discussion, analysis, and problem solving rather than on lecture, memorization, and quiz taking. These classes provide a strong foundation for excellence in undergraduate, graduate, and professional pursuits. Participation in the program does not add or change any requirements for graduation.

Honors courses introduce students to the methodologies of conducting original research and producing a polished, discipline-appropriate report of their work. For instance, in Composition I courses, students may not only write essays but also work on the methods for developing a research project, such as devising a central question and mastering the annotated bibliography. In World History, some students may read a recent biography of one of the leaders of the various "third world" independence movements from the 1950s and 1960s and compare the leadership style of such a person to the leadership styles of Thomas Jefferson and Kaiser Wilhelm II of Germany. Other students may write on a range of topics, including Saddam Hussein, Tsar Nicholas II, the Battle of Poltava, and the French Wars of Religion. This sampling of the work done by students underscores a central tenant of the Honors Program: providing enriching opportunities to develop fundamental skills in critical thinking, original research, and effective communication. Each year, students have the opportunity to present their best work at GSC, state, regional, or national conferences. The Honors Program sponsors CIRCA: The Conference for Innovation, Research, and the Creative Arts. This Conference allows students to showcase their work.

Over 100 students are usually enrolled in Honors courses at GSC. The GSC Foundation continues to support academic excellence through its Honors Program Scholarships for academic excellence and study abroad opportunities. The GSC Foundation also supports other activities, including CIRCA.

For more information, see Honors Program under the Academic Affairs part of the GSC Web site. Or contact Dr. Mary Carney, Director of the Honors Program at mcarney@gsc.edu.

CHAPTER THREE

Department Policies

FIRST-YEAR COMPOSITION PROGRAM ENGLISH COMPOSITION I (ENGL 1101)

Syllabus

(Revised Summer 2012)

General Course Information: Each instructor will provide, on a separate sheet, information concerning his/her office number, office telephone number, office hours, e-mail address, and important dates during the semester.

Texts: *Guide to First-Year Composition* from Fountainhead Press *is* required. English 1101 instructors may require their students to purchase a rhetoric/reader, a grammar/style handbook, and supplemental texts.

Course Description: English Composition I (ENGL 1101) is the first of two three-semester-hour composition courses required of every student in Area A of the Semester Core Curriculum. The broad goal of ENGL 1101 is to help our students recognize that writing is a complex, labor-intensive process that involves active reading, critical thinking, multiple-draft writing, and precise editing. To be eligible to take ENGL 1101, a student must meet English Department placement criteria or have a grade of C or better in ENGL 0099 (Learning Support English). To be exempt from ENGL 1101, a student must make a score of 3 on the AP Examination or 50 on the CLEP Examination and write a two-hour essay that at least two of three English Department faculty pass. In accordance with Gainesville State College regulations, a student must have a grade of C or better in English 1101 or English 1101H (Honors Composition) before taking English Composition II (ENGL 1102). ENGL 1101 carries three semester hours of transfer credit.

Course Objectives: In keeping with the College's mission, ENGL 1101 prepares students for college and career writing experiences by directing them in the basic organization and development of essays of various lengths. The specific objectives of the course address an integral part of the College's general education outcomes. These include:

- Becoming aware of one's writing process and knowing terms related to this process: prewriting, peer review, revising, and editing.
- Reading a variety of challenging texts with assistance as needed; recognizing and evaluating the rhetorical choices made in a text.
- Expanding critical thinking abilities by exploring context and assumptions in various issues, learning to deal with multiple perspectives, and relying on established authorities.
- Becoming aware of various audiences and genres.
- Learning rhetorical strategies to develop ideas and increasing rhetorical awareness of how text is manipulated to meet purpose and audience needs.
- Writing essays with analytical and interpretive components, including analysis of written texts.
- Organizing essays logically.
- Writing coherent, unified paragraphs and essays in both timed and untimed settings.
- Using outside sources (library, Internet, other electronic media) to explore an idea, question, or thesis; integrating sources into a text, handling quotations, and using MLA style to give appropriate credit to sources.
- Improving grammar, mechanics, development, and organization in context as needed.
- Demonstrating competence with the following word processing concepts: margins, spacing, fonts, font size, paragraph formatting (first-line and hanging indents), block quotations, and headers.

Course Calendar: See instructor's materials.

Course Policies:

- In addition to other writing assignments, each student will write at least five essays, one of which will be a documented essay requiring library and/or Internet-based research. Essays should focus primarily on academic skills such as summary, synthesis, and analysis. At least one of the essays will be written in class; the majority will be written out of class.
- ENGL 1101 students should have a basic understanding of English grammar and a familiarity with the rules of standard English. A student demonstrating grave composition and/or grammar deficiencies may be referred to the Writing Center at the Academic Computing Tutoring and Testing Center (ACTT Center) on the Gainesville campus or the Writing Lab at the Oconee campus where tutors are available. Any student may seek help in clearing up problems, but some students may be assigned work to improve their skills in problem areas.
- Plagiarism—accidental or intentional—will be dealt with in accordance with the Student Conduct code, which can be found in the Student Handbook at the Student Life Web site. The *MLA Handbook for Writers of Research Papers* (7th ed.) defines plagiarism as follows:
    - To use another person's ideas or expressions in your writing without acknowledging the sources is to plagiarize.... A writer who fails to give appropriate acknowledgment

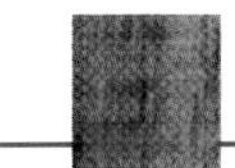

when repeating another's wording or particularly apt term, paraphrasing another's argument, or presenting another's line of thinking is guilty of plagiarism. (Section 1.7)

- ENGL 1101 meets three lecture hours per week. Attendance at all scheduled classes and conferences is expected. Each instructor will establish an attendance policy for the class.
- Instructors will establish their own policies for making up missed work. The student is responsible for making up missed work, if allowed to do so by the instructor, and the student should see the instructor as soon as possible to arrange how and where to complete missed assignments.

Course Grading: Essays are not graded on content alone. Errors in spelling and grammar will also be considered in the evaluation of writing assignments. The English Department has approved a rubric for use in ENGL 1101; instructors are free to construct their own rubrics, but they should reflect the approved guidelines. In addition to the approved rubric, the documented research essay should also be graded according to the departmental research skills rubric.

Final Portfolio: A Final Portfolio emphasizing the importance of revision is strongly recommended, though not required. Instructors may substitute a final paper, project, or exam for the Final Portfolio at their discretion.

Grading: Instructors may weigh the various essays and other assignments for the course as they choose, but no less than 75 percent of the final grade will be based on the essays and Final Portfolio. At least 25 percent of the total semester grade will be reported to students prior to the midpoint of the semester.

Explanation of Grades:

A	Excellent, signifies an overall average of 90-100.
B	Above average, signifies an overall average of 80-89.
C	Passing, signifies an overall average of 70-79.
D	Needs improvement, signifies an overall average of 60-69. The student must repeat ENGL 1101.
F	Failing, signifies an overall average of 0-59. The student must repeat ENGL 1101.
W	Withdrew, signifies that the student withdrew from the class without penalty prior to the midpoint of the semester. An instructor may not assign a grade of W unless the student has initiated the withdrawal process.
WF	Withdrew Failing, signifies that the student withdrew from class after the midpoint of the semester. A WF counts the same as an F.
I	Incomplete, signifies that the student has not completed assignments. Instructors can assign this grade to students who have been unable to complete one or two assignments because of an extraordinary health- or work-related situation. Students who fail to complete the missed assignments in one semester will receive a grade of F.

Disruptive Behavior Policy: Students who exhibit behaviors that are considered to obstruct or disrupt the class or its learning activities will be considered under the Board of Regents Policy on Disruptive Behavior. Behaviors that are considered to be inappropriate in the classroom include: sleeping, drinking, eating, coming in late, interrupting others, talking out of turn, inappropriate behavior during group work, verbal behavior that is disrespectful to other students or the instructor, use of cell phones or laptops, or any other behavior that may be disruptive. Students who exhibit such behavior will be given a verbal warning by the class instructor, then will be given a written warning in a meeting with the Dean of Humanities and Fine Arts, and then will be subject to disciplinary procedures as outlined in the Gainesville State College Student Handbook on the Student Life Web site.

Severe Weather Policy: When there is a threat of severe weather conditions in the College's service area, the safety of the GSC students and employees will be the first consideration. If a decision is made to close the campus, all personnel will be notified as expeditiously as possible. On campus and public communications will be used to alert the public and staff to plans resulting from unusual conditions. Faculty, staff, and students should tune to one of the following radio or TV stations for up-to-date GSC Closing information: WSB-TV, FOX5-TV, WXIA-TV, WSB-Radio, WGST-Radio, WDUN 550 AM-Radio, WLET 106.1 FA, 103.7 FM, 102.1 FM, 1340 AM, WGAU 960 AM, WIFC, WJJC 1270 AM, WCON 99.3 FM, and 1450 AM. Text messages will also be sent through Laker Alert.

Smoking/Tobacco Policy: Because of the harmful effects of smoking and use of other tobacco products on an individual's health and for the protection of non-smokers from the harmful effects of second-hand smoke, the College has established the following policy: Gainesville State College does not allow the use of any tobacco products in the buildings or on the grounds of the institution. This policy applies to the Gainesville and Oconee campuses.

Disability Accommodations Policy: Any student who feels he or she may need an accommodation based on the impact of a disability should contact Disability Services at the Gainesville or Oconee campus.

Additional Information: See instructor's materials.

SPECIFIC DETAILS OF THIS SYLLABUS ARE SUBJECT TO CHANGE.

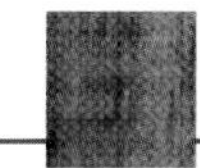

FIRST-YEAR COMPOSITION PROGRAM
ENGLISH COMPOSITION II (ENGL 1102)

Syllabus
(Revised Summer 2012)

General Course Information: Each instructor will provide, on a separate sheet, information concerning his/her office number, office telephone number, office hours, e-mail address, and important dates during the semester.

Texts: *Guide to First-Year Composition* from Fountainhead Press *is* required. English 1102 instructors may require their students to purchase a grammar/style handbook and other supplemental texts.

Course Description: English Composition II (ENGL 1102) is the second of two three-semester-hour composition courses required of every student in Area A of the Semester Core Curriculum. The aim in English 1102 is to expand students' understanding of how an idea, an era, or an experience can find expression in multiple forms and genres and move them toward greater independence in their own academic writing. To be eligible to take ENGL 1102, a student must have a grade of C or better in ENGL 1101 or ENGL 1101H (Honors Composition I). If a student receives a 5 on the AP English Examination, the student may be exempt from ENGL 1102. In accordance with Gainesville State College regulations, a student must make a grade of C or better to earn credit for ENGL 1102. The course carries three semester hours of transfer credit.

Course Objectives: In keeping with the College's mission, ENGL 1102 prepares students for college and career writing experiences by directing them in the basic organization and development of essays of various lengths. The specific objectives of the course address an integral part of the College's general education outcomes. These include:

- Taking control of one's own writing process and learning to adjust the process for the purpose.
- Critically engaging multiple perspectives, identifying established authorities, and recognizing bias.
- Reading a variety of complex texts independently, with an emphasis on evaluating sources.
- Increasing understanding of academic discourse, with more emphasis on thesis-driven essays.
- Independently choosing rhetorical strategies best suited to purpose or audience.
- Developing abilities to analyze a variety of texts.
- Incorporating independent research (library, Internet, and other electronic media) into an essay that takes a position. Incorporating multiple sources with distinct perspectives into a single

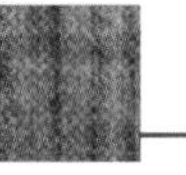

paper. Increasing mechanical skills in integrating sources into a text, handling quotations, and using a standard documentation style to give appropriate credit to sources.

- Demonstrating competence with the following word processing concepts: inserting and labeling images, creating outlines, attaching Word documents to e-mail.
- Recognizing and understanding grammatical and mechanical terms.

Course Calendar: See instructor's materials.

Course Policies:

- In addition to other writing assignments, each student will write at least five essays. Most English 1102 essays should include multiple sources, and at least one will be a documented essay requiring substantial library and/or Internet-based research. English 1102 essays are expected to grapple with a wide range of texts (written, filmic, etc.) based around a core theme. The compositional emphasis is on writing thesis-driven essays that demonstrate independent thinking and critical evaluation of texts.
- ENGL 1102 students should have a basic understanding of English grammar and a familiarity with the rules of standard English. A student demonstrating grave composition and/or grammar deficiencies may be referred to the Writing Center at the Academic Computing Tutoring and Testing Center (ACTT Center) on the Gainesville campus or the Writing Lab at the Oconee campus where tutors are available. Any student may seek help in clearing up problems, but some students may be assigned work to improve their skills in problem areas.
- Plagiarism—accidental or intentional—will be dealt with in accordance with the Student Conduct code, which can be found in the Student Handbook at the Student Life Web site. The *MLA Handbook for Writers of Research Papers* (7th ed.) defines plagiarism as follows:
    - To use another person's ideas or expressions in your writing without acknowledging the sources is to plagiarize.... A writer who fails to give appropriate acknowledgment when repeating another's wording or particularly apt term, paraphrasing another's argument, or presenting another's line of thinking is guilty of plagiarism. (Section 1.7)
- ENGL 1102 meets three lecture hours per week. Attendance at all scheduled classes and conferences is expected. Each instructor will establish an attendance policy for the class.
- Instructors will establish their own policies for making up missed work. The student is responsible for making up missed work, if allowed to do so by the instructor, and the student should see the instructor as soon as possible to arrange how and where to complete missed assignments.

Course Grading: Essays are not graded on content alone. Errors in spelling and grammar will also be considered in the evaluation of writing assignments. The English Department has approved a rubric for use in ENGL 1102; instructors are free to construct their own rubrics, but they should reflect the guidelines in the approved rubric. In addition to the approved rubric, the documented research essay should also be graded according to the departmental research skills rubric.

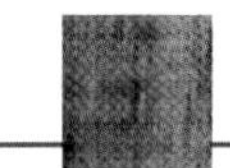

Final Portfolio: A Final Portfolio emphasizing the importance of revision is strongly recommended, though not required. Instructors may substitute a final paper, project, or exam for the Final Portfolio at their discretion.

Grading: Instructors may weigh the various essays and other assignments for the course as they choose, but no less than 75 percent of the final grade will be based on the essays and Final Portfolio. At least 25 percent of the total semester grade will be reported to students prior to the midpoint of the semester.

Explanation of Grades:

A	Excellent, signifies an overall average of 90-100.
B	Above average, signifies an overall average of 80-89.
C	Passing signifies, an overall average of 70-79.
D	Needs improvement, signifies an overall average of 60-69. The student must repeat ENGL 1102.
F	Failing, signifies an overall average of 0-59. The student must repeat ENGL 1102.
W	Withdrew, signifies that the student withdrew from the class without penalty prior to the midpoint of the semester. An instructor may not assign a grade of W unless the student has initiated the withdrawal process.
WF	Withdrew Failing, signifies that the student withdrew from class after the midpoint of the semester. A WF counts the same as an F.
I	Incomplete, signifies that the student has not completed assignments. Instructors can assign this grade to students who have been unable to complete one or two assignments because of extraordinary health- or work-related situation. Students who fail to complete the missed assignments in one semester will receive a grade of F.

Disruptive Behavior Policy: Students who exhibit behaviors that are considered to obstruct or disrupt the class or its learning activities will be considered under the Board of Regents Policy on Disruptive Behavior. Behaviors that are considered to be inappropriate in the classroom include: sleeping, drinking, eating, coming in late, interrupting others, talking out of turn, inappropriate behavior during group work, verbal behavior that is disrespectful to other students or the instructor, use of cell phones or laptops, or any other behavior that may be disruptive. Students who exhibit such behavior will be given a verbal warning by the class instructor, then will be given a written warning in a meeting with the Dean of Humanities and Fine Arts, and then will be subject to disciplinary procedures as outlined in the Gainesville State College Student Handbook on the Student Life Web site.

Severe Weather Policy: When there is a threat of severe weather conditions in the College's service area, the safety of the GSC students and employees will be the first consideration. If a decision is made to close the campus, all personnel will be notified as expeditiously as possible. On campus and public communications will be used to alert the public and staff to plans resulting from unusual conditions. Faculty, staff, and students should tune to one of the following radio or TV stations for up-to-date GSC Closing information: WSB-TV, FOX5-TV, WXIA-TV, WSB-Radio, WGST-Radio, WDUN 550 AM-Radio, WLET 106.1 FA, 103.7 FM, 102.1 FM, 1340 AM, WGAU 960 AM, WIFC, WJJC 1270 AM, WCON 99.3 FM, and 1450 AM. Text messages will also be sent through Laker Alert.

Smoking/Tobacco Policy: Because of the harmful effects of smoking and use of other tobacco products on an individual's health and for the protection of non-smokers from the harmful effects of second-hand smoke, the College has established the following policy: Gainesville State College does not allow the use of any tobacco products in the buildings or on the grounds of the institution. This policy applies to the Gainesville and Oconee campuses.

Disability Accommodations Policy: Any student who feels he or she may need an accommodation based on the impact of a disability should contact Disability Services at the Gainesville or Oconee campus.

Additional Information: See instructor's materials.

SPECIFIC DETAILS OF THIS SYLLABUS ARE SUBJECT TO CHANGE.

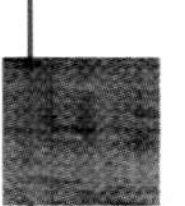

English 1101/1102 Grade Definitions for Research Skills in Documented Research Paper

In order to understand the essay grade expectations of Gainesville State College English instructors, the English Department offers the following definitions. However, students should be aware that an individual instructor can and may design a unique rubric for his/her writing assignments, based upon the particular requirements/demands of that assignment.

	A Mastery	B Competent	C Developing	D Emerging	F Undeveloped
Argument:	Identifies research problem and key details clearly	Identifies research problem clearly; knowledge of some key details and nuances apparent in argument	Summarizes research issue or problem; nuances & key details may be understated	Identification of research question is inaccurate or poorly summarized. Key details missing	Fails to identify problem or summarize accurately
Critical Thinking:	Approach reveals clear sense of context (historical, cultural, political); acknowledges bias and questions assumptions; addresses multiple perspectives from a variety of sources	Approach adequately explores contexts and assumptions regarding the issue. Relies on established authorities, and begins to recognize bias. Recognizes and addresses multiple perspectives adequately	Approach explores contexts and assumptions regarding the issue, though in a limited way. Relies on established authorities. Deals with multiple perspectives, but may do so roughly	Approach is ego- or socio-centric; minimal acknowledgement of own biases; deals with a single perspective only	No critical thinking skills apparent; deals poorly with a single perspective
Research Skills:	Demonstrates exemplary search, selection or source evaluation skills. Identifies uniquely salient resources	Demonstrates strong search, selection, or source evaluation skills to meet needs of the assignment	Demonstrates adequate search, selection, or source evaluation skills; research appears to have been routine, but sources are appropriate to assignment	Demonstrates minimal search, selection, or source evaluation skills; sources inadequate to assignment	No evidence of search, selection, or source evaluation skills; data or evidence is simplistic or inappropriate
Source Integration:	Examines evidence and sources; questions accuracy, relevance, and completeness	Examines most evidence and sources; questions accuracy, relevance, and completeness	Evidence used is qualified and selective	Repeats research information without question or dismisses evidence without adequate justification	No evidence of research evaluation

English 1101 Paper Grade Definitions

In order to understand the essay grade expectations of Gainesville State College English instructors, the English Department offers the following definitions. However, students should be aware that an individual instructor can and may design a unique rubric for his/her writing assignments, based upon the particular requirements/demands of that assignment.

	A Mastery	B Competent	C Developing	D Emerging	F Undeveloped
Content:	A significant, memorable central idea seemingly effortlessly defined, supported with original, unique examples and vivid detail	A significant central idea clearly defined, supported by concrete, substantial, and consistently relevant detail	Central idea apparent, straightforward, supported with concrete detail, but detail that is occasionally repetitious, irrelevant, or trite	Central idea lacking, confused, or trivial; unsupported with concrete details and examples	No discernible central idea; off-topic; poor development overall
Organization:	Creatively crafted essay, logically structured and ideally reflective of purpose, with seamless transitions	Thoughtfully crafted essay; structure is complementary to purpose; paragraphs are unified and coherent; transitions are smooth and effective	Plan of theme apparent; paragraphs are unified and coherent, but may be rather general in development; transitions between paragraphs are smooth, if occasionally repetitive or formulaic	Plan and purpose not apparent; paragraphs incoherent and/or lacking in unity; transitions abrupt, unclear or ineffective	No plan or purpose; illogical paragraphing; no transitions
Style:	Sophisticated sentences effectively and distinctively expressed; vivid, fresh, precise diction	Skillfully constructed sentences; distinctive, economical, and idiomatic diction	Sentences clearly constructed but lacking distinction; diction is appropriate, clear and idiomatic	Sentences incoherent, incomplete, monotonous; diction inappropriate, repetitive, and vague	Sentences garbled, fused, incomplete: diction unidiomatic or substandard
Grammar and Mechanics:	Consistent standard English usage, spelling, and punctuation	Consistent standard English usage, spelling, and punctuation	Clarity and effectiveness of expression weakened by occasional deviations from standard grammar, punctuation, and spelling	Communication obscured by frequent deviations from standard grammar, punctuation, and spelling	Multiple major errors in grammar, punctuation, and spelling

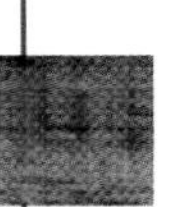

English 1102 Paper Grade Definitions

In order to understand the essay grade expectations of Gainesville State College English instructors, the English Department offers the following definitions. However, students should be aware that an individual instructor can and may design a unique rubric for his/her writing assignments, based upon the particular requirements/demands of that assignment.

	A Mastery	B Competent	C Developing	D Emerging	F Undeveloped
Content:	A significant, memorable central idea seemingly effortlessly defined, supported with detailed, comprehensive examples from the texts	A significant central idea clearly defined, supported by concrete, substantial, and consistently relevant details from the texts	Central idea apparent, straightforward, supported with concrete detail, but textual detail that is occasionally repetitious, irrelevant, or trite. Details from the texts are present but may be unclear or awkwardly integrated	Central idea lacking, confused, or trivial; unsupported with concrete textual details and examples	No discernible central idea; off-topic; poor development overall. No attempt at textual analysis
Comprehension:	Exemplary comprehension of what was read and creative or engaging insight into deeper meanings in the text	Strong comprehension of what was read and much insight into deeper meanings in the text	Adequate comprehension of what was read and some insight into deeper meanings in the text	Minimal comprehension of what was read, and only superficial insight into deeper meanings of the text	Does not comprehend what was read
Organization:	Creatively crafted essay, logically structured and ideally reflective of purpose, with seamless transitions	Thoughtfully crafted essay; structure is complementary to purpose; paragraphs are unified and coherent; transitions are smooth and effective	Plan of theme apparent; paragraphs are unified and coherent, but may be rather general in development; transitions between paragraphs are smooth, if occasionally repetitive or formulaic	Plan and purpose not apparent; paragraphs incoherent and/or lacking in unity; transitions abrupt, unclear or ineffective	No plan or purpose; illogical paragraphing; no transitions
Style:	Sophisticated sentences effectively and distinctively expressed; vivid, fresh, precise diction	Skillfully constructed sentences; distinctive, economical, and idiomatic diction	Sentences clearly constructed but lacking distinction; diction is appropriate, clear and idiomatic	Sentences incoherent, incomplete, monotonous; diction inappropriate, repetitive, and vague	Sentences garbled, fused, incomplete: diction unidiomatic or substandard
Grammar and Mechanics:	Consistent standard English usage, spelling, and punctuation	Consistent standard English usage, spelling, and punctuation	Clarity and effectiveness of expression weakened by occasional deviations from standard grammar, punctuation, and spelling	Communication obscured by frequent deviations from standard grammar, punctuation, and spelling	Multiple major errors in grammar, punctuation, and spelling

Essay Evaluation

Student ________________________________

	Excellent	Good	Acceptable	Unacceptable	Very Weak
Assignment Requirements					
Originality					
Title					
Attention Getter					
Thesis Clarity					
Introduction					
Sub-Points					
Topic Sentences					
Transitions					
Support Quantity					
Support Quality					
Conclusion					
Ending					
Focus					
Organization					
Tone					
Wording					
Diction					
Grammar					
Punctuation					
Spelling					
Paper Format					
Works Cited					
Internal Citations					
Quality of Sources					

Grade: ________

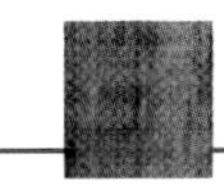

Grading Scale and Standards Sheet for ENGL 1102

I. Content

___clear, original, and significant thesis ___main points that engage the audience ___valid logic ___convincing argument and sufficient evidence (clear & specific details, examples to support claims) ___lack of plot summary ___eye-catching and informative title ___at least three direct quotations

Excellent Above Average Average Weak Poor

II. Organization

___unifying main idea for the whole essay ___valid beginning (engagement and thesis statement) ___valid middle (topic sentence, support, analysis) ___valid end (application, relevance of the topic) ___ focused topic sentences ___unified paragraphs ___meaningful breaks between paragraphs ___unforced transitions between paragraphs ___logical transitions between sentences ___quotations introduced and not just dropped into text

Excellent Above Average Average Weak Poor

III. Sentence Style & Diction

___engaging writing style and vocabulary for audience and purpose ___correct word order ___varied sentence structure ___logical transition words ___avoidance of repetition/ wordiness ___active voice used ___smooth incorporation of quotations ___accurate and clear word usage ___correct word forms ___correct spelling ___easily identified pronoun antecedents

Excellent Above Average Average Weak Poor

IV. Grammar & Mechanics

___clearly separated sentences ___complete sentences ___unmixed grammar constructions ___clearly linked clauses ___avoidance of comma splices ___subject-verb agreement ___verb tenses and forms ___pronoun agreement ___logical and correctly placed modifiers ___clear comma usage ___clear punctuation ___apostrophes ___correct MLA citation

Excellent Above Average Average Weak Poor

90-100=A 80-89=B 70-79=C 60-69=D 0-59=F Total points________

Things you did well: **Things to work on / see me about:**

Name________________________________ Date ____________________Essay________________

English 1101/1102

ESSAY EVALUATION FORM

CONTENT

_____ no clear main idea
_____ details/examples/quotations too general/insufficient/inappropriate to prove points
_____ extraneous material
_____ contains summary unconnected to a major point
_____ details/examples/quotations context not clear or firmly connected to point to be proven

ORGANIZATION

Introduction:

_____ unclear/weak/simplistic thesis statement
_____ introduction is not long enough/does not engage interest

Conclusion:

_____ implications(s) of thesis missing
_____ provides only a summary
_____ introduces new information/not memorable

_____ informative and engaging title missing
_____ lacks clear and specific topic sentences
_____ missing transitional words or phrases between paragraphs or points of paragraphs
_____ body paragraph(s) not fully developed
_____ body paragraph development strays from the point
_____ contains incoherent passages (logic difficult to follow)

STYLE

Sentence Structure

_____ lacks varied length and type of sentences
_____ quotations used inappropriate/not integrated within sentences (dropped quotations)
_____ uses primer style, repetitive structures, awkward sentences, etc.
_____ lacks transition words or phrases between sentences

Diction

_____ diction not specific or clear (too vague and general)
_____ too many "to be" verbs and passive voice
_____ words that are incorrect or carry the wrong connotations
_____ uses unnecessary words
_____ incorrect use of "you"
_____ clichés/ambiguous language/jargon

GRAMMAR/ PUNCTUATION/SPELLLING/FORMAT

Fragment	_____	Comma Splice	_____	Agreement	_____
Fused Sentence	_____	Pronoun Ref	_____	Spelling	_____
Verb Form	_____	Apostrophe	_____	Punctuation	_____
Instructions not followed		_____		Grammar	_____
Improper MLA Documentation		_____			

GRADE:__________

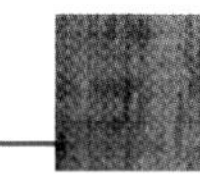

HOW IS COLLEGE DIFFERENT FROM HIGH SCHOOL? (from the website of Southern Methodist University)

FOLLOWING THE RULES IN HIGH SCHOOL	CHOOSING RESPONSIBLY IN COLLEGE
* High school is *mandatory* and usually *free.*	* College is *voluntary* and *expensive.*
* Your time is structured by others.	* You manage your own time.
* You need permission to participate in extracurricular activities	* You must decide whether to participate in co-curricular activities.
* You can count on parents and teachers to remind you of your responsibilities and to guide you in setting priorities.	* *You* must balance your responsibilities and set priorities. You will face moral and ethical decisions you have never faced before.
* Each day you proceed from one class directly to another, spending 6 hours each day—30 hours a week—in class.	* You often have hours between classes; class times vary throughout the day and evening and you spend only 12 to 16 hours each week in class
* Most of your classes are arranged for you.	* You arrange your own schedule in consultation with your adviser. Schedules tend to look lighter than they really are.
* You are not responsible for knowing what it takes to graduate.	* Graduation requirements are complex, and differ from year to year. You are expected to know those that apply to you.
*** Guiding principle: You will usually be told what to do and corrected if your behavior is out of line.**	*** Guiding principle: You are expected to take responsibility for what you do and don't do, as well as for the consequences of your decisions.**

GOING TO HIGH SCHOOL CLASSES	SUCCEEDING IN COLLEGE CLASSES
* The school year is 36 weeks long; some classes extend over both semesters and some don't.	* The academic year is divided into two separate 15-week semesters, plus a week after each semester for exams.
* Classes generally have no more than 35 students.	* Classes may number 100 students or more.
* You may study outside class as little as 0 to 2 hours a week, and this may be mostly last-minute test preparation.	* You need to study at least 2 to 3 hours outside of class for each hour in class.
* You seldom need to read anything more than once, and sometimes listening in class is enough.	* You need to review class notes and text material regularly.
* You are expected to read short assignments that are then discussed, and often re-taught, in class.	* You are assigned substantial amounts of reading and writing which may not be directly addressed in class.
* **Guiding principle: You will usually be told in class what you need to learn from assigned readings.**	* **Guiding principle: It's up to you to read and understand the assigned material; lectures and assignments proceed from the assumption that you've already done so.**

HIGH SCHOOL TEACHERS	COLLEGE PROFESSORS
* Teachers check your completed homework.	* Professors may not always check completed homework, but they will assume you can perform the same tasks on tests.
* Teachers remind you of your incomplete work.	* Professors may not remind you of incomplete work.
* Teachers approach you if they believe you need assistance.	* Professors are usually open and helpful, but most expect you to initiate contact if you need assistance.
* Teachers are often available for conversation before, during, or after class.	* Professors expect and want you to attend their scheduled office hours.

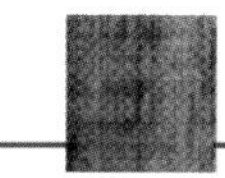

* Teachers have been trained in teaching methods to assist in imparting knowledge to students.	* Professors have been trained as experts in their particular areas of research.
* Teachers provide you with information you missed when you were absent.	* Professors expect you to get from classmates any notes from classes you missed.
* Teachers present material to help you understand the material in the textbook.	* Professors may not follow the textbook. Instead, to amplify the text, they may give illustrations, provide background information, or discuss research about the topic you are studying. Or they may expect *you* to relate the classes to the textbook readings.
* Teachers often write information on the board to be copied in your notes.	* Professors may lecture nonstop, expecting you to identify the important points in your notes. When professors write on the board, it may be to amplify the lecture, not to summarize it. Good notes are a must.
* Teachers impart knowledge and facts, sometimes drawing direct connections and leading you through the thinking process.	* Professors expect you to think about and synthesize seemingly unrelated topics.
* Teachers often take time to remind you of assignments and due dates.	* Professors expect you to read, save, and consult the course syllabus (outline); the syllabus spells out exactly what is expected of you, when it is due, and how you will be graded.
* Teachers carefully monitor class attendance.	* Professors may not formally take roll, but they are still likely to know whether or not you attended.
* **Guiding principle: High school is a teaching environment in which you acquire facts and skills.**	* **Guiding principle: College is a learning environment in which you take responsibility for thinking through and applying what you have learned.**

TESTS IN HIGH SCHOOL	TESTS IN COLLEGE
* Testing is frequent and covers small amounts of material.	* Testing is usually infrequent and may be cumulative, covering large amounts of material. You, not the professor, need to organize the material to prepare for the test. A particular course may have only 2 or 3 tests in a semester.
* Makeup tests are often available.	* Makeup tests are seldom an option; if they are, you need to request them.
* Teachers frequently rearrange test dates to avoid conflict with school events.	* Professors in different courses usually schedule tests without regard to the demands of other courses or outside activities.
* Teachers frequently conduct review sessions, pointing out the most important concepts.	* Professors rarely offer review sessions, and when they do, they expect you to be an active participant, one who comes prepared with questions.
* **Guiding principle: Mastery is usually seen as the ability to reproduce what you were taught in the form in which it was presented to you, or to solve the kinds of problems you were shown how to solve.**	* **Guiding principle: Mastery is often seen as the ability to apply what you've learned to new situations or to solve new kinds of problems.**

GRADES IN HIGH SCHOOL	GRADES IN COLLEGE
* Grades are given for most assigned work.	* Grades may not be provided for all assigned work.
* Consistently good homework grades may raise your overall grade when test grades are low.	* Grades on tests and major papers usually provide most of the course grade.
* Extra credit projects are often available to help you raise your grade.	* Extra credit projects cannot, generally speaking, be used to raise a grade in a college course.

* Initial test grades, especially when they are low, may not have an adverse effect on your final grade.	* Watch out for your *first* tests. These are usually "wake-up calls" to let you know what is expected—but they also may account for a substantial part of your course grade. You may be shocked when you get your grades.
* You may graduate as long as you have passed all required courses with a grade of D or higher.	* You may graduate only if your average in classes meets the departmental standard—typically a 2.0 or C.
* **Guiding principle: *Effort counts.* Courses are usually structured to reward a "good-faith effort."**	* **Guiding principle: *Results count.* Though "good-faith effort" is important in regard to the professor's willingness to help you *achieve* good results, it will not *substitute* for results in the grading process.**

HOW TO BE SUCCESSFUL IN FRESHMAN COMPOSITION:

Eight Common-Sense Tips

1. Come to class!

Woody Allen has famously said, "Eighty percent of success is showing up." The majority of the activities you will need to participate in to improve your writing skills are centered on class meetings. Most instructors take class participation into account for your overall grade, so you can make significant progress toward being successful just by showing up.

2. Come prepared.

Want to make major points with your professor? Do the reading and come to class prepared. It is just that simple. Students who come to class ready and able to participate in discussions and activities will get the most out of class time and their professor's expertise. Those who come unprepared are not fooling anyone, especially their professor.

3. Keep up with your syllabus.

Your professor expects you to take control of your time and preparation, and he or she has given you a blueprint of the semester on your syllabus. Consult your syllabus often to make sure you know your professor's policies, timelines for assignments, contact information, and grading priorities.

4. Turn in all of your work, and turn it in on time.

This may seem obvious, and it should be! However, it is especially important in composition courses that you do all of the assigned work as each writing assignment builds on the previous assignment to improve your skills progressively.

5. Talk with your professor.

All professors hold office hours when they are available to help students. Take advantage of the opportunity to spend some one-on-one time with your professor to clarify any material you find confusing or to get extra help. If you are unable to meet your professor in the office, send an e-mail. Your professor is an important resource for you, so don't be afraid to ask for help.

6. Write your drafts early.

Many English professors are willing to review early drafts of your essays to give you some feedback, but you will need to give yourself enough time to ask for help by getting started early. Again, use good time management practices so that you can take advantage of some extra help and ensure a good grade!

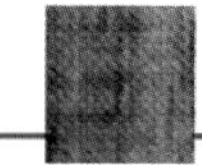

7. Present good-looking work.

Proofread your pages carefully; don't depend on electronic spell checkers and grammar checkers! Make sure the format you have used is correct; check spacing and margins. In a composition course, the presentation of your ideas is almost as important as the ideas themselves.

8. Use all of your resources.

At Gainesville State College, you can also get extra help in the Writing Centers on both campuses. Writing tutors are willing to brainstorm with you to help you get started, review rough drafts with you, or answer grammar questions. In addition, you can get research assistance from the reference librarians in the library as you prepare for research assignments.

CHAPTER FOUR

College Policies

We're glad you have joined the Gainesville State College community. All communities have rules to make life easier and more pleasant, and we are no exception. This chapter will cover some of the basic college policies that all members of the community—you, the college faculty and staff, and even the administrators—are expected to be aware of. The key overall is to treat others with the same courtesy, civility, and respect that you wish for yourself.

DISRUPTIVE BEHAVIOR POLICY

No one wants to waste time in a chaotic or uncontrolled classroom. What your professors expect is simple good manners and civility—language appropriate to a public place, behavior that does not disturb others, and in general an attitude and demeanor that contribute to the day-to-day activities of the campus.

Students who exhibit behaviors that obstruct or disrupt the class or its learning activities will be considered under the Board of Regents Policy on Disruptive Behavior. Behaviors which may be inappropriate in a classroom include sleeping, coming in late, talking out of turn, leaving a cell phone on, texting or talking on the phone while class is in session, inappropriate use of laptops, verbal behavior that is abusive or disrespectful of other students or the faculty member, or other behaviors that may be disruptive. Students who exhibit such behavior may be temporarily dismissed from the class by the instructor and will be subject to disciplinary procedures outlined in the Student Handbook.

CLASSROOM PROTOCOL

You can do some things that will enhance your learning and your classroom experience. These are for the most part simple matters of courtesy. When you are in a GSC classroom, keep these in mind:

- Be on time. Your instructors may penalize tardy students, so make every effort to arrive before class actually begins. We know that parking is often a problem at the busiest time of the day, so plan ahead and drive to school a little early just in case you face a long walk to your first class.
- Turn off cell phones while in class. If you have a laptop or notebook computer, you may use it to take notes; but don't chat online, play games, or distract yourself or those around you with inappropriate use of the computer.
- Pay attention. Professors usually don't mind if you ask them to clarify a point, but do keep up with the lecture or discussion.
- Be prepared. Bring your textbooks and note-taking materials with you. Don't rely on your memory alone.
- Take part in class discussions, but don't dominate and don't let your emotions get the better of you. Even if the class is discussing a highly charged subject about which you feel strongly, people can still disagree without losing their tempers or becoming aggressive in their language.

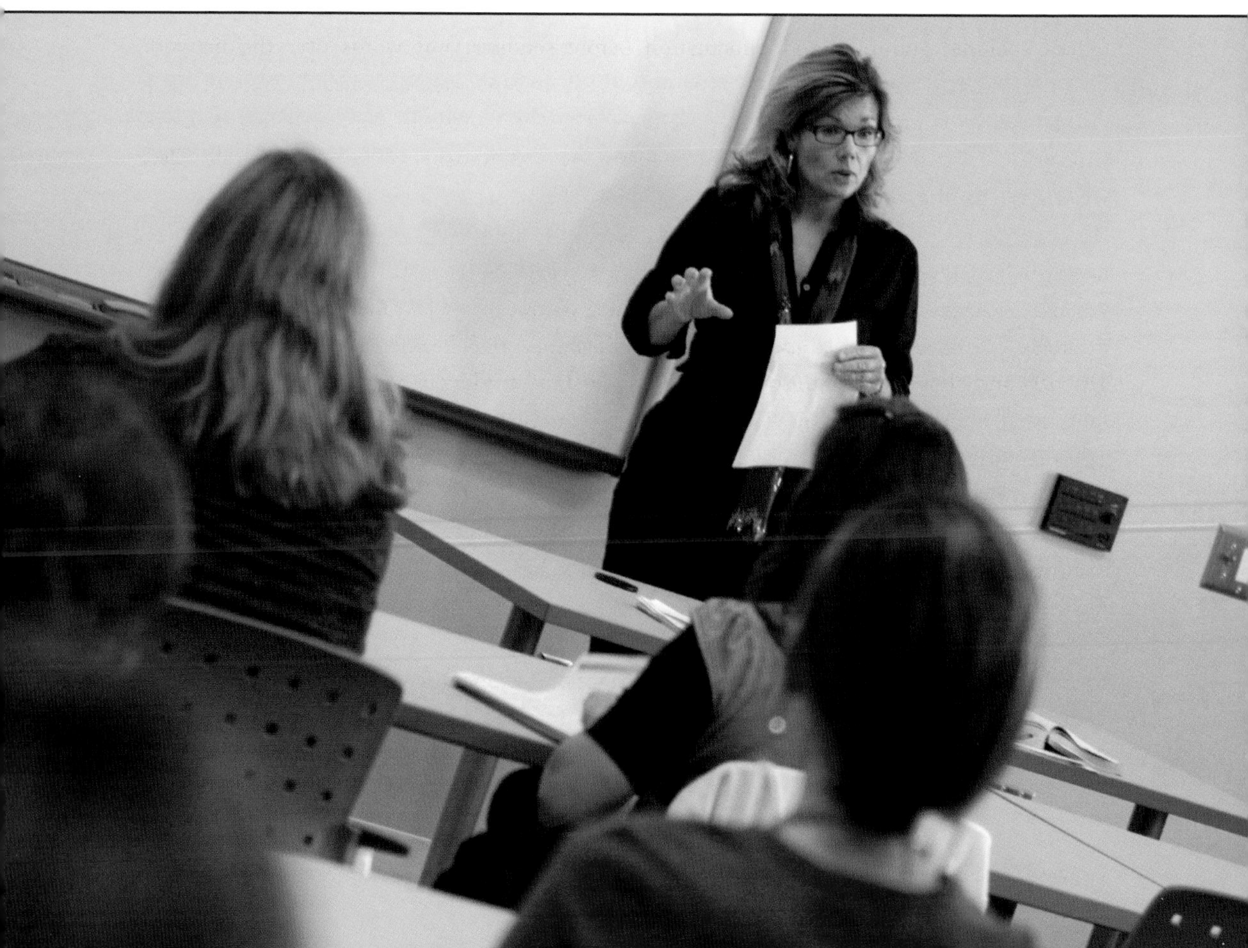

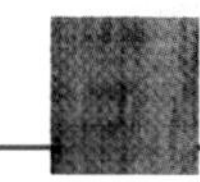

- Be considerate of other students and of the teacher. It's better not to eat meals during class or to bring in soft drinks or snacks.
- Be aware of the teacher's policies. These may vary. Generally, you will find specific guidelines and policies on your teacher's syllabus for the course.

COMPUTER PROTOCOL

At Gainesville State College, students and faculty exchange a great deal of information by Internet connections (like eLearning) and by e-mail. As in any community, it's best when everyone understands how to engage each other with civility and respect. This involves something called Netiquette, short for Internet etiquette. Netiquette refers to practices that help make the Internet experience pleasant for everyone. Like other forms of etiquette, netiquette concerns matters of courtesy in communications.

General Netiquette for E-mail, Discussion Boards, and Chat Rooms

- Check spelling, grammar, and punctuation before sending your words over the network. Chatting and posting are more like speaking, but they are still academic when done for a course. Abbreviated writing that might be appropriate when text messaging a friend might *not* be appropriate in an e-mail to a teacher or classmate. Also, avoid using all lower case words. Clear writing is a form of common courtesy and good manners.
- Be aware that e-mail and Internet communications lack the nuances of speech. Being online will not allow you to use non-verbal cues that are common in face-to-face discussion, your tone of voice, facial expression, or body language. Something you mean as a joke might be read as a sarcastic attack. Use common sense and avoid saying things that *might* be offensive to others.
- Teachers and classmates might or might not understand emoticons or acronyms. If they don't, then you cannot communicate with them. Use straightforward language, and in a formal setting, don't use emoticons or acronyms such as LOL or AFAIK. And remember, ALL CAPS is often perceived as SHOUTING.
- Use civil language. Think about e-mail, chatting, and posting in the same way as making a verbal comment in a classroom. Any words you post or e-mail are public. When in doubt, leave it out. Decorum is crucial in any online correspondence.
- If you attach documents or photos, be sure they are appropriate and follow the standards of respectful classroom behavior. Avoid attaching images or documents copyrighted by other people.
- When sending attachments, use standard formats for GSC: Word, Excel, PowerPoint, and Adobe PDF.

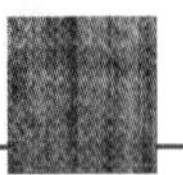

E-mail Netiquette

- Your GSC e-mail account is the preferred way for your teachers to communicate with you. It is the only e-mail account, for example, approved for your teachers to discuss grades with you. Always use your GSC e-mail account, not your home account, for official or class-related business.
- Always provide the purpose of the e-mail in the subject line.
- Use an appropriate salutation or greeting to begin an e-mail. "Hey, Dude!" may be an appropriate greeting for a friend, but it is not the type of respectful salutation that you should use when e-mailing a professor. Professors and staff should be addressed with appropriate title: Dr., Professor, Mr./Mrs./Ms., President, Vice President, etc. Most of your teachers won't be offended if you use Mr. or Mrs. Instead of Dr., but if you're in doubt, use Professor.
- Conclude your message with complete identification and contact information at the bottom of the e-mail. If you want your teacher to send you something by surface mail or to telephone you, be sure to give your address or your telephone number.
- Be brief. Separate ideas into clear, concise paragraphs with spaces in between; do not write one long paragraph containing diverse points and information.
- Do not address several issues in one e-mail; limit e-mails to one, two, or three related points on the topic in your subject line.
- Use distribution lists sparingly. You may use the student Notice Board when there is a mass e-mail to the entire campus community.
- Double check the "To" line in your replies to make sure that the e-mail goes to the right party. Avoid "Replying to All" when you do not mean to—that can result in embarrassing and sometimes legally marginal situations.
- When appropriate, use the "Options" icon in Outlook to mark messages as personal, private, or urgent or to request that the message has been received or read.
- When your teachers receive an e-mail, they will try to reply within 48 hours, excluding weekends or holidays. GSC teachers are asked to set the auto response "Out of Office" if away for an extended time period, in which case you will receive a message telling you when your teacher will be available again.

Discussion Board Netiquette

Teachers may use discussion boards as a supplement to in-class discussions. If your teacher sets up a discussion board through eLearning or another method, here are some guidelines.

- Pay attention to the discussion question posed by the instructor. Read it carefully to make sure you understand it and answer the question in your posting.
- Label your posting appropriately to fit your message; an automatic reply keeps the instructor and class from looking down the list to find your message quickly. For example, if you're posting your speech topic for approval, could you find your group members' postings out of a list of

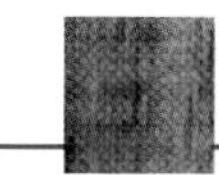

30 subject lines that say "Re: Speech Topic"? It would be better to label the message "Global Warming Persuasive topic acceptable?"

- Respond not just to the teacher but to other student postings; after all, this is a discussion that is occurring in an online format. To engage in the discussion, read other postings and respond to them directly.
- If other students reply to your posting, respond to their questions or comments. As you would in a face-to-face conversation, acknowledge the person speaking to you.
- If you don't have anything substantial or constructive to say for your reply, please do not reply. Responses like "that's nice" or "what JM said" do not keep the discussion going.
- For long responses, attach a document and type a message in the discussion box indicating what is in the attachment.

Chat Room Netiquette: Chat Rooms Created by a Professor

- Log on before the scheduled time for the chat room session to begin.
- If you do log on after the session has started, try not to waste class time asking about what you have missed in the discussion.
- Keep your statements on topic with the discussion—talking with a keyboard can be exciting, but eLearning chat rooms are still academic environments. Stay focused and try not to derail a discussion with a side issue.
- Remember that you are part of an academic environment. Type as you would speak in a traditional classroom, not on a blog. Before sending what you type, read it over a couple times to make sure you will not be sending something you might regret. Once you hit "send" in a chat room, you can't change what you have written and you can be sure that your classmates and teacher will "hear" it. Even when the instructor is not a participant in the chat room, he or she will have a transcript of the assigned chat to read.
- Concise language allows you to make your point more quickly and allows others to read what you have to say more quickly.
- Repetition should be avoided in favor of moving the discussion forward.
- Avoid attacking a classmate for a point of view you disagree with. Debate should be civil. Resorting to personal attacks is a form of intellectual irresponsibility. This means no name-calling or personal insults, even if someone else provokes you.
- If you are offended by some words typed by another student, please explain how you feel to that student, but do not try to be offensive in return. If the problem continues, please talk to your teacher about it.
- Avoid dominating an online conversation. Give everyone a chance to type. Reading in a chat room is just as important as listening in a classroom.
- Avoid lurking. If you simply read what others are typing and never contribute your own thoughts, you will not benefit from having others respond to you. Typing in a chat room does not require a loud voice, so you don't have to be shy.

- If you are replying to a particular person, you can indicate so (i.e., @smith). The class can decide how to manage multiple conversations.

Chat Feature in Who's Online

- If you send an invitation to someone to chat inside eLearning, please wait for a response. If you simply want to send a message to someone and plan to check for a reply later on, please use e-mail instead.
- If you are logged on and would not like to reply to chat invitations, please make yourself invisible or unavailable. Otherwise, please respond to chat invitations in a timely manner.
- Remember who your audience is. If you send a chat invitation to a classmate, you are free to use less formal language. But if you contact your teacher about an assignment, take time to edit your writing and compose complete sentences.

ATTENDANCE AND ABSENCES

Attending class is important for you. Don't cut class unless you are ill or have a real problem attending class. If you must be out, it's usually a good idea to get in touch with your professors to learn how you may make up the missed work. Attendance policies vary from professor to professor, so be sure you understand what is expected in each class (this information is available in your course syllabus). Be aware that if you are having trouble attending class, you may be better advised to withdraw from the class by midterm than to remain in it and make a low or failing grade. If you withdraw, you will receive a grade of W, which does not count against your grade-point average. However, if you simply stop attending a class, you will receive a grade of WF, which counts the same as an F and will bring your GPA down.

INCOMPLETES

Occasionally an emergency or illness late in a term may prevent a student from finishing a course. The student may then request a grade of I or Incomplete, from the professor. In order to do this, the student should be able to document the reason for the request (a doctor's note for an illness or verification of a family emergency such as an automobile accident or a house fire, for example). The professor may then arrange with the Dean of the School to grant the I.

A student who has received an I in a course must complete the course requirements within the next regular academic term to have the I removed and changed to a passing grade. If the student receives an I for fall semester, the student must complete the course requirements by the end of spring semester; if the student receives the I at the end of either spring or summer terms, the student must complete the course requirements by the end of fall semester.

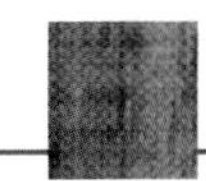

If you receive an I, you have the responsibility of arranging a schedule with your teacher for making up the work. If you fail to complete the course requirements by the end of the next regular term, the grade of I will be changed to F.

GRADE APPEALS

Rarely, students may believe that they have received an unfair grade because their teacher violated GSC policy or procedures or did not grade according to the course syllabus. In that event, the college has established this as the formal process of appealing a grade:

Grade-related appeals will be restricted to alleged violations of institutional policy and stated classroom procedures. The syllabus should be considered a contractual agreement between instructor and student; the classroom procedures and policies stated on the syllabus must affirm institutional policies. If a discrepancy exists, the institutional policy will supersede the syllabus.

When a student believes that an instructor has not followed proper procedure and wishes to appeal, the student will proceed as follows:

A. The student will discuss the contested grade(s) or symbol(s) with the course instructor within the first 30 calendar days of the Full Session of the following semester. If the student is unable to contact the instructor, the student should seek the aid of the instructor's Division or Department Chair (or the Director of Learning Support). When the course instructor is the Division or Department Chair, then the student should seek the aid of the instructor's Dean. The Division or Department Chair will facilitate a dialogue between the student and instructor which must be completed within 14 calendar days of the first contact between the student and the instructor or the student and the Division or Department Chair.
B. If the student-instructor dialogue has not resolved the issue, the student will then request the assistance of the Division or Department Chair. The Division or Department Chair will collect information and serve as a mediator between the student and instructor.
C. If the matter cannot be resolved at the Division/Department level through mediation in a timely fashion (within 14 calendar days), the student will complete a Grade Appeal Form (available from the Academic Affairs Web site). This form, along with any supporting documents, must be submitted to the Dean's office of the notifying school within 14 calendar days of the Division/Department Chair's notifying the student that mediation has failed.
D. The Dean will request written responses to the student's appeal from the course instructor. The course instructor has up to 14 calendar days to submit his/her written responses.
E. The Dean, in consultation with the Division or Department Chair, will select a three-member ad hoc Grade Appeals Committee comprised of two faculty members from the school (one from each campus) and a faculty member from outside the school.
F. The Grade Appeals Committee will review the information provided by the student in the Grade Appeal Form and written responses from the course instructor. If the Grade Appeals

Committee feels that more information is needed, they may submit questions directly to the instructor and/or the student. The instructor and/or student will submit the additional information requested in writing. All information should remain completely confidential. The Grade Appeals Committee will make a recommendation to the Dean with justification within 30 calendar days. If an element of the grade dispute involves any form of academic dishonesty, the Grade Appeals Committee may also make a recommendation to the Dean about disciplinary actions. The Dean will make her/his decision and provide official notice of the decision to the student and instructor.

G. In the event that the Dean is the instructor, then the entire process will begin with the Dean's immediate supervisor. The President has delegated final decisions on grade appeals to the Vice President for Academic Affairs or her/his designee, in this case, the Dean.

LATE WORK

It's always best to be aware of deadlines and to turn work in promptly. Many professors at GSC encourage students to submit their work electronically, while others ask for paper copies of essays and assignments. In either case, make every effort to turn your work in on time. If you miss turning in an assignment without a valid reason, your professor may penalize you (or may even decline to accept the assignment at all). Be prepared to document any reason for being late with an assignment.

The syllabus for each course will give you information about your professor's policy on late work. Be sure to read it and to abide by it. If you have a real reason for missing an assignment, most teachers will work with you—but again, the best policy is to be on time.

None of these policies are meant to be punitive if you make a conscientious effort to participate in the campus community as a courteous and contributing individual. Gainesville State College is all about students, and if you will meet your peers, the faculty, the staff, and the administration halfway, you will be on your way to success in college.

CHAPTER FIVE

Academic Support

GSC is a student-centered institution; therefore, we pride ourselves on aiding students in their educational success. This chapter outlines some of the many academic resources available to students.

WRITING CENTER

In the Writing Center, a student can have an individual conference with a writing instructor, an expert on both the writing process and the mechanics of an academic paper. The writing

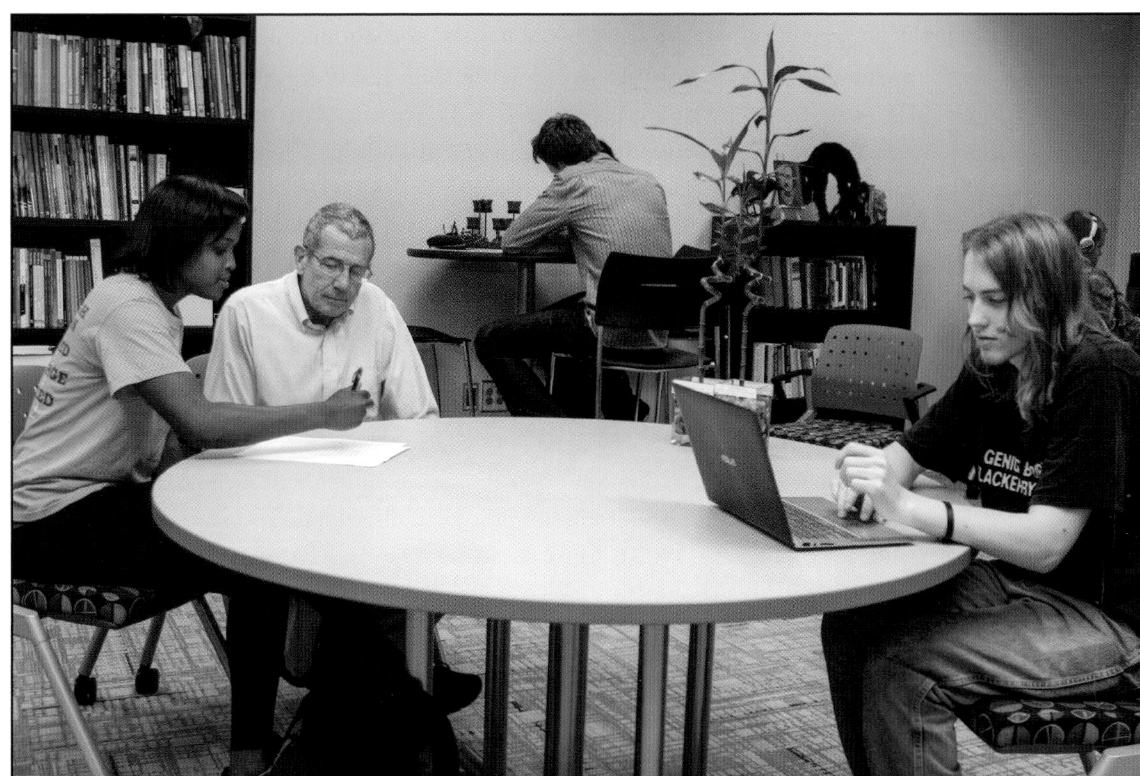

Writing Center in Nesbitt Building (Academic IV)

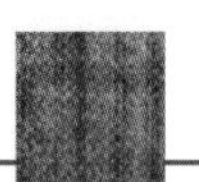

instructor can help a student writer generate ideas for an essay, write well-developed paragraphs and a well-structured essay, revise the essay, and find the answers to grammar questions as well as to questions of format for MLA or APA research papers and other research standards. Students can receive help for all levels of English papers, from ESL to freshman composition to literature, and also for writing projects for Nursing, Biology, Economics, Art, Music, Computer Science, Business, Communication, Physical Education, Philosophy, Film, Sociology, Psychology, and many other courses taught at Gainesville State College. Good writing is central to all of the college curriculum. It is our goal to teach student writers to become better writers and to give students the tools to judge and edit their own writing. We are expert readers, and our job is to provide another pair of eyes and offer feedback and suggestions.

The Writing Center has three professional writing instructors and several student writing instructors. These instructors can answer questions about academic writing and provide student writers with other resources where they can learn more about methods of writing academic papers and see models of what professors are looking for in the assignments they give student writers. The instructors can also help students who are working on stories, poetry, and other personal writing, such as resumes, personal statements for college and scholarship applications, and business letters.

Located in Room 2103 of the Academic IV Building, the Writing Center is open Monday through Thursday from 8:00 am to 8:00 pm and on Friday from 8:00 am to 3:00 pm. Students can either make an appointment or simply drop by. The Writing Center has computers, study tables, couches, and easy chairs where students can read and relax. The Writing Center also has a Smart Board-equipped study room where students can work on PowerPoint presentations, group projects, speeches, and other presentations.

CALM—CENTER FOR ADULT LEARNERS AND MILITARY

As an Adult Learner and Military student, it is pivotal for you to get the information needed in making your goals and dreams a reality. Here at GSC we strive to offer all the services you need to make this happen. You will find in every student service office a staff member that is there to help you answer your questions and lead you in the right direction. Also our adult learning and military outreach coordinator, Christy Orr is located in Dunlap/Mathis room 143 and available to assist you in achieving your goals. Visit us online at http://www.gsc.edu/academics/acadenrich/calm/Pages/default.aspx.

You could also visit The Military Resource Center. It is a dedicated place for Student Veterans, Service members and their Family with common backgrounds, experiences and goals where they can study, connect, and support each other. This center is equipped with four computer workstations, a lounge area with satellite television, two study areas with whiteboards, and resource materials. The center is located in Dunlap/Mathis room 119.

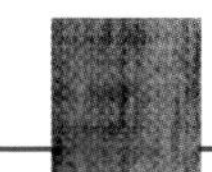

AMERICANS WITH DISABILITIES ACT

GSC views disability as an important aspect of a richly diverse student population and welcomes students with disabilities who are otherwise qualified for college. The Office of Disability Services (ODS) serves as a resource for students and coordinates a variety of academic and support services. ODS collaborates with students, faculty, staff, and community members to facilitate access and increase awareness toward the goal of full participation and equal opportunities for success for students with disabilities.

Students who require accommodations should meet with an ODS representative as early as possible. ODS coordinates the provision of reasonable accommodations for students with disabilities, as defined by the Rehabilitation Act of 1973 and the Americans with Disabilities Act of 1990. Accommodations are provided on an individual basis, and current documentation is required.

What is a Disability?

A disability is a physical or mental impairment that substantially limits one or more major life activities—such as learning, walking, seeing, hearing, speaking, or breathing.

Examples of disabilities include (but are not limited to):

- Acquired Brain Injury
- Attention Deficit Hyperactivity Disorder
- Autism/Asperger Syndrome
- Blindness and Visual Impairment
- Chronic Health Impairment
- Deaf and Hard of Hearing
- Learning Disability
- Mobility Impairment
- Psychological Disability
- Other disabilities covered by the ADA & Section 504 of the Rehabilitation Act

What are some accommodations that a student with a disability might be eligible for?

Examples of accommodations include (but are not limited to):

- Alternative media, such as:
    - electronic text
    - enlarged print
    - Braille
- Assistive technology, such as:
    - screen reading (text-to speech) software

    - voice activation (speech-to-text) software
    - screen magnification software
- Extended time on tests
- Quiet testing room
- Use of a non-programmable (simple four-function) calculator
- Note-taking support
- Sign language interpreter or C-print captioning ("real time" speech-to-text transcription)
- Scheduled breaks during testing
- Adjustable seating or tables

Is there a program to promote a smooth transition to college life for first year students with disabilities?

Yes, the Gainesville Campus has a program called First Year Foundation. The First Year Foundation (FYF) program is designed to increase academic success and improve retention and completion rates for students with disabilities at GSC. FYF has two components: a two-day summer workshop for first-year students with disabilities and a ten-month peer mentor program. During the summer workshop, new students learn about campus resources and practice effective learning strategies. Peer mentors participate with students during the workshop and coordinate monthly meetings during the school year. Through this program, new students develop personal connections and begin to acquire the knowledge and skills to be confident and successful college students.

Students should contact the ODS with any questions or concerns regarding accommodations, available resources and support, or to volunteer to be a peer mentor or a note taker.

Gainesville Campus: Dunlap-Mathis, room 107, (678) 717-3855
Nicola Dovey, *Director of Disability Services*: ndovey@gsc.edu
Oconee Campus: Administration, room 112, (706) 310-6204
Jesse Abbott, *Coordinator of Disability Services*: jabbott@gsc.edu

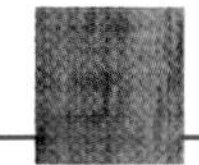

The John Harrison Hosch and Oconee Libraries

<www.gsc.edu/academics/libraries/Pages/default.aspx>

The Hosch and Oconee Libraries provide access to a collection of over 160,000 items in support of course work and research. Knowledgeable library faculty work with students and faculty one-on-one at the Information Help Desks, and teach full-and half-semester courses and one-hour workshops in research, critical inquiry, and the use of library resources. Library collections include books, electronic books (look for the e-book link and icon in the catalog), DVDs, periodicals, electronic databases (many available through GALILEO) and the borrowing privileges provided by GIL Express, which allows for interlibrary loan for GSC patrons from any school in the University System of Georgia.

In Gainesville, the library provides the second largest computer lab on campus, with PCs installed on desks and in study carrels. Individual and group work are accommodated throughout the library at carrels and in study rooms, and comfortable chairs, couches and tables are present throughout the library so patrons may read, study, and use laptops connected to the library's wireless network. A "smart" study room offers space and hardware to practice presentations.

Books in the circulating collection support students as they research and explore concepts covered in class, and area liaison librarians (library faculty with specialized knowledge of content areas) are eager to assist with research and locating materials. Students may request research advisory appointments with librarians to get one-on-one support through the research process.

The libraries are open Monday through Thursday 7:30 am-10:00 pm, Fridays 7:30 am-3:00pm. Hosch Library is open Sundays 1:00 pm-6:00 pm.

To contact Hosch Librarians, please call (678) 717-3653:

STEM: Amanda Nash
BEHW: Deborah Prosser
Social Sciences: Scott Kantor
HFA: Teresa Pacheco

To contact Oconee Librarians, please call (706) 310-6238

BEHW/HFA: Angela Megaw
STEM/Social Sciences: Sean Boyle

For course reserves, library accounts, or inter-library loan, contact John Ash, Circulation Manager in Gainesville, and Asia Hall, Information Help Desk Manager in Oconee.

The Oconee Library

The Oconee Library combines the tutoring and make-up testing services of the ACTT Center and the Writing Center with those of a traditional library, such as instruction, research assistance and reserves, as well as access to books, DVDs and periodicals. To support these services, the Oconee Library features a large computer lab and group study space. The Libraries offer a campus exchange service facilitated through the Library's Catalog, GIL, to request materials housed at the other campus. The Oconee Library also shares all electronic resources such as databases and e-books.

Where to Begin

On the GSC Libraries Web site (<www.gsc.edu/academics/libraries/>), look for the **Research Tools**.

What to Search

Library catalogs will help you find books and videos on your topic. There are two catalogs you'll need to use in your research: **GIL-Find** and **GIL Universal**. The databases in **GALILEO** will help you find articles.

GIL-Find will point you to materials in the Gainesville and Oconee Libraries.

GIL Universal lets you search for books in the libraries of all 30+ USG colleges and universities.

GIL *Express* lets you borrow them.

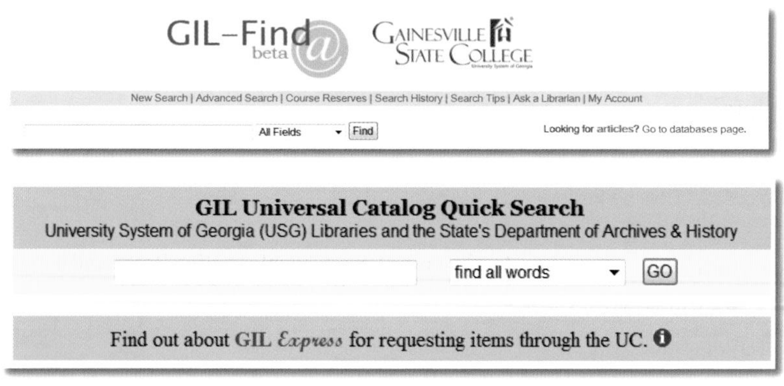

The databases in **GALILEO** link you to articles from magazines, newspapers, and scholarly journals.

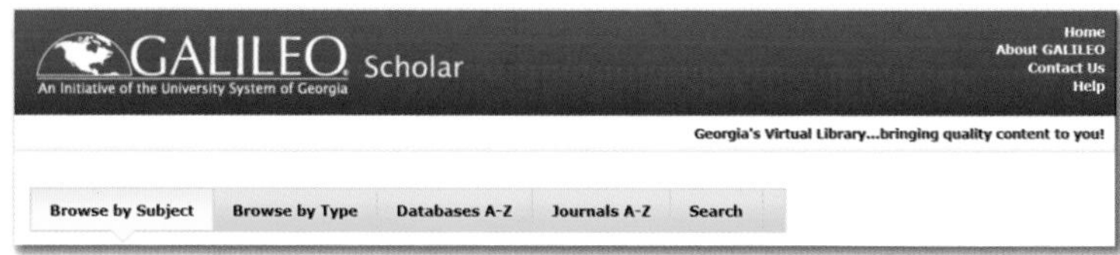

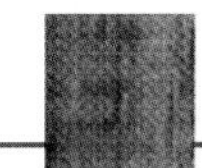

How to Search

GIL-Find

- Search using keywords—words or short phrases that describe your topic.
- Use the **Advanced Search** and combine keywords for a more focused search. **Don't search by long phrases.** Remember: More keywords = fewer results (and vice versa).
- You can limit your search results by Format, Location, Language, etc.
- You can Print/E-mail/Text your results.
- Go to **My Account** for Favorites, Renewals, and Requests.

GIL Universal

- Use the **Keyword Search**.
- Print or E-mail your results.
- Make a GIL *Express* request to borrow materials.

GALILEO

- Try a multidisciplinary database like ***Academic Search Complete, Research Library,*** or ***CQ Researcher*** to start; use the Databases A-Z menu to find these databases.
- Try a subject database for more specialized coverage of your topic; use the Browse by Subject menu to find databases in your subject area.
- Use **Advanced Search** and search using keywords.
- Combine keywords for a more focused search. **Don't search by long phrases.** Remember: More keywords = fewer results (and vice versa).
- You can often limit your search results by Source Type, Date, Full-Text, etc.
- You can Print/E-mail/Cite your results.

What Next?

Off-campus access to **GALILEO** requires a password. Look it up in your GIL-Find account, or use Virtual Lab to turn your computer into a GSC computer.

Evaluate the materials you find—give them the *CRAAP* test! Think about the *C*urrency, *R*elevance, *A*uthority, *A*ccuracy, and *P*urpose of any book, article, or Web site before you use it in your research.

Help!

Library Services

Have questions? ASK A LIBRARIAN!

Schedule an Individual Research Appointment

If you need any help with your research, just ask!

You can stop by the Information Desk, send us an e-mail, or schedule an appointment for one-on-one assistance.

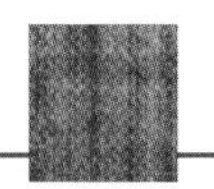

TURNITIN.COM

Turnitin.com is an online grading platform utilized by many professors at Gainesville State College due to its ability to offer students more feedback in a faster manner. Essentially, professors can use *Turnitin* to assign draft assignments and revisions, final essays, portfolios, and even peer-revision assignments. After professors create these assignments, students simply sign up for their professor's course (see student *Turnitin.com* guide), and then submit their essays accordingly. *Turnitin,* a web-based function, also allows professors to occasionally offer more time for their students to complete drafts as students don't have to turn in essays in class. When students upload essays to *Turnitin*, the Web site automatically checks the originality of the essay against its warehouse of stored essays as well as content on the Internet. This assures students that their content is unique and double checks that students do not receive credit for turning in work that is not their own.

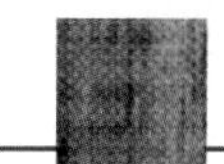

Once students upload their essays to *Turnitin*, the professor can then grade the essays using the Grademark feature. As mentioned above, this feature allows professors to grade from any computer with access to the Internet and often allows them to turn papers around more quickly. Again, because *Turnitin* is online, professors can return essays after class hours or on the weekend. Additionally, the remarks and comments left via Grademark are much more legible than the comments hand written on student essays. These comments also offer more information and even links to help students improve errors and continue growing as writers.

In addition to these positive aspects, *Turnitin* is "green;" no paper is necessary, making it environmentally responsible. Also, the platform offers easy accessibility for students. Since *Turnitin* warehouses all of a student's graded essays, he or she can easily look back at a professor's comments from any computer. In addition, if professors assign final portfolios or revision assignments, students can easily locate previous essays and comments. Finally, students can be assured that their own work will not be plagiarized as *Turnitin.com* submits all student work to its repository.

Gainesville State College is very excited to offer students the ability to use *Turnitin* as it offers them further tools to reach their academic goals.

STUDENT GUIDE TO USING TURNITIN.COM

Class ID:______________

Password:________________

Register with Turnitin

- First, navigate to <www.turnitin.com> and click on the **Create Account** button on the top right hand corner of the page (under username box).
- On the next page look down below the fill-in boxes to where it says **Create a New Account.** Click on **Student**.
    - Note: if you have used turnitin.com for any other course, you may simply log into your account and then follow the instructions for **Enroll in a Class** (see below).
- Follow the instructions and fill in the information. The Class ID is listed above along with the password.
- Certify that you are at least thirteen, and click **I Agree**.
- Congratulations—you're registered!

Enroll in a Class

- To login to Turnitin, go to <www.turnitin.com>.
- At the top right, enter your **e-mail address** and user **password.**
- Click **Log In.**
- Click the **Enroll in a Class** tab at the top of the screen.
- On the next screen, enter the **Class ID** and **enrollment password**
- Click **Submit** to enroll in the class and add it to your homepage.

Submit a Paper

- Log in and select our class.
- Click the **Submit** button next to the desired assignment in your class portfolio.
- Enter a title for your paper in the **Submission Title** box.
- Select **Single File Upload** from the submission drop down menu.
- Click **Browse** and find the file you want to submit. While you may submit in a number of formats, using a .rtf file or a .doc or .docx file will best preserve your formatting.
    - **Note:** You can cut and paste your paper into the white text box instead by choosing **Cut and Paste Upload**; however, your formatting will be lost.
- Double-click on the file name and the file path should appear in the file field.
- Click **Submit.** On the following page you will be asked to confirm the text of your submission.

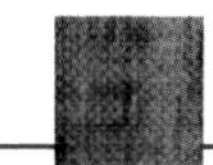

- Click **Yes to Submit** your final paper.
    - Note: Once essays are submitted, students are unable to resubmit. Therefore, please check carefully that you are uploading the correct version of your essay.
- Make a note of the **digital receipt ID** that confirms your submission.
- Click **Logout**.

Questions? Click on the **Help!** button at the top of any Turnitin page for easy-to-follow directions and video tutorials.

CHAPTER SIX

Sample Student Essays

INFORMAL ESSAYS

Rosalyn Love

Dr. Worrall

ENGL 1101 *This I Believe* Essay

15 February 2012

Daddy's Hands

When I was a little girl, I wanted my daddy to be like all the dads on television. I wanted him to go to work in an office wearing a fancy suit and tie and to be home every night by six o'clock for dinner. I thought that would make him happy, and I was sure it would make me happy, but my daddy was not a white-collar man. He worked with his hands every day of his life. His office was a backhoe, and his suit and tie were a t-shirt and overalls. He was a blue-collar man, and his hands were callused.

I did not like the way my daddy's hands felt. They were rough and cracked. He used lotions and salves to soften them, but the roughness never went away. His hands were always callused. These hands steadied the back of my bicycle after he took the training wheels off. The same hands brushed away the dirt from my scraped knee and dried the tears that slid down my cheek. Then, without fail, he would pick me up and set me back on the bicycle time and time again, until I no longer needed his callused hands to steady me.

As time passed, he began to work less, but his hands remained callused. Once I asked him if he wanted to have them removed, and he said, "No." He told me those calluses were reminders of the things he had done throughout his life. They were the result of hard work, like picking cotton and building tree houses. They held his children, his grandchildren, and his wife. "Oh no," he said, "I've earned 'em and I plan to keep 'em."

My dad died suddenly in 2002, and his death left a gaping hole in our family. My heart was broken, and I was certain I could never smile again, but I did. One day when I was feeling particularly sad I went to visit his grave. While I was there, I heard the sound of a bulldozer off in the distance, and the familiar smell of tractor fuel drifted through the air. As my heart swelled inside my chest and the tears streamed down my face, I saw my daddy sitting in the cab of that tractor, waving goodbye with his callused hand. In that moment, I realized he would have wanted me to celebrate his life, not mourn it.

Eventually, I began seeing bits and pieces of my dad's handiwork around the house, and when I did, my heart grew lighter. Grief was beginning to loosen its tight grip on my heart. As I slowly began to accept his death, I accepted his callused hands. These hands were of a man who loved his family and worked hard to provide a happy home. In his life and in his death, my daddy taught me there is no shame in callused hands, only honor. I believe in callused hands.

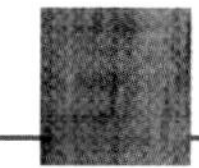

Dalton Marsh

Dr. Leslie Worthington

ENGL 1101

13 September 2010

The Day I Decided I Wanted to Grow Wings

The day I first realized what I wanted to do with my life was when I was ten years old. I was holding hands with my grandfather, waiting at the Gainesville airport for our plane to arrive. The wind chill struck down to the bone, my legs trembled, and my face tingled. I knew what was about to happen, but for some reason, the event of flying hadn't yet hit me. We were about to experience something magnificent; an associate of my grandfather, Carlton, was allowing us the opportunity of a lifetime. He lowered the door on his single-wing, propeller-driven, personal airplane and invited us in. The cabin was five feet wide and ten feet in length, just enough for a few passengers. There were six seats in three rows, covered in leather and with double seat belts. The plane was cozy, set to around eighty degrees Fahrenheit, enough to fight off the winter chill. Even with the heat bearing down on my face, I couldn't fight off the chattering of my teeth or the shaking of my legs. My grandfather sat in the passenger and I sat in the diagonally rearmost seat. We patiently waited on Carlton for lift off. As I locked down my belt, I was unaware of the new world of airplanes and what terrifying adventures would come from it.

Carlton looked back and briefed us on the preflight instructions. "Keep your seat belts on until we are at a steady altitude and I will take care of the rest," he said. He then contacted air traffic control:

"This is Carlton Reeves to air traffic control. Come in air traffic control, over."

"This is air traffic control, over Gainesville.

How are you doing today, Mr. Reeves, over," they replied.

"Grand. I would like permission to take off on the Gainesville runway over," Carlton responded.

"Permission granted; you will be on air strip number two. Have a good flight sir. Watch out for the changing turbulence, over and out."

The radio went silent, and Carlton turned to my grandfather and me, nodded and started up the engine. He put the plane into reverse and aimed us toward the runway entrance while pulling knobs and pushing buttons on his control panel. The plane drove similar to a tractor with a sail: it rocked slowly left and right and putted softly toward the strip. The runway was fogged over, and the pavement was slick with the previous night's rain. The propeller began spinning rapidly, and I clenched onto my grandfather's hand as if it was my lifeline. We began speeding down the runway, the front of the plane leaning upwards toward the sky.

My stomach sank; the view from the front window was nothing but a blue sky dotted softly in clouds. Looking out the window, I could see the world in a crooked dimension. Leveling out, I gazed out into the distance with the

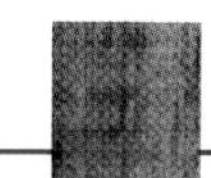

most beautiful scene of my life. It was truly breath taking. The cars reminded me of small insects, and the buildings were two dimensional, revealing only their foresides and roofs. Never in my life had I been so astonished that something could be so beautiful. My fingers sweating from diverting the heater's flame away from my face, now laid at the base of the window, just hoping that I could push it out, and climb out into this new world. I viewed how curved the horizon was due to the mountainous terrain of Northeast Georgia. That is when I knew that this day would be forever monumental, a true stepping stone in my life. For many people this day would have been just ordinary, flying from one place to another, but for me flying was my home. It was my escape from it all. Nothing in the world mattered up until this point, and nothing would matter for some time to come.

We flew north bound toward the mountain range. After twenty minutes or so, we were contacted by air traffic control. This time Carlton set the conference to his headset only, so that we couldn't listen in. Carlton's tone became worrisome, and his grip tightened on the controls. He looked back and said, "It's about to get bumpy." Those words bounced around in my head. "How does the air become bumpy?" I asked myself. Without hesitation, the plane began to shake. Carlton leaned back and yelled, "Strap on your seat belts." Before I could reach for my seatbelt, the wind lashed against the side of the plane, bouncing us about and tossed me from my chair. I grasped the strap with two fingers, pinching it like a fish victim to a crab's claw.

The plane bounced me in between the seats, like I was the pinball in a 70s pinball tournament. My grandfather turned to me and used one hand to grab me and toss me back to my seat, latching my seatbelt shut all in one motion. Grasping my bruised ribs and rubbing my knee, I trembled in fear. The heaven that I was in immediately turned to hell. Never before had I experienced life and death all in the same day. The plane shook violently; Carlton pulled down on the controls and twisted it with all of his might, turning the plane around. We navigated out of the turbulence and made our way back toward town.

It was a very interesting adventure on the airplane, but it was finally time to head home, after such a painfully interesting trip. Flying back to the airport, we flew over Lake Lanier, its water pristine, and nothing like the bitter taste of gasoline that I find when in it. As we prepped to land, Carlton acquired landing permission from air traffic control. Tilting the plane down toward the earth and fiddling with the various widgets, Carlton slowed the plane for its descent. Carlton leveled out the plane as we entered the runway and then pulled back on the controls to gain more wind resistance. The plane touched down on the runway, screeching to a halt. That's the day I realized I wanted to be an airline pilot. The thrill of flying changed my life forever.

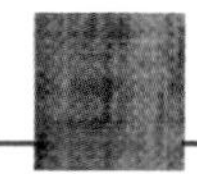

RESEARCH ESSAYS

Leah Reed

Dr. Patricia Worrall

ENGL 1101

18 April 2012

Finding Nutrition in a Fake Food World

The most important part of any civilization is its ability to thrive. America advanced in technology and knowledge throughout the years; however, in the midst of these advancements, nutrition has been lost. Despite medical advances, America is facing more obesity, heart disease, and diabetes than ever before because of our chemically modified food.

Throughout the years as the United States population has grown, a higher volume of produce and meats has been needed to satisfy the large numbers of people. To do this, meat companies, "put them [animals] in buildings, made them eat corn, among other things, which made them fat but also sick, gave them no room to move and allowed them not a stitch of sunlight" (Zenn 61), all in the name of keeping America fed. But they didn't stop there: "to make these sickly animals even fatter, they injected them with growth hormones and female hormones, and to keep them alive they pumped them full of antibiotics" (Zenn 61). These antibiotics are being pumped into the food that almost all Americans are eating. We are consuming sickly animals that are filled with antibiotics and hormones; this "'increases the prevalence of antibiotic-resistant pathogens, and those germs can cause infections in humans that are difficult or impossible to treat,' says CSPI Executive Director Michael F" (qtd. in "FDA Scraps 12-year-old Petition"). Not only are we filling our bodies with harmful toxins that can cause disease, we're also exposing ourselves to new pathogens that could cause a serious epidemic. The effects of this poison meat can be seen in infectious disease, obesity, and other health-related issues that America, as a country, is currently facing.

The problem we now face is how to get away from the genetically modified foods that are causing health issues. Although we can monitor what we eat as individuals, the crisis is much more serious for those who can't afford to buy organic food or are uneducated about the risks involved in eating processed food. The Food and Drug Administration is responsible for establishing regulations on what companies can sell. For example, looking for foods that are labeled natural is one way consumers are trying to choose healthy alternatives. However, "The U.S. food and drug administration has yet to define the term natural on food labels. Although they do not object to companies using the term if food does not contain added color, artificial flavors or synthetic substances" ("Defining 'Natural'"). For us to be able to make conscientious decisions on what products to buy, the FDA needs to give detailed definitions for what companies can label their products.

Since the FDA has not set guidelines for most food products, individuals should work towards petitioning the current nutritional issues. However, authority figures have more influence than individuals. For us to

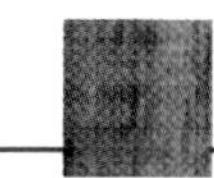

make a difference, we must first influence those who are in political and social standing to also petition current FDA guidelines for food products. Restrictions that need improvement include: hormones and antibiotics being injected into meat products and labeling of natural foods.

One problem we face when trying to get a petition against the FDA is spreading awareness. Obtaining knowledge about the negative side effects of these processed foods is difficult. One way to spread awareness is by contacting individuals who are in influential positions. An example is Michelle Obama. As First Lady, she has a great deal of influence in this country, and she has used that influence to spread awareness about health. In one interview, the First Lady noted, "Nearly one in three of our children are overweight or obese, at risk for illnesses such as diabetes, heart disease and cancer that cost our economy billions of dollars each year to treat" (Obama). Because of this startling statistic, Mrs. Obama started a program that spreads awareness about childhood obesity and works to promote health called *Let's Move*. With Mrs. Obama's efforts, *Let's Move* has successfully brought fitness and nutrition to many communities throughout the United States.

Another problem we face is the ability to get people in authority to care about nutrition. Ignorance is easily cured by merely sharing knowledge; however, knowledge is not enough to make people passionate about being healthy. In order to reach people in a personal way, we should trace family health issues back to nutrition. Revealing how loved ones have been affected in their own lives will spur people into taking their health into their own hands.

The more people in authority that take a personal stance on nutrition, the more influence we have on the FDA. Petitioning the FDA isn't going to make a difference unless we have people in authority on our side.

For America to continue to grow and thrive, we must first start helping individuals thrive. Life is not meant to be filled with disease but with vitality. Nutrition must become a priority in order to stop the progression of disease in America. Just as technology advances so does the understanding of how the body works and how we can keep it functioning at its best.

Works Cited

"Defining 'Natural' on Food Labels." *Environmental Nutrition.* Feb. 2012. Web. 18 April 2012.

"FDA Scraps 12-year-old Petition to Pull Antibiotic Approvals for Food Animals." *DVM: The Newsmagazine of Veterinary Medicine.* Jan 2012. Web. 18 April 2012.

Obama, Michelle. "Working Together for the Health of America's Children." CNN. Feb. 2012. Web. 18 April 2012.

Zenn, Michael J. *The Self Health Revolution.* New York: One Revolution, 2008. Print.

 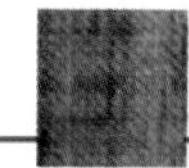

Ryan George

Dr. Turner

English 1101

16 October 2011

It's Up to You

Everyone knows that the two leading operating systems for cell phones in The United States are Apple's IOS and Google's Android. Although most people favor one over the other, their leading sales percentages prove that these two cell phone operating systems are both very well done. People choose their phones based on a few different determinants; some of these include what phones are available under their current plan, what applications can be used with their phones, and how it operates. People choose a combination of determinants that appeal most to them when looking at phones. Now, as of October 14, 2011, the iphone running IOS and Android are available within all cell phone service providers. With this being said, the decision is solely based on choice instead of whether or not a user is able to attain one or the other based on what cell phone service provider he/she has. Debate rages over which of the two out performs the other, as always happens between two competing technologies. However, I have come to the conclusion that there is no way to accurately determine which of the two is better, but that it comes down to user preference. More specifically, focusing on IOS and Android from a United States basic user perspective, there are pros and cons to three differing aspects between the two operating systems that most basic users focus on; these include the App Store and the Market, the accessibility of the operating system, and the option of cell phone brands (Blodget).

First, Apple's App Store has many pros, but also many cons. Beginning with the pros, Apple is a strict company that is selective of the applications they let into the App Store. As a result, the buyers can be very confident that any application they buy is going to be of high quality and surely will not contain any viruses. Quality is an important characteristic that every consumer wants in a product. However, Apple's tendency to be strict is also the cause of the cons of the App Store. In today's U.S. economy, money is tight for most people, which means that consumers are looking for cheaper prices. In the App Store, many of the applications can be pricey. The quality is there, but a bigger cost follows it. Also, downloads on IOS are limited solely to the App Store. The IOS does not allow users to download applications from online websites (Wauters).

Android's Market is made for the same purpose as the App Store, but its pros and cons are almost in reverse compared to the App Store. In Android's Market, there are a greater number of free apps than in the App Store. A greater selection of free applications will always be a pro in any circumstance. Another pro for Android's Market is that a greater number of people can create applications for it. Android does turn down some applications, but definitely much less than Apple. Android also lets users download applications from sources other than the Market. This is where cons come in due to Android's versatility. The quality is not as consistent in applications as the App Store

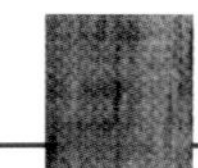

because of the freedom that Android gives its application developers. Also, if a user chooses to download an application from a source other than the Market, there is a chance that the application may include a virus or harmful software. The App Store and the Market are overall very successful at their job, which is to make applications available to users. As a result of the pros and cons, a conclusion cannot be drawn to state that one is better than the other; in the end, user preference is what makes the difference (Distimo).

Accessibility of a phone is important to users whether they realize it or not. Again, beginning with the pros, Apple's IOS is well known for the simplicity of the operating system. It is very clean and runs smoothly. As a result, users are able to easily navigate through the phone with little to no trouble. The con to this simplicity is lack of customization within the phone. IOS is an operating system based around what the general public prefers. However, what the general public prefers might not meet the standards of someone else. This is where Android's accessibility pros stand out. The customization of the Android operating system is superb; the user is able to customize everything from what applications or widgets the user wants on which screen, to how far apart the user wants the letters on the touch screen QWERTY keyboard. Undoubtedly, this does complicate the accessibility of the operating system, which is a con to Android. Users will not find Android as easy as IOS to maneuver through from the start. Android is by no means too complicated to learn, but it does require effort to completely understand the operating system. These operating system differences are the factors that users will take into consideration when deciding which to invest in (Dachis).

Lastly, one must consider the pros and cons of the cell phone brands that support the two operating systems. Apple is the only company that makes phones that support IOS. The pro to this is that Apple is a very prestigious company that is known for quality. This makes for an easier decision for the user because the only decision he/she has to make is how much internal storage to get on the iphone. The con to this is that if someone likes the IOS but does not like the look or feel of the iphone, he/she is stuck with only one phone choice. Apple is also a more expensive company whose prices may not be affordable to everyone. The pros of Android are the multiple cell phone brands that support the operating system. This brings the advantage of having a decision when it comes to what phone a buyer wants. This also helps further accommodate users because of the range in phone prices. However, the con to this is some phones may not run the Android operating system as well as others. The brand of the phone also usually adds a few characteristics of its own on top of Android, which has caused minor complications within the operating system. Depending on what is most important to the user, he/she will make the decision of which operating system is the best fit (Hiner).

Ultimately, the user is the deciding factor on whether or not Apple's IOS or Google's Android is the best phone operating system. There is no way to successfully prove that generally one is better than the other. By comparing and contrasting the three main aspects of the operating systems in regards to a basic

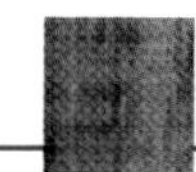

user, each operating system has its pros and cons that collectively make the operating systems different from one another. In no way does this determine that one is better than the other, but that user preference is what makes one operating system better for one user than the other.

Works Cited

Blodget, Henry. "Android Is Destroying Everyone, Especially RIM." *BusinessInsider.* BusinessInsider, 2 Apr. 2011. Web. 18 Oct. 2011.

Doctorow, Cory. "Android and IOS both fail, but Android fails better." *Theguardian.* Theguardian, 9 Aug. 2011. Web. 18 Oct. 2011.

Hinder, Jason. "Android vs. Apple: The 2011 Cage Match." *Zdnet.* Zdnet, 18 Jan. 2011. Web. 18 Oct. 2011.

Wauters, Robin. "There Are Now More Free Apps For Android Than For The iPhone: Distimo." *Techcrunch.* AOL tech, 27 April. 2011. Web. 18 Oct. 2011.

Dachis, Adam. "Top 10 Ways IOS Outdoes Android." *Lifehacker.* Lifehacker, 21 May 2011. Web. 18 Oct. 2011.

Carrie Reilly

Dr. Shannon Gilstrap

English 1101

21 April 2012

America's War on the Bully Breed: Is Your Dog "Man's Best Friend" Or "Man's Best *Killer*?"

One afternoon last week, I found myself babysitting my eight-year-old cousin, Brooklyn, who was visiting from Mississippi. We had spent about an hour at the kitchen table, drawing on some printer paper. "Can you draw me a picture of a dog?" I asked. She nodded, picked up a purple marker, and— in that blasé, eight-year-old manner of hers— scribbled for a minute or two. When she finished, she held up a sketch of a circular dog with floppy ears, a wagging tail, and one of those dopey smiles with the tongue hanging out. I gave her a thumbs-up and said, "Awesome. Can you draw a pit bull, too? I'm writing about dogs for my class, so I'm just curious." Brooklyn hesitated a little, but then grabbed a new sheet of paper and started scribbling again. When she finished this time, however, she held up a drawing of something that looked like a bloody square with pointy teeth and devil horns (which, to my surprise, turned out to be ears). I asked her if she didn't like pit bulls, to which she shrugged and replied, "No, but they're those mean kind of dogs that fight everybody and eat other dogs. That's what my friend told me."

Interestingly enough, Brooklyn's notion that pit bulls are "bloody squares with pointy teeth and devil horns" is a notion that she now shares

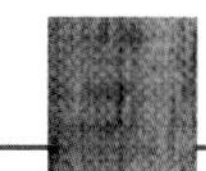

with people of nearly every age and disposition in the United States. In lieu of an estimated total of 31 American dog-related deaths in 2011 alone (22 of which involved pit bulls) and seven already reported in 2012, it is no shock that people are pushing their state and local governments for more stringent dog restrictions and becoming increasingly terrified of anything labeled, or even resembling, a "bully breed" dog (*DogsBite*). The fact that a substantial portion of these dog fatalities involved infants and children continues to keep people, especially parents, precariously on their toes about dog-related dangers in their communities (Atkins). Furthermore, the often-debauched media publicity of dog violence relating to "dangerous dogs" (usually pit bulls) has not helped to soothe America's rising bully breed anxiety. However, the huge waves of praise for stricter, mostly breed-specific, dog regulations have not remained unscathed by opposition. As more people support the addition of "teeth" to dog-related legislation, others vehemently argue that adding "teeth" takes the "heart" out of bully breed dog ownership, while state and local governments find themselves muddled amidst a very emotionally charged conflict.

Before examining the conflict in depth, however, understanding the canines that are instigating the conflict in the first place is important—the bully breeds. Most Americans tend to believe that all "bully breed" dogs are pit bull terriers, but in actuality, multiple (often surprising) breeds also fall into the "bully" category, including Boston terriers, Boxers, and all of the chunky, drooling English bulldogs. People pay most attention to the stronger, "scarier" members of the breed group that are involved in most publicized dog

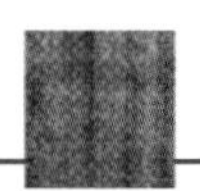

attacks, however, which include—alongside the well-known American pit bull terriers—breeds like bullmastiffs, banter bulldogges, Staffordshire terriers, and sometimes Rottweilers (*Bulldog Breeds*). Many of these breeds have analogous physical traits, such as "block heads" or bulky figures, and consequently most are stereotyped as American pit bulls because of their similar appearances, whether they are actually American pit bulls or not. Furthermore, although yes, many of the bully breeds were *eventually* bred to fight other dogs (particularly American pit bulls, their descendants, and other more "stocky" breeds in the group), the *original* purpose for breeding them was generally for hunting or herding livestock on farms. Thus, apart from their common aggressive nature toward other animals, they were specifically bred to be nimble, athletic, dedicated, resourceful, and most importantly, extremely loyal to their owners and other "pack members" (*Pit Bull Rescue Center*). Many bully breed experts contend that bully breeds are not instinctively hostile toward humans and are actually quite loving, yet warn owners that special precautions *must* be taken to fulfill the energetic needs of most "bully" dogs, in order to avoid any possible aggressive "outbursts" by them (*Bulldog Breeds*). Furthermore, all of the people I interviewed who currently own or have previously owned a bully breed dog shared stories about how—though their dogs would sometimes lash out at other animals—they are generally very compassionate and "silly" dogs when provided with a loving home and a proper, athletic environment.

Examining the generally "tough" traits and appearances of bully breed dogs helps one better understand why such a large amount of existing

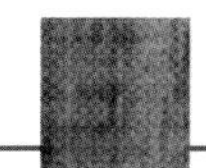

legislation often not only restricts people from owning bully breed dogs, but also restricts these specific breeds from being in certain public or private places, bans them from specific cities and towns altogether, or regulates them in other, various ways. Be it because of the "imposing threat" that seems to loom from these dogs and their violent past, or the enormous pressure exerted upon the government by angry families who have lost loved ones to vicious dogs, state and local governments have been passing and amending dog-related regulations at an increasingly rapid pace.

In Georgia, for instance, more dog statutes exist in and around the community than many people ever realize. A large portion of these regulations is on a micro-local level. Most neighborhood associations enforce general rules like leash laws (any neighborhood dog outside of a house must be leashed or chained at all times) or dog fencing and containment regulations. In addition, many have more specific regulations too, including mandatory dog-muzzling rules for certain breeds (it is easy to guess which ones), forced neighborhood registration and/or extra fees for owning various bully breeds, or even regulations which state that homeowners who own a "dangerous dog"—defined as anything from vicious attack poodles to Rottweilers, depending on the neighborhood—must live a certain distance away from households with children and/or school bus stops, which is the case in the neighborhood where Brooklyn's family lives. Other common regulations at the micro-local level are enforced at many private businesses, such as at veterinary clinics, breed-specific dog-boarding facilities, or company stores such as PetSmart (where I

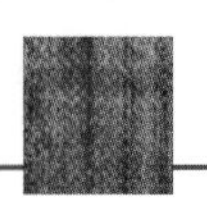

have now worked for over a year) that have policies banning pit bull-type dogs from playing with the others dogs in "Doggy Day Camp," or from even being caged in the same area as other dogs when they are boarded at the in-store "PetsHotel."

Although local and state governments have many dog laws resembling those aforementioned, they usually apply to a much broader spectrum of dogs and dog owners and are often more difficult to enforce because they are either too specific, too ambiguous, or just poorly constructed (Hunt). An example of a citywide dog ordinance includes Dawson, Georgia's law that all pit bulls must *only* be kept in outdoor, concrete "kennels" on the homeowner's property (Williams). Also in Georgia, the city of College Park requires anyone within city limits who owns a "potentially dangerous dog" (a bully breed, Doberman, or a German Shepherd) to pay for "Dangerous Dog" insurance, register their dog with the city, and pay an annual 25-dollar ownership fee (Dixon). As far as statewide dog-related legislature is concerned, examples include two recent and controversial "Dangerous Dog" laws in Georgia, House Bill 685 and its partner, House Bill 717. The two regulate, among other things, allowing homeowners to have only one "vicious dog" at a time, forcing specific "vicious" breeds to be spayed and implanted with microchips and requiring owners of "vicious" dogs to purchase "dangerous dog" licenses that *must* be renewed annually in order to avoid felony charges (HB 685, 179-190).

These dog laws and the hundreds of others like them generate such a large amount of controversy across America. Those who are against the high

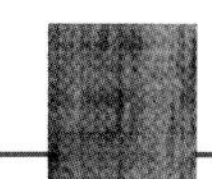

number of dog restrictions are mainly those who believe that the government unfairly targets specific breeds, such as bully breed dogs. Jennifer Cooper, a professional dog trainer at PetSmart who owns two previously abused pit bulls, says that people's general fear of pit bull-type dogs is what gives birth to all of this "unfair" legislation. Bentley, her now eight-month-old pit bull, was found starved and battered, crumpled up in a plastic container on the highway. She whole-heartedly insists that he is "the sweetest shyest dog you'll ever meet [sic]", but because the apartment complex she lives in bans any and all pit bull-type dogs, she has to hide him and her other dog every day, at all costs. "Why should I be in danger of losing my apartment just because my dog *looks* like those 'murderous' dogs you see in the news?" she says, adding, "I mean I feel like a prisoner in my own home [sic]" and that if anyone should get in trouble, it should be the men who abused her two dogs. Others who in similar situations to Jennifer's also argue that the bully breeds are misunderstood, and instead of creating more legislation targeting them, the government should just educate adults and children about them. Some people also argue that most dog-related regulations are outright ridiculous, are unfairly "one-size-fits-all," and are invasive of property (if one considers dogs as property) because they feel as though their respective governments have not considered "the dog owner's side" of the conflict (Hunt).

Thousands of other people praise the rise in dog-related regulations in recent years, however. They contend that if one considers the massive, average number of dog bites and attacks that involve children each year (a number which climbs over one-hundred thousand), enforcing more dog laws is a no brainer (Atkins, fig 3). Especially for people who have lost loved ones to fatal dog attacks, such as the attack by two pit bulls that killed Georgia native Misti Wyno last year, there is a huge need for dog restrictions (*Valdosta Daily Times*). Many feel as though these laws *must* be breed-specific because only specific breeds kill. Indeed, nearly all dog-related deaths in America are predominately caused by three breeds: American pit bull terriers, Rottweilers, and German Shepherds ("U.S. Dog Bite"). As one Valdosta sheriff put it, "Pit bulls were meant to kill and that's what they're going to do. They must be stopped at all costs" (*Valdosta Daily Times*).

The bully breed has stirred up a vicious storm of conflict around the country. Be they seen as sweet dogs like Bentley, or "killer" dogs like the one in Brooklyn's drawing, they are turning out to be something that is very difficult for people and governments alike to handle. As dog-related legislation continues to grow ever more complicated and emotional, it is tough to say what truly is right or wrong.

Works Cited

Atkins, Lauren, Dana Cole, and Marianne Vello. "Animal Bite Surveillance in Georgia, 2004-2006." *Georgia Epidemiology Report*. 23.11 (2007). Web. 17 Apr. 2012.

BullDog Breeds. PetGuide Network. 2002. Web. 17 Apr. 2012.

Cooper, Jennifer. Personal interview. 15 Apr. 2012.

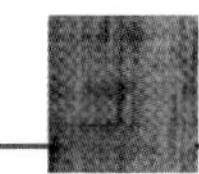

Dixon, Duffie. "New Law Targets 'Potentially Dangerous' Dogs." *11alive News* [College Park, GA] 06 Jun 2011. Web. 17 Apr. 2012.

Georgia. State House of Representatives. Judiciary Non-Civil Committee. *HB 685 - Dogs; Dangerous and Vicious; Extensively Revise Provisions*. Georgia General Assembly, 29 Mar. 2012. Web. 3 Apr. 2012.

Georgia. State House of Representatives. Judiciary Non-Civil Committee. *HB 717 Dogs; Criminal Penalties for Certain Owners failing to Secure; Provide.* Georgia General Assembly, 7 Mar. 2012. Web. 3 Apr. 2012.

Hunt, April. "Dog Law Debate Persists: Measure Might Not Clear Up Confusion in State Definitions." *Atlanta Journal Constitution* 15 Feb. 2012: B3. Print.

"Pit Bull Kills Valdosta Woman." *Valdosta Daily Times* 09 Dec 2011. Web. 17 Apr. 2012.

Pit Bull Rescue Central. Pit Bull Rescue Central Incorporated. 2010. Web. 17 Apr. 2012.

"U.S. Dog Bite Fatalities January 2006 to December 2008 ." *DogsBite: Some Dogs Don't Let Go*. DogsBite, 20 Apr 2009. Web. 17 Apr 2012.

Williams, Sharinda. "Pit Bull Ordinance Passed in Dawson." *WALB News* [Albany, GA] 13 Jan 2012. Web. 17 Apr. 2012.

LITERARY ANALYSIS ESSAYS

Cristian Delgado

Dr. Turner

ENGL 1102

19 March 2012

Within The Granite

A global conflict such as the Vietnam War does not come and go without placing a heavy toll on the people who experience it. Whether the losses are political, monetary, or psychological, they do a great deal of damage to the affected population. For veterans in particular, the emotional price paid is an enduring one, often taking a lifetime to overcome. "Facing It" presents such a case, describing the experience of a Vietnam War veteran as he visits the memorial dedicated to the international struggle. Author Yusef Komunyakaa pays little effort to introduce characters and instead explores inside the mind of the nameless narrator from the start of the poem. Lack of a name, however, does not render the veteran indescribable, as the emotions stirring inside the weathered soldier prove to be dreadful ones. Kumonyakaa uses somber imagery to reveal the intense grimness felt by a war veteran upon visitation of the Vietnam Veterans Memorial.

Themes of darkness make their first appearance in "Facing It" as early as the first couple of lines. The color black used to describe the granite gives the opening of the poem an eerie sense of despair (line 2). Komunyakaa depicts the narrator with the matching color, which stresses both a bond

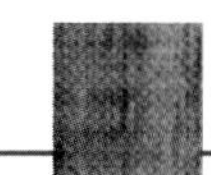

between the man and the wall, as well as a consistency in moods. Throughout the progression of the poem, the author further strengthens the relationship between the veteran and the memorial. The sentence, "I turn this way--the stone lets me go," portrays the narrator's struggle to separate from the wall (line 8). In contrast, other characters in the poem have the free will to depart from the landmark, as hinted in lines 19 through 21: "Names shimmer on a woman's blouse / but when she walks away / the names stay on the wall." In the line "I am stone" (line 5), the veteran even claims he is a fragment of the wall.

The narrator's tie with the wall roots further than a simple obsession for its sleek design and architecture. The black granite signifies death and sorrow, more specifically that which transpired during the Vietnam War. The Veteran's partaking in the war renders him a permanent piece of the memorial, along with the painful memories from the conflict it represents. 58,022 names make a presence on the wall, heightening the already overwhelming power of the memorial. The wall's strength engulfs the veteran's free will and leaves him "depending on the light / to make a difference," the difference being freedom from the anguish and emotional scars the war imprinted on him (lines 12-13). All of these points elevate the conjoined nature of the protagonist with the wall and ultimately illustrate the feeling of suffocation most likely felt by him during the entire poem.

"Facing it" also consists of imagery that resembles flashbacks and other characteristics of post-traumatic stress disorder (PTSD). PTSD notoriously causes high levels of anxiety and depression. The line "I said I wouldn't damnit: No tears" proves that the speaker has difficulty restraining his sorrow in the presence of the memorial (line 3). Line 6 of the poem reveals that the marble wall functions poorly as a mirror for the protagonist, creating a "clouded reflection." The distorted image elevates the sense of uneasiness and also doubles as a bridge to the veteran's thought cloud. Like cartoons found in the Sunday paper, the thought cloud of the veteran uncovers his memories, in this case, his grim remembrances of the battlegrounds of Vietnam. The phrase "A bird of prey, the profile of night / slanted against morning" symbolizes the enemy air force the veteran encountered during his military service (lines 7-8). The "Night / slanted against morning" symbolizes the fine line separating life and death in the battlefield and the enemy plane's ability to instigate harm on those wearing the wrong uniform. The poem mentions another combat reference as the protagonist scans through the names on the black wall. He partially believes he will find his own in "letters like smoke" (line16). Considering smoke's swift nature to disappear quickly and its affiliation with firearms, the smoke mentioned in the poem uncovers how lucky the veteran feels to be alive, and how easily and quickly an enemy combatant from the war could have created a spot for him on the wall of death. As the veteran continues to search the wall, his fingers come across the name Andrew Johnson. The name holds no notoriety and most likely belonged to a common soldier. Whether the man was a dear friend, or simply an acquaintance of the protagonist, remains a question unanswered throughout the poem; however, line 18's depiction of

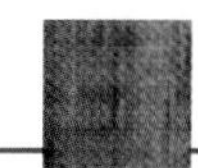

"the booby trap's white flash" confirms the veteran's presence in the site where Andrew Johnson was killed. The enemy plane returns to haunt the mind of the veteran in lines 22 through 24, this time making a less ambiguous appearance. The image eases into the poem symbolized by a bird once again, but the next line subsequently ends any guessing with, "The sky. A plane in the sky." The Veteran clearly has a strong connection with fighter planes; perhaps he was part of the air force or fell victim to various enemy air strikes. "Wings cutting across my stare" clues a possible intimidation factor retained by the veteran, as the plane leaves him motionless and dazed.

The concluding lines of the poem present the dichotomy of a person extremely affected by the war against a person not very affected at all. The phrase "A white vet's image floats / closer to me" presents the case of one who suffered directly from the war (lines 25-26). The color white used to describe the image does not necessarily describe the person's race; instead, the paleness of the figure amplifies the physical and emotional fatigue that the war and its memories placed on him and countless other sufferers. The stranger's loss of an arm further emphasizes the physical cost that the stone, which symbolizes the war, took away from individuals: "He's lost his right arm / inside the stone" (lines 28-29). Line 27 claims that the protagonist is a window that the ghostly figure is looking through. The personal relationship between the speaker of the poem and the white vet could perhaps be nonexistent, but their shared torment allows them to understand each other clearly, like a window. The image projected on the other side of the window most likely shows a past shared by two veterans in the ruthless warzones of Vietnam. The narrator also eyes another weeper around him. This time, the company is a woman "trying to erase names" (line 30). The woman first appears to be part of the narrator's gloomy world that the black marble envelops. In reality, however, the woman visits the memorial only as a tourist, feeling little emotion as she brushes her son's hair. The woman represents the majority of people who have fully coped with the losses of the war. Through the image of this woman, the narrator escapes the trancelike state of grief he fell victim to during the entirety of the poem, allowing him to interpret the woman's brushing of the boy's hair as simply that.

Komunyakaa shines light on the powerful emotions veteran's feel when they internally revisit a conflict such as the Vietnam War. The Vietnam veteran's memorial takes on a life of its own as it carries the veteran through a journey into the past. Komunyakaa exposes the dramatic emotions that, like the veteran featured in the poem, all veterans experience when remembering the role they played in history. The imagery in "Facing It" asserts the discomfort felt by the veteran in this situation and sends a message of enlightenment to all veterans that they are not alone.

Works Cited

Komunyakaa, Yusef. "Facing It." *Internet Archive.* University of North Carolina Press. 2006. Web. 12 March 2012.

 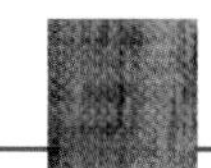

Faith Evans

Dr. Patricia Worrall

ENGL 1102

22 March 2012

A Dynamic Relationship Revealed

In any exceptional story, a relationship is examined. These relationships could encompass a multitude of possibilities—lovers, friends, or as seen with Sherlock Holmes and John Watson, a teacher-student relationship. Arthur Conan Doyle explores this relationship through his novels *The Hound of Baskervilles* and *A Study in Scarlet* in a variety of facets. The relationship between Sherlock Holmes and Dr. John Watson tends to be a teacher-student relationship; Holmes acts as the teacher who interacts with student, Watson, with lessons, reprimands, and eventually, trust.

In Doyle's *A Study in Scarlet*, the introduction of Holmes and Watson presents a change in both of their lives. Watson, just returning from Afghanistan, is in desperate need of a roommate and needs to "take up quarters in some less pretentious and less expensive domicile" (18). This catalyst leads Watson to eventually find Holmes by way of Stamford who was "a dresser under [Watson] at Bart's" (18). Holmes does not waste time in starting his lessons. They present themselves as soon as Watson is introduced to Holmes by Stamford who reminds Watson that he is not to be held responsible for the outcome of the meeting. Just the fact that Stamford feels the need to pre-warn Watson displays that not everyone has the ability to get along with Holmes'

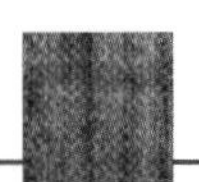

unique behavior. With the obligatory introductions out of the way, Holmes deduces within seconds that Watson has been in Afghanistan by a "train of thoughts that ran so swiftly through [Holmes'] mind, that [he] arrived at the conclusion without being conscious of intermediate steps" (29). Holmes later breaks down how he arrived at that conclusion to a bewildered Watson who realizes for the first time the entirety of what he has to learn. In reality, it would be easy to "compare Sherlock Holmes' inner space to an encyclopedia, not only for its variety and vastness of knowledge, but also for the impossibility of having them all under control to the same degree" (Caprettini 328). His extensive thought process quickly goes past the intellectual capability of the reader and Watson. The fact that Holmes takes the time to show Watson this thought process illustrates the teacher role that Holmes begins to assume.

In Doyle's novel *The Hound of Baskervilles*, Holmes and Watson's relationship continues to blossom as Watson puts his skills to the test. As the story begins, Watson's futile attempt to duplicate Holmes' deductive reasoning skills portrays how he tries to learn certain traits at his friend's knee. As a test, Holmes questions Watson about who could have left a walking stick in his office based on "the thick iron ferrule" and its "dignifying, solid, and reassured" state (9-10). When Sherlock Holmes asks Watson to present his theories on the walking stick, Watson delves into various ideas. Holmes then responds that these ideas are "perfectly sound" and that Watson has "habitually underrated [his] abilities" (10). This leads to Watson to feel "proud . . . to think [he] mastered his system as to apply it in a way which earned his approval" until

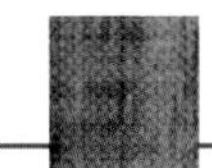

Holmes shoots his concepts down (10). Watson's theories are all disbanded by Holmes as he remarks that "in noting [Watson's] fallacies, [he] was occasionally guided towards the truth" (10). Watson desperately tries to live up to the extremely high standards that Holmes has and prematurely assumes himself to be accurate. In W.H. Auden's poem "Detective Story," he states, that a "feud between the local common sense and intuition" exists, and Watson does not seem to have the knack of knowing what is going on like Holmes does (17-18). In this instance, Watson remains somewhat Holmes' inferior, an amateur in comparison.

In Doyle's novel *The Hound of Baskervilles*, Holmes shows Watson how he lets his guard down and trusts his judgment. When discussing who will accompany Sir Henry and Dr. Mortimer back to Baskerville Hall, Holmes politely declines the invitation and recommends that they take Watson. He assures them that "there is no man who is better worth having at your side when you are in a tight place" (48). In fact, "Holmes . . . faithful friend is one of Conan Doyle' masterly ways of fostering identification with Watson" since he is a trusted colleague to Holmes who is offered up in his place in this situation (Fowler 358). Holmes' confidence in Watson is not extended toward many people, and Watson is a special case to Holmes. Another case when Holmes lets his guard down is when following a lead with a cab driver. Holmes normally has a witty answer for any surprise thrown his way. However, when the cab driver, John Clayton, who drove the mystery spy trailing Sir Henry, says that the spy said his name was Sherlock Holmes, Watson had never "seen [his] friend more completely taken aback" (50). Holmes' ability to show Watson how he was really feeling displays how he trusts Watson. The façade that Holmes normally seems to emulate fades away when with Watson.

As relationships progress, they change. New facets are formed, and original perceptions are altered. Relationships are a vital part in any story, and Holmes and Watson are no exception. Their interactive, learning friendship serves as a basis for the stories in which they appear. A teacher-student relationship is always there to remind the reader of the professional and impressive Holmes who is always aided by the faithful John Watson.

Works Cited

Auden, W.H. "Detective Story." *The Longman Anthology of Detective Fiction.* Ed. Deana Mansfield-Kelley and Lois A. Marchino. New York: Pearson Education, Inc., 2005. Preface. Print.

Caprettini, Gian Paolo. "Sherlock Holmes: Ethics, Logic, and the Mask." *Sherlock Holmes: The Major Stories with Contemporary Critical Essays.* Ed. John A. Hodgson. Boston: Bedford/St. Martin, 1994. 328-334. Print.

Doyle, Arthur Conan. *The Hound of the Baskervilles.* Clayton, Delaware: Prestwick House, 2006. Print.

---. From *A Study in Scarlet. Sherlock Holmes: The Major Stories with Contemporary Critical Essays.* Ed. John A. Hodgson. Boston: Bedford/ St. Martin's, 1994. 17-31. Print.

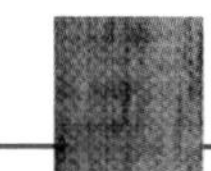

Fowler, Alastair. "Sherlock Holmes and the Adventure of the Dancing Men and Women." *Sherlock Holmes: The Major Stories with Contemporary Critical Essays.* Ed. John A. Hodgson. Boston: Bedford / St. Martin's, 1994. 353-367. Print.

CHAPTER SEVEN

Rhetoric

WHAT IS RHETORIC?

The word ***rhetoric*** is a good example of a word whose meaning has changed dramatically over time. You have probably heard someone say of a politician's speech, "Oh, that's just rhetoric," meaning that the politician's words are just empty verbiage or hot air. The politician was attempting to sound impressive while saying nothing that had real meaning or perhaps making promises he or she had no intention of keeping—essentially engaging in verbal deception. However, in the field of composition and writing studies, rhetoric has a much different meaning. Though definitions vary from one practitioner to another, rhetoric generally means the study and use of persuasion, a meaning that traces its roots back to the original use of the term by ancient Greeks and Romans.

During the golden age of Greece and Rome, from 500 BCE to 100 CE, art, architecture, and literature thrived. Rhetoric, in the form of oratory, was essential to both societies, as Greeks and Romans employed rhetoric to resolve disputes in the law courts and to promote political action. Philosophers such as Socrates, Plato and Aristotle, and the Roman rhetoricians Quintilian and Cicero were aware of the possible abuses of rhetoric, but to them, rhetoric was an integral part of public life, as well as the primary means of educating young people in their future roles as citizens. Philosophers in ancient Greece and Rome wrote books about rhetoric which became the basis of the teaching of writing and other essential subjects that have influenced the educational process ever since.

Aristotle defined rhetoric as "the faculty of discovering, in a given instance, the available means of persuasion," which we might paraphrase as the power to see the means of persuasion available in any given situation. Each part of this definition is important. Rhetoric is power; for the person who is able to speak eloquently, choosing the most suitable arguments about a topic for a specific audience in a particular situation, is the person most likely to persuade. In both Greece and Rome, the primary use of rhetoric was oratory, persuasion through public speaking. However, texts of many famous speeches were recorded and studied as models by students, and prominent rhetoricians wrote treatises and handbooks for teaching rhetoric. To Greeks and Romans, a person who could use rhetoric effectively was a person of influence and power because he could persuade his audience to action. The effective orator could win court cases; the effective

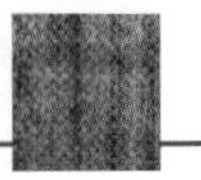

orator could influence the passage or failure of laws; the effective orator could send a nation to war or negotiate peace.

Skill with rhetoric has conveyed power through the ages, though in our contemporary world, rhetoric is often displayed in written text such as a book, newspaper or magazine article, or scientific report, rather than as a speech. Persuasive communication can also be expressed visually, as an illustration that accompanies a text or a cartoon that conveys its own message. Indeed, in our high visual society with television, movies, video games, and the Internet, images can often persuade more powerfully than words alone.

Using rhetoric effectively means being able to interpret the rhetoric we are presented with in our everyday lives. Knowledge of persuasive communication or rhetoric empowers us to present our views and persuade others to modify their ideas. Through changes in ideas, rhetoric leads to action. Through changes in actions, rhetoric affects society.

Selected Definitions of Rhetoric

Aristotle, 350 BCE—Rhetoric is "the faculty of discovering, in a given instance the available means of persuasion."

Cicero, 90 CE—Rhetoric is "speech designed to persuade." Also, "eloquence based on the rules of art."

Quintilian, 95 CE —Rhetoric is "the science of speaking well."

Augustine of Hippo, ca. 426 CE —Rhetoric is "the art of persuading people to accept something, whether it is true or false."

Anonymous, ca. 1490–1495—Rhetoric is "the science which refreshes the hungry, renders the mute articulate, makes the blind see, and teaches one to avoid every lingual ineptitude."

Heinrich Cornelius Agrippa, 1531—"To confess the truth, it is generally granted that the entire discipline of rhetoric from start to finish is nothing other than an art of flattery, adulation, and, as some say more audaciously, lying, in that, if it cannot persuade others through the truth of the case, it does so by means of deceitful speech."

Hoyt Hudson, 1923—"In this sense, plainly, the man who speaks most persuasively uses the most, or certainly the best, rhetoric; and the man whom we censure for inflation of style and strained effects is suffering not from too much rhetoric, but from a lack of it."

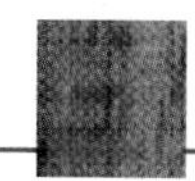

Richards, 1936—"Rhetoric, I shall urge, should be a study of misunderstanding and its remedies."

Sister Miriam Joseph, 1937—Rhetoric is "the art of communicating thought from one mind to another, the adaptation of language to circumstance."

Kenneth Burke, 1950—"[T]he basic function of rhetoric [is] the use of words by human agents to form attitudes or to induce actions in other human agents."

Gerard A. Hauser, 2002—"Rhetoric, as an area of study, is concerned with how humans use symbols, especially language, to reach agreement that permits coordinated effort of some sort."

THE ELEMENTS OF RHETORIC

From the time of the ancient Greeks and Romans to our present day, someone has always attempted to alter the lives of others through words; witness the eloquent phrases in the Declaration of Independence, Lincoln's Gettysburg Address, Martin Luther King's "I Have a Dream" speech, John F. Kennedy's inaugural address, or even the demagoguery of Adolph Hitler and Saddam Hussein. The major power of their words is the power of rhetoric, the art or discipline of writing effectively and persuasively, used to inform or motivate an audience. While Aristotle defined rhetoric as discovering the best means of persuasion in any given situation, this definition might include not only the argumentative but the expository or informative mode of discourse as well. In fact, rhetoric operates in almost every form of writing we find. For this reason, rhetoric is still an important concern of each of us today, primarily because none of us can escape it—not the lawyer, the teacher, the politician, the computer analyst, or the student. We all indulge in and are exposed to rhetoric daily. Therefore, the goal of the class in which you are enrolled and the goal of this text are to raise your awareness of the rhetorical components all around you so you might be more effective in expressing your own ideas as well as more alert to others' use and misuse of rhetoric. This text, through its instructions and exercises, can serve as a guide for you in your move toward communicating your thoughts and feelings through words.

Your tasks as a writer can range from giving the directions for planting a garden to persuading an audience that capital punishment should or should not be abolished. Whether you choose to use the expository or persuasive method, you should understand and be able to use certain rhetorical elements in order to make your ideas more convincing or persuasive. These elements include the writer's purpose, audience, voice, and the situation. While all four elements play a role in every composition, they do not always have equal roles. For example, audience would obviously assume a greater place in process analysis and persuasive essays than in a comparison and contrast essay, and voice might play a minimal role in definition and a major role in narration and description. Nevertheless, each principle must be present for you to achieve

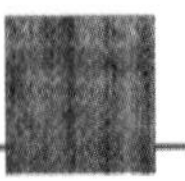

your goal of communicating your ideas. However varying their presence in an essay, all four elements must be included.

FIGURE 1-A

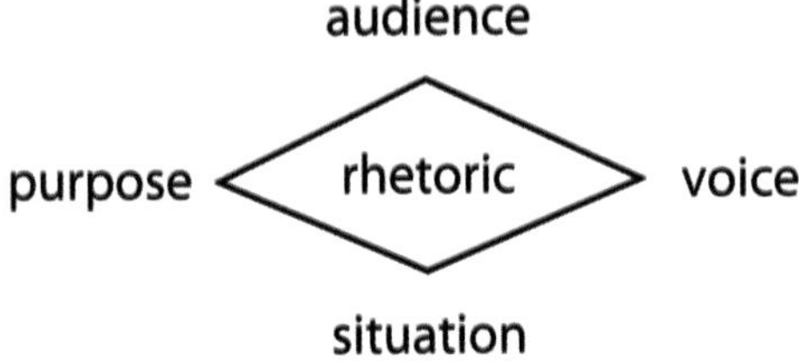

Purpose

Writing always has a purpose. Every writer must have a reason for writing, and that reason, or purpose, determines which of the other three elements of rhetoric will be emphasized. The general purpose of various writing methods is to know what we think and how best to communicate those thoughts. Therefore, we must always determine what particular message we want to convey and what method would likely be most effective. Do we wish simply to report or inform, to explain, or to persuade? During your college career and afterwards, you might be required to report on a given project or to inform your audience as to the progress of a particular project. In addition, you might be expected to explain to a coworker the step-by-step procedure for seeking advancement in the company, or you may wish to persuade your supervisor that your particular ideas warrant attention over the proposals of a co-worker. Whichever rhetorical mode you select to write your essay, it must have a purpose, and the purpose must be clearly evident to the reader.

The rhetorical purpose is sometimes determined by the specific assignment. If a topic is assigned, your task of deciding on a purpose may already have been done for you. However, often you will have to determine the purpose yourself. If it cannot be discovered immediately, the purpose can emerge from your preliminary brainstorming of the assigned general topic and from the early stages of organizing your random thoughts. Until a purpose is clearly in your mind, though, it is best not to begin writing the essay, else you will likely waste time and effort. Time spent in determining your purpose is far better used than time spent in wandering from point to point without direction. Knowing your purpose helps you sharpen your focus. Make certain, too, that your goals are reasonable and that you can manage what you tell your audience you will accomplish in your statement of purpose, or your thesis. Then you can decide which method of presentation is the most efficient and can best accomplish your purpose.

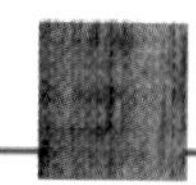

Audience

Your audience is your intended listener or reader. Every word we utter is directed toward something or someone, even if we are only talking to ourselves. When we speak to someone, we have the advantage of immediate feedback, of noting the reaction, either verbal or nonverbal, and so we are able to determine whether or not he understands us. When speaking, therefore, we can adjust our voice, gestures, or language to accommodate our listener, thus increasing our chances of being understood. In writing, however, the advantages of instant feedback and subsequent adjustments are not available to us. Therefore we must be more aware of who our audience is and what he or she knows. If we want to achieve an intended effect (purpose), we must be able to make certain assumptions about our audience. In adapting your ideas to meet your particular audience, you must bear in mind the interests and values of those you want to reach. Estimate what their backgrounds are, their education, age, sex, political and religious inclinations, and experiences. What can they expect to gain by reading your ideas? These concerns help you establish which approach to use in presenting your ideas and what to stress or to omit in your essay. Identifying the audience will assist you in anticipating questions and in being prepared to address those questions in your essays. This procedure is not unlike a job applicant's research into a company with whom he intends to interview.

Students are correct in assuming that their audience is their instructor. But most writing instructors will want you to specify a variety of audiences, real or imagined, in order to sharpen your rhetorical skills to meet the demands of different situations. This task is not always easy. Addressing a variety of audiences in a variety of essays places restraints on students, but these situations more than likely reflect the situations you may encounter in life. You will always be confronted with different audiences, different situations, and different subjects. It is best, then, to keep in mind that you will likely have more than one audience for your essay—your instructor and some other designated audience. This dual audience requires you to adapt to each one's needs and expectations, just as a newspaper reporter must write a news item with his editor as well as the general reading public in mind. Knowing your audience and writing to them does not mean you have to sacrifice your own beliefs in order to accommodate those of your audience. You must not feel you have to choose between your integrity and reader appeal. If you are skillful in the use of rhetoric, you can maintain an honest and authentic voice and at the same time still be a successful strategist.

Voice

Having defined your audience, you must now determine the role that you want to assume with your audience. This stance, or voice, that you must assume is much like the different masks you prepare daily. You present yourself one way when attending class, and you present yourself quite differently when you are on a date or visiting your in-laws. While these masks are different, your identity is still the same. Each role is sincere, but each allows you the flexibility to select

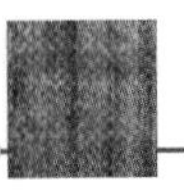

the appropriate demeanor and words for a specific occasion and audience. This role-playing is similar to the role you assume in presenting your ideas in your essay to a given audience. Consider how you would express yourself in a personal letter to a friend as compared to how you would express yourself in a letter of application for scholarship funds. Authenticity and sincerity are imperative. They guide the voice in its attempt to demonstrate you are serious about your subject and respectful of your audience. Be genuine in whatever voice you assume. You can be sympathetic, neutral, angry, or humorous, but most of all be yourself. What you say and how you say it, therefore, are determined by your purpose, audience, and subject matter.

Situation

The fourth element of the rhetorical process is the situation. It is the most important of all four elements because without it you would have no basis for an essay. The remainder of this text is concerned with the steps in putting together your ideas and deciding on the appropriate method of presenting those ideas to a designated audience in a given situation. Which arrangement to use in presenting your essay depends upon the situation, your audience, your voice or the stance you take in offering your ideas, and your purpose. The rules for the art and craft of rhetoric are not written in stone, nor are they "writ in water." A great deal of rhetorical flexibility in regard to these rules is available to writers of compositions, but sometimes the refusal to concern yourself with these rules can have disastrous consequences. In the classroom the results can be an inferior grade, while in the marketplace they can mean unemployment.

The rules that are discussed in the following pages represent the methods of writing that are time-proven that have served people in almost every endeavor—mostly, but not always, for good purposes. We can only hope that you use your rhetorical skills for the general good, never to be abused or misused.

So now we arrive at our starting place; through language and the expression of ideas we begin to understand our world and ourselves.

ARGUING RHETORICALLY

Rhetorical Arguments Survive the Test of Time

The Declaration of Independence is not only an historical document; its assertions serve as a benchmark for the status of freedom in the United States and in countries around the world. For example, Dr. Martin Luther King, Jr. stood in front of a crowd of thousands at the Lincoln memorial in 1963 to present his "I Have a Dream" speech, which refers specifically to the Declaration of Independence. He said,

> When the architects of our republic wrote the magnificent words of the Constitution and the Declaration of Independence, they were signing a promissory note to which

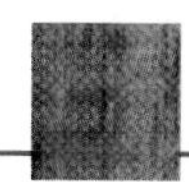

> every American was to fall heir. This note was a promise that all men, yes, black men as well as white men, would be guaranteed the "unalienable Rights" of "Life, Liberty and the pursuit of Happiness." It is obvious today that America has defaulted on this promissory note, insofar as her citizens of color are concerned. Instead of honoring this sacred obligation, America has given the Negro people a bad check, a check which has come back marked "insufficient funds."

According to Dr. King, America had not lived up to the promise made in the Declaration of Independence that all men were created equal and entitled to the "unalienable Rights" of "Life, Liberty and the pursuit of Happiness." But King was not content with blame and accusations; he had a dream that America would someday make good on that "bad check" and that Negro people would be equal to whites.

Then, in November 2008, President-elect Barack Obama stood in front of another crowd of thousands as he gave the "Victory Speech," and reminded America that the "preacher from Atlanta" [King] had said, "We will overcome [prejudice]." Just by his physical presence as an African-American president-elect, Obama evoked the heritage both of King's speech and of the Declaration of Independence. Obama said, "If there is anyone out there who still doubts that America is a place where all things are possible; who still wonders if the dream of our founders is alive in our time; who still questions the power of our democracy, tonight is your answer."

The Declaration of Independence, as author Stephen E. Lucas shows in the following document, brilliantly served its purpose of declaring the independence of the thirteen American colonies. Moreover, as the examples from the speeches by President-elect Obama and Dr. King attest, the Declaration has stood the test of time and is still relevant in asserting the occasion and the necessity for the nation's freedom and equality.

The Rhetorical Triangle

The act of speaking or writing encompasses three elements: the writer (or **speaker**), the purpose (or **subject**), and the **audience.** In the case of the Declaration of Independence, Thomas Jefferson wrote the basic draft, though the document was signed by all the members of the Continental Congress. The purpose of the document was to declare independence and, as Stephen E. Lucas points out, to show such a declaration was "necessary" or inevitable, given the offenses of the British government. Otherwise, the Americans were merely rebels in a civil war. The document had several immediate audiences: the colonists themselves who may or may not have supported such a declaration, the British government, and foreign powers such as France whom the Continental Congress hoped to entice into entering the war. Without foreign support, the war was likely to fail. Over time, however, the Declaration has acquired other audiences, such as generations of Americans and people around the world who hold the United States accountable for the promises it made when it declared that "all men are created equal, that they are endowed

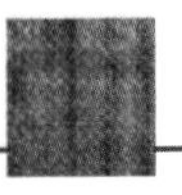

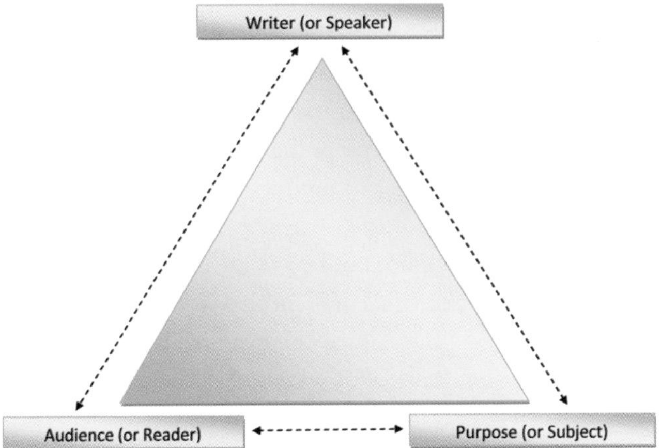

by their Creator with certain unalienable Rights, that among these are Life, Liberty and the pursuit of Happiness." Like the occasion for the writing of the Declaration of Independence, every speaking or writing situation has the same three elements, though some situations may be more urgent or persuasive than others. A good way to visualize the three interacting rhetorical elements is as a triangle.

The writer's or speaker's charge is to project an ethos or image of credibility and reliability that is persuasive to the audience. An effective writer is always aware of the audience's characteristics, including demographics, level of knowledge about the subject, prejudices, values, and emotions. The writer may inform the reader of information or express thoughts about a topic, but all rhetorical purposes are, in some way, persuasive. For example, Stephen E. Lucas points out that the introduction of the Declaration of Independence

> identifies the purpose of the Declaration as simply to "declare"—to announce publicly in explicit terms—the "causes" impelling America to leave the British empire. This gives the Declaration, at the outset, an aura of philosophical (in the eighteenth-century sense of the term) objectivity that it will seek to maintain throughout. Rather than presenting one side in a public controversy on which good and decent people could differ, the Declaration purports to do no more than a natural philosopher would do in reporting the causes of any physical event. The issue, it implies, is not one of interpretation but of observation.

So, the Continental Congress may not have voiced their intent to argue independence but to declare it, so that they would not be inviting argument in return. There, indeed, may have been no need to persuade the British of their intent, as fighting had already begun; but no matter what they stated, the signers of the Declaration desperately needed to persuade both American colo-

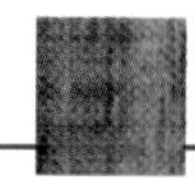

nists and the French (potential allies) of the seriousness and validity of American independence. By signing their names to the document, members of the Continental Congress thus declared themselves traitors to the British. There was no turning back, for them, or for anyone who supported the cause of American independence.

Aristotle's Persuasive Appeals

Some theorists associate the rhetorical triangle directly with Aristotle's **appeals** (or proofs): *ethos, pathos,* and *logos*. ***Ethos*** refers to the writer's (or speaker's) credibility, ***pathos*** to emotion used to sway the audience; and, finally, purpose (or subject) to ***logos***, for an effective argument will include evidence and other supporting details to back up the author's claims.

Aristotle wrote:

> Of those proofs that are furnished through the speech there are three kinds. Some reside in the character (*ethos*) of the speaker, some in a certain disposition (*pathos*) of the audience and some in the speech itself, through its demonstrating or seeming to demonstrate (*logos*).

Contemporary theorist Wayne C. Booth said something similar:

> The common ingredient that I find in all writing that I admire—excluding for now novels, plays, and poems—is something that I shall reluctantly call the rhetorical stance, a stance which depends upon discovering and maintaining in any writing situation a proper balance among the three elements that are at work in any communicative effort; the available arguments about the subject itself (*logos*), the interests and peculiarities of the audience (*pathos*), and the voice, the implied character of the speaker (*ethos*).

Arguments from *Logos*

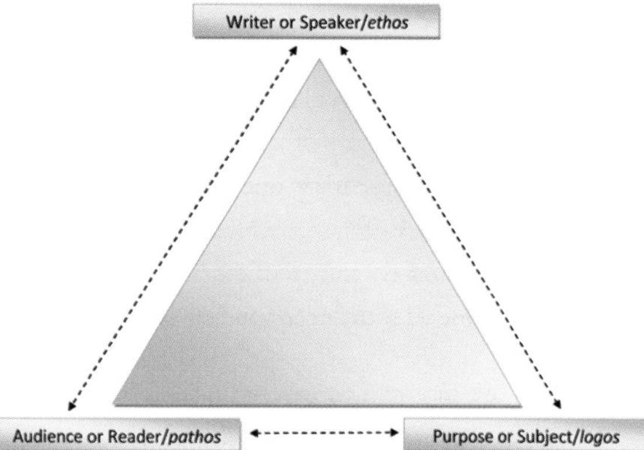

Logos, or reason, was Aristotle's favorite of the three persuasive appeals, and he bemoaned the fact that humans could not be persuaded through reason alone—indeed that they sometimes chose emotion over reason. Aristotle also used the term *logos* to mean rational discourse. To appeal to *logos* means to organize an argument with a clear claim or thesis, supported by logical reasons that are presented in a well-organized manner that is internally consistent. It can also mean the use of facts and statistics

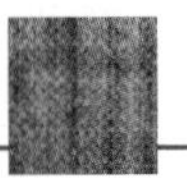

as evidence. However, logos without elements of pathos and ethos can be dry, hard to understand, and boring.

Deductive Reasoning

Aristotle was the first person in Western culture to write systematically about logic, and he is credited with developing and promoting syllogistic or **deductive reasoning** in which statements are combined to draw a **conclusion**. He wrote, "A statement is persuasive and credible either because it is directly self-evident or because it appears to be proved from other statements that are so." This logical structure is called a **syllogism**, in which premises lead to a conclusion. The following is perhaps the most famous syllogism:

Major premise:	All humans are mortal.
Minor premise:	Socrates is human.
Conclusion:	Socrates is mortal.

The **major premise** is a general statement accepted by everyone which makes an observation about all people. The second statement of the syllogism is the **minor premise,** which makes a statement about a particular case within the class of all people. Comparison of the two premises, the general class of "all humans" and the particular case of "Socrates" within the class of "all humans" leads to the conclusion that Socrates also fits in the class "mortal," and thus his death is unavoidable. Thus, the logic moves from the general to the particular.

Similarly, if you try the pumpkin bread at one Starbucks and like it, you infer that you will like the pumpkin bread at another Starbucks. The argument would look like this:

Major premise:	Food products at Starbucks are standardized from one Starbucks to another.
Minor premise:	You like the pumpkin bread at one Starbucks.
Conclusion:	You will like the pumpkin bread at another Starbucks.

However, if your major premise is wrong, and the owner of one Starbucks substitutes an inferior stock of pumpkin bread, then your conclusion is wrong. Deductive reasoning is dependent upon the validity of each premise; otherwise the syllogism does not hold true. If the major premise that food products are standardized at all Starbucks franchises does not hold true, then the argument is not valid. A good deductive argument is known as a valid argument and is such that if all its premises are true, then its conclusion must be true. Indeed, for a deductive argument to be valid, it must be absolutely impossible for both its premises to be true and its conclusion to be false.

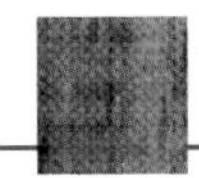

Inductive Reasoning

Aristotle identified another way to move logically between premises, which he called "the progress from particulars to universals." Later logicians labeled this type of logic as **inductive reasoning**. Inductive arguments are based on probability. Even if an inductive argument's premises are true, that doesn't establish with 100% certainty that their conclusions are true. Even the best inductive argument falls short of deductive validity.

These are examples of inductive reasoning:

Particular statement:	Milk does not spoil as quickly if kept cold.
General statement:	All perishable foods do not spoil as quickly if kept cold.
Particular statement:	Microwaves cook popcorn more quickly than does conventional heat.
General statement:	All foods cook more quickly in a microwave.

For the first example, inductive reasoning works well because cold tends to prolong the useable life of most perishable foods. The second example is more problematic. While it is true that popcorn cooks more quickly in a microwave oven, the peculiarities of microwave interaction with food molecules does not produce a uniform effect on all foodstuffs. Rice, for example, does not cook much, if any, faster, than cooking on a stovetop. Also, whole eggs may explode if cooked in their shells.

A good inductive argument is known as a strong (or cogent) inductive argument. It is such that if the premises are true, the conclusion is likely to be true.

Logical Fallacies

Generally speaking, a **logical fallacy** is an error in reasoning, as opposed to a factual error, which is simply being wrong about the facts. A deductive fallacy (sometimes called a formal fallacy) is a deductive argument that has premises that are all true, but they lead to a false conclusion, making it an invalid argument. An inductive fallacy (sometimes called an informal fallacy) appears to be an inductive argument, but the premises do not provide enough support for the conclusion to be probable. Some logical fallacies are more common than others, and, thus, have been labeled and defined. Following are a few of the most well known types:

Hasty Generalization. An argument that draws a conclusion based on insufficient or inappropriate samplings: "My Oldsmobile is a real lemon; therefore, General Motors manufactures inferior automobiles." "Students at the University of Houston are rude. Last night the guys in the room

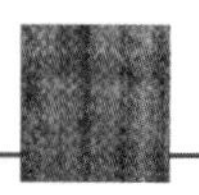

next to mine played their stereo at full blast until two in the morning, and as I was on my way to class this morning a bicyclist almost ran me down."

Red Herring. In hunting, a strongly scented object drawn across a trail will distract hounds and cause them to follow the new scent. In argument, a red herring is a different issue raised to lead attention away from the issue being debated or argued. Usually the new issue arouses an emotional response that creates a digression. "According to the newspapers, sexually transmitted diseases are climbing at an alarming rate among children in their teens. This raises a serious question about the wisdom of teaching sex education in middle school."

Begging the Question. An argument based on an assumption that has yet to be proven: "The immoral experimentation on animals for research must be abolished;" "My narrow-minded English instructor seems to have forgotten how difficult it is to be a student."

Either/or Reasoning. An argument that suggests that only two alternatives exist when more than two actually exist. "If you quit college, you will never succeed in anything you do." "We can recognize that athletes who participate in major sports must be given special consideration at Texas A&M, or we can let the university sink into athletic oblivion."

Faulty Analogy. An argument based on a comparison of two things that share few or no common and relevant features. An analogy should be carefully examined to be sure that the things being compared are alike in ways essential to the conclusion being drawn. The fact that they are alike in some ways is not enough. "Since he was a good actor, I'm sure he will make a good president." "Bill, you are a superb computer technician. You seem to have a natural talent for analyzing system problems and remedying them. Surely, then, you should be able to analyze the problems in the rough drafts of your papers and turn them into polished essays."

Argumentum ad Hominem. The Latin phrase means *argument against the man* and names the fallacy of attacking the person rather than his argument. Such an attack may be legitimate when someone presents no argument but his own unsupported testimony. For example, the procedure is frequently used in courts to impeach witnesses who are testifying as experts. If it can be shown that they are not experts or that their testimony cannot be relied on, their trustworthiness as witnesses is seriously challenged. However, if someone presents evidence to support a claim, simply attacking his character is illegitimate. "Mr. Grumpky should not be allowed to serve on the school board because he is a non-Christian." "I went to a meeting on gender issues last night. The speakers were about as homely a group of women as I've ever seen. No wonder they hate men. Maybe if they dressed a little better and put on some makeup they wouldn't have to be concerned about gender issues."

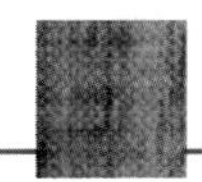

Argumentum ad Populum. This "appeal to the people" is used particularly by politicians and advertisers. This fallacy ignores the issue at hand to appeal to the in-group loyalties and fears of the audience. Appeals to prejudice and self-interest are also part of this appeal. For example, one might argue that people should be against any form of government regulation of business since America was founded on the principle of freedom from oppression.

Appeal to Ignorance. This argument implies that since no one has proved a particular claim, it must be false or, since no one has disproved a claim, it must be true. This fallacy usually involves a matter that is either incapable of being proved or has not yet been proved. "Since no one has convincingly disproved Darwin's theory, it must be valid."

Tokenism. This fallacy occurs when one makes only a token gesture (does very little of what is required), but then shouts or brags about it as loudly as one can. For example, a company might point to a highly placed executive who is female to show how well they treat and promote women when, in fact, she is the only woman in an executive position in the whole company.

The Straw Man. This fallacy occurs when a person misinterprets or distorts an opponent's position to make it easier to attack, or when he attacks weaker opponents while ignoring stronger ones. For example, when opponents of gun control characterize those who support some limitations on the ownership and use of weapons as radicals who would do away with hunting and Americans' constitutional right to bear arms, they are attacking a straw man.

Bandwagon. An argument that claims that something cannot be true (or false) because a majority of people support (or oppose) it. Based on popular opinion, the argument appeals to prejudice and ignores the facts. For example, "it is obvious that any caring parent would not want his/her child attending school where a classmate has HIV."

Slippery Slope. An argument based on an unlikely chain reaction; it rests on an alleged chain of events, and there is not sufficient reason to believe that the implied effect will actually occur. For example, "If we legalize marijuana, the United States will become a nation of addicts and criminals." (If . . . then . . .)

Selective Sampling. Proof offered that contains part of, but not the whole truth. Since not all the facts are stated, the claim can be true and false (misleading?) at the same time (half-truths). For example, "Three out of five dentists surveyed preferred Brand X toothpaste."

Unreliable Testimony. An argument based on an untrustworthy, biased, or unqualified authority. (Fame/celebrity doesn't qualify as authoritative or expert opinion). For example, "Several of my neighbors support the termination of our school's head coach."

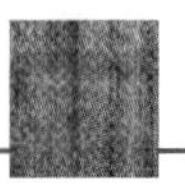

Circular Reasoning. An argument based on the repetition of an assertion as a reason for accepting it: "Drugs are harmful because they injure the body." "The president would never lie to the public because he is an honest man."

False Cause. An argument that confuses a causal relationship. For example, one might mistake a contributory cause for a sufficient one, or assume that because one event occurred before a second event, the first caused the second (an example of the *Post Hoc, ergo Propter Hoc* fallacy, a Latin phrase meaning "after this; therefore because of this.") "Because the city council outlawed firearms, the crime rate declined." "Research shows that successful people have large vocabularies; therefore one way to become successful is to develop a large vocabulary."

Arguments from *Pathos*

Pathos makes use of emotion to persuade an audience. Aristotle wrote: "Proofs from the disposition of the audience are produced whenever they are induced by the speech into an emotional state. We do not give judgment in the same way when aggrieved and when pleased, in sympathy and in revulsion."

Effective rhetors know their audiences, particularly what emotions they hold that are relevant to the issue under consideration. What motivates them? What are their fears, their hopes, their desires, and their doubts? If the audience has the same emotions as you do, fine. However, if they do not already hold those emotions, you need, through the stories you tell, the statistics you cite, and the reasoning you offer, to bring them to share the hurt, the anger, or the joy that will persuade them to share your viewpoint.

For example, when Martin Luther King, Jr., in his "I Have a Dream" speech referred to the "hallowed spot" of the Lincoln Memorial, he was appealing to his audience's feelings of patriotism and reverence for the accomplishments of President Lincoln. Subtly, he was also garnering this emotion toward Lincoln in contemporary support of civil rights. Lincoln had issued the Emancipation Proclamation that declared all slaves to be free, yet, according to King, America had not lived up to Lincoln's promise.

Arguments from *Ethos*

No exact translation exists in English for the word *ethos*, but it can be loosely translated as "the credibility of the speaker." This credibility generates good will which colors all the arguments, examples, and quotes the rhetor utilizes in his text. Rhetors can enhance their credibility by evidence of intelligence, virtue, and goodwill and diminish it by seeming petty, dishonest, and mean spirited. In addition, a speaker or writer can enhance his or her own credibility by references to quotes or the actions of authorities or leaders.

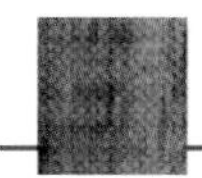

Aristotle wrote:

> Proofs from character [*ethos*] are produced, whenever the speech is given in such a way as to render the speaker worthy of credence—we more readily and sooner believe reasonable men on all matters in general and absolutely on questions where precision is impossible and two views can be maintained.

For example, Martin Luther King, Jr. pointed out in his "I Have a Dream" speech that according to the framers of the Constitution and the Declaration of Independence, the "unalienable Rights" of "Life, Liberty and the pursuit of Happiness" apply equally to black men and white men. He was, in effect, borrowing the *ethos* of Thomas Jefferson and the framers of the Constitution in support of the unalienable rights of blacks.

Combining *Ethos, Pathos,* and *Logos*

Did you notice that the triangle earlier in this chapter representing Aristotle's three appeals is equilateral, meaning that all sides are equal in length? This is to illustrate that the *ethos, pathos,* and *logos* elements are equally important and merit equal attention in the writing process. No text is purely based on one of the three appeals, though more of the argument in a particular text may be based on one appeal rather than another. In each writing situation, however, an effective rhetor will think about how each plays into the structure of the argument.

In today's world, for example, a public speaker's effectiveness is affected by the ability to use a teleprompter or, if one is not available, to memorize a speech well enough so he or she has to refer to notes infrequently. If a speaker's eyes flit from left to right across the text of a teleprompter, it shows on television and reduces the credibility, or ethos, of the speaker, no matter how well the other appeals are executed in the speech. The equivalent of presentation for a written text would be to produce a document that is essentially free from surface grammatical errors, is spell-checked, and is printed on good paper stock with the correct margins and type size. If the document does not look professional, it will lose credibility or ethos no matter what it says.

To give another example, E. Benjamin Skinner's essay "People for Sale" relies on the highly emotional image of a child being sold into slavery for its major appeal. However, if you read back through the essay, you will see that it has a clear thesis, which could be stated as the following: slavery exists in the present time, even in the United States, and it is not even that difficult to buy a slave. The essay is well organized and offers a variety of evidence, including statistics and first-person observation. *Logos* may not stand out as the primary appeal in Skinner's essay, but it is nevertheless strong in its appeal to *logos*.

If you want to develop your writing skills, it is essential that you pay attention to each of Aristotle's appeals—*ethos, pathos*, and *logos*.

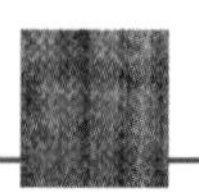

DETERMINING THE KAIROS OF THE WRITING SITUATION

Finding the Kairos of the Argument

Each time a rhetor (a writer or speaker) constructs an argument, he or she is working within a context of a certain moment, a particular time and place. This moment, which the ancient Greeks called **kairos** (a word which has no exact English translation) may include audience and culture in addition to time and place. Kairos both constrains and enables what a rhetor can say or write effectively in a context. For example, when Martin Luther King, Jr., gave his "I Have a Dream" speech, his words were carefully crafted to take into consideration the setting in front of the Lincoln Memorial. He said, "Five score years ago, a great American, in whose symbolic shadow we stand today, signed the Emancipation Proclamation." The words "five score" recall the "four score and seven years ago" of Lincoln's words in the Gettysburg Address. And King also pointed out that he and his audience that day stood in the "symbolic shadow" of Lincoln who signed the Emancipation Proclamation. In these ways, he made use of Lincoln's shadow to legitimize what he was saying about civil rights.

In other ways, however, the kairos of the moment limited what he could say. His audience included both the thousands of people in front of him who were dedicated to the cause of racial equality and also the audience of those millions watching on television who may or may not have agreed with his message. Thus, the tone of his message needed to be subtly measured not to antagonize those among his audience, particularly the television audience, who may have opposed aspects of the civil rights movement such as school integration. However, he spoke to let both his supporters and his opponents know, "The whirlwinds of revolt will continue to shake the foundations of our nation until the bright day of justice emerges." Yes, King advocated non-violent demonstrations, but they were demonstrations nonetheless; he was putting opponents on notice that the disruptions caused by demonstrations would continue "until justice emerges." King consistently took the high road, while maintaining the power of the kairotic moment when he spoke. This is one reason that his words continue to be studied decades after his death.

Consider the Elements of *Kairos*

Not every speech is given in front of the Lincoln Memorial, but every speech or written text has a *kairos*, and the effective rhetor takes advantage of factors relating to the audience and the situation which could not happen just any time and any place. Following are some suggestions for maximizing the advantages of *kairos*.

- *Determine the kairotic moment.* What is the timeliness of the issue? Has something happened recently regarding this issue that can be emphasized in an argument? For example, if you are

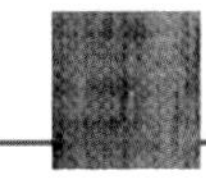

writing about the death penalty, focusing on a recent case or a recent protest would emphasize the timeliness of the issue.

- *Know your audience.* What are the characteristics of the audience? Do they agree with your position on the issue or not? What is their educational level and extent of their knowledge about the subject? For example, if you are writing about immigration policy reform, does your audience believe there is a need for reform? Do they have personal experience with illegal or legal immigrants? You can judge the amount of background information you need to provide based on the characteristics of your audience. Also, the most important members of the audience, so far as an argument is concerned, are not those who already agree with you but those who are neutral or even slightly opposed to your position but willing to listen. As King did, be careful not to phrase your argument in ways that are insulting to people who do not agree with you, for if you do so, they will stop listening to you.
- *Establish your personal ethos.* As a rhetor, do you have a personal connection to the topic? For example, if you are writing about the pros and cons of using medication to treat ADHD, do you yourself have that condition or know intimately someone who does? If so, it may be appropriate to include a mention of your story, along with other background information in your essay. If you have no personal connection to your topic, find the stories of others that do have such a connection and become their advocate.
- *Find ground to stand on.* This may not work for every essay, but is there something about the place where you stand, literally or figuratively, that adds ethos to your argument, as Martin Luther King, Jr. stood at the Lincoln Memorial? If, for example, you live in a border community, you stand at an important juncture for issues such as immigration, free trade, and national security. In the essay that follows, "How Clean, Green Atomic Energy Can Stop Global Warming," the authors begin with the sentence, "On a cool spring morning a quarter century ago, a place in Pennsylvania called Three Mile Island…" Thus, they place themselves figuratively at that critical place in the atomic energy debate—Three Mile Island.

Include Images to Increase Kairotic Appeal

Kairos is about making use of the context of an argument—a particular moment in a specific time and place. If you were, for example, writing an essay about the causes of the 2008 "mortgage meltdown" and the resulting crisis in the United States, you could give your audience a more immediate sense of the time and place by including an illustration, such as the one on the next page from *The Economist.*

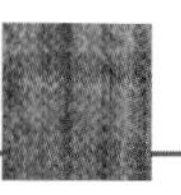

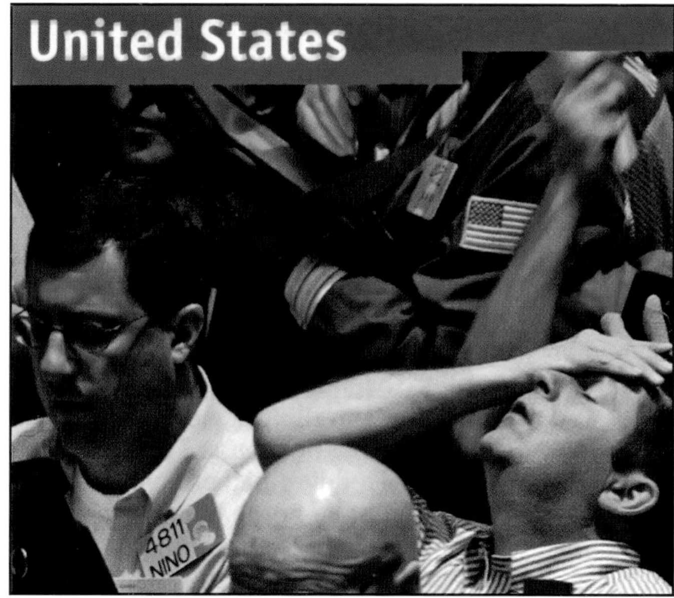

Source: *The Economist*, Sept. 20, 2008

This *Economist* photo vividly illustrates the reaction of one man on the floor of the New York Stock Exchange to one of the downturns in the stock market, and in one glance will make clear to your reader the seriousness of the financial crisis from the perspective of Wall Street.

Although such an image is copyrighted, you can scan and import it into your essay without formal permission because it is a class assignment for educational purposes. You cannot, however, put it up on a web page or otherwise publish it without permission. You should credit the image by putting "Source: *The Economist*, Sept. 20, 2008" above or below your photo caption, and you should also include the image in your works cited page or list of references.

Social Networking Sites Utilize Text and Images

Social networking sites such as Facebook and Twitter are used daily by millions of people to keep in touch with busy friends, business associates, and those who share common interests. Most social network sites allow members to create a profile for themselves and then have additional pages for contacts with friends or other topics. Some members choose to have closed or internal social networking that is members or "friends" only. Other sites allow open membership. Social scientists and rhetoricians have begun studying social networking sites because they are a new and different communication medium, but considering the millions using the sites on a daily basis, the sites seem destined to continue.

Facebook members interact, but not face-to-face nor even usually in real time. You leave messages for friends, and friends respond when they have the time. One easy-to-access option

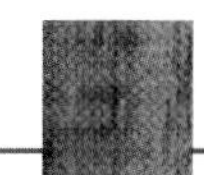

lets you say what you are doing now, whether it is baking a cake or touring the old city in Jerusalem. Members post pictures of grandchildren, their pets, and recent travels. The *kairos* of Facebook is undemanding, stay-in-touch communication, with the option of sharing what you want of your personal life. The loss may be "face time" but the gain is personal contact—of a sort. As Lisa Selin Davis explains, if you have friends who have become Facebook hermits, your choice is lose a friend or join Facebook.

ORGANIZATION

In his *Rhetoric,* Aristotle discusses the five parts of the deliberative discourse (a discussion of what we should or should not do to bring about some future goal), only two of which, *invention* and *disposition,* are relevant to the organization of the written essay.

Invention

Invention is the process or method writers use to discover arguments. Aristotle divided the process into two parts: finding arguments and devising arguments from scratch.

Non-Artistic Proofs. What Aristotle called non-artistic proofs are arguments that have already been formulated by others. We call this process research. Properly conducted research will lead to an abundance of information on, and authoritative discussion of, the topic you are writing about.

Artistic Proofs. Artistic proofs are arguments you develop on your own; that is, they are arguments you devise through your own ability, your own art, without reference to outside sources. They include the logical appeal, the emotional appeal, and the ethical appeal.

Topics. Topics are proofs grouped under common headings. Under **common topics** Aristotle discusses such topics as definition, comparison-contrast, causal analysis, and the proper use of testimony or authority. Under **special topics** for a deliberative discourse, Aristotle points out that an argument can attempt to persuade the reader that a particular solution to a problem is a common good that it is moral, just, or right. If a writer can do that, readers will more easily offer their assent. In making this kind of an appeal, a writer may refer to our religious beliefs (adultery may be condemned because it is forbidden in the Bible), to our sense of fair play (eliminating the capital gains tax will unfairly benefit the very rich who already pay few taxes), to our belief in law (we should not smoke marijuana because it is illegal), to our sense of loyalty to an ideal (political action committees should be severely curtailed because they are inherently undemocratic), or to our empathy for fellow humans (all people deserve to have food and shelter).

The power of this appeal comes from its assumption of moral authority. If a writer's audience is composed of strong believers in some holy text, for instance the Bible or the Qur'an, the writer can use scripture as a source of authority. However, someone who does not accept

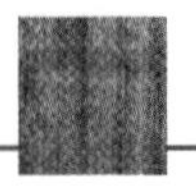

the moral force of a holy text will hardly be convinced by references to it. The same is true of other groups.

Some of the most intractable of contemporary conflicts derive from the fact that different groups have different moral bases for their beliefs. Again, to echo Aristotle, in making this kind of plea, writers appeal to what their audience considers to be good or right over and above what they consider useful or in their own interest. For example, Jane Goodall, in "Some Thoughts on the Exploitation of Non-Human Animals," makes an essentially ethical appeal when she states that "all except the most primitive of non-human animals experience pain, and [. . .] 'higher' animals have emotions similar to the human emotions that we label pleasure or sadness, fear or despair." She implies that, since animals have feelings just as we do, it is no more right for us to subject them to suffering than it would be for us to subject other humans to suffering. Rhetorically, she asks: "How can we, the citizens of civilized, western countries, tolerate laboratories which—from the point of view of animal inmates—are not unlike concentration camps?" Her point is that no matter what benefits we receive, it is simply wrong to experiment on animals.

Finally, one can attempt to persuade readers that a particular solution to a problem will benefit them in some way. Not only will quitting smoking promote one's health, for example, since health is a common good, it will also save one money.

Disposition

Disposition is the way one disposes, or organizes, one's argument. According to Aristotle, there are six parts, or sections, to an argument:

Introduction. In your introduction you need to supply an attention-getting opener to your topic and then a statement of your claim (the stand you intend to take).

Narration. The narration is a discussion of the background of the issue under consideration. Readers, for example, may not know that there is a problem to be solved. The amount of background material you provide depends upon the knowledge of your audience and the complexity of the issue you are dealing with.

Division. In the division you list the arguments you will advance in support of your proposition/claim.

Confirmation. The confirmation is the longest and most important part of your argument. Here you give the evidence to support your proposition/claim arranged in the order you have listed in the division.

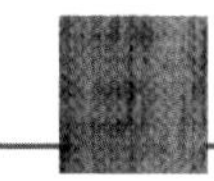

Refutation. The refutation is a discussion and rebuttal of your opponent's counterarguments. See below.

Conclusion. In your conclusion make a strong appeal for acceptance of your argument.

Refutation

In a face-to-face argument, we have the advantage of responding directly to an opponent. In writing, however, we lack this advantage. Therefore, we must depend on refutation when we argue our ideas in writing. In your **refutation** section, you anticipate your opponent's arguments and prove they are, to some degree, wrong, invalid, or fallacious. Methods of refutation include pointing out an opponent's faulty premise, an error in deductive logic, a deficient definition, a logical fallacy, any inappropriate or inaccurate evidence, insufficient evidence, or a questionable authority, to name a few. For the most part, refutation involves undermining an opponent's argument. You might deny that he has proved his claim. You might refute the truth of his premises or object to the inferences drawn from the premises. You might say, "I admit the truth of your conclusion, but I challenge its appropriateness in this particular instance because [. . .]." Let good judgment and common sense rule. Consider your audience and their emotional biases, the occasion, the subject, and your own personality to help you determine the best course of action regarding refutation.

Some instructors prefer that you refute the opposition before beginning your confirmation. There is reasonable cause for such placement, especially if your opponents' views are shared strongly by your audience. However, if your opponent's arguments are weak, you can afford to delay refutation until the end of your own argument, using your discussion to build a case against your opponent's views. If your audience is hostile to your views, it might work to your advantage, psychologically, to delay your refutation until the end of your argument, to keep the direct attack of your opposition out of sight as long as possible. You need not remind your audience at the outset of your opposition, thus closing their ears to the remainder of what you have to say. By placing the refutation at the end, you may dispose your audience momentarily to hear what you have to say without compounding their hostility. Finally, you can also incorporate refutation wherever it is needed in each paragraph, rather than placing it in a separate section.

Outline for an Essay Based on Deductive Argument

I. Introduction
- A. Lead-in to your topic
  - Startling statistic and/or
  - Interesting example
- B. Statement of the conclusion of your syllogism; the proposition or claim you are going to defend

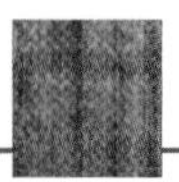

II. Narration

A. Background information to clarify your topic and illustrate the problem for which you are proposing a solution. You might need to include here definitions of terms relevant to your argument.

B. Statement of the major premise and the minor premise that lead to your conclusion.

(*Note: One option to this method is to combine paragraphs I and II into a single paragraph. Consult with your instructor.*)

III. Statement of major premise as topic sentence

A. Evidence #1 supporting the truth of your major premise.

Examples

Statistics

Authority

B. Evidence #2 supporting the truth of your major premise

Examples

Statistics

Authority

IV. Statement of minor premise as topic sentence

A. Evidence #1 supporting the truth of your minor premise

Examples

Statistics

Authority

B. Evidence #2 supporting the truth of your minor premise

Examples

Statistics

Authority

V. Restatement of conclusion of syllogism as topic sentence

A. Evidence #1 supporting the benefits to your audience of accepting your conclusion

B. Evidence #2 supporting the benefits of your audience of accepting your conclusion

VI. Refutation (optional—see discussion of refutation above)

A. Statement of counterargument (alternative conclusion) #1

Evidence #1 to refute or mitigate the force of A

Evidence #2 to refute or mitigate the force of A

B. Statement of counterargument (alternative conclusion) #2

Evidence #1 to refute or mitigate the force of B

Evidence #2 to refute or mitigate the force of B

VII. Conclusion A strong appeal for acceptance of your conclusion and/or a call to action.

While this format is the standard method of organizing a deductive essay, it offers options to the student in the construction of the introductory paragraph (you may wish to combine paragraphs

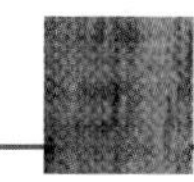

I and II in the above outline), and you may prefer to insert your refutation into each of the body paragraphs rather than have a separate section for refutation at the end of the essay. Consult your instructor for guidelines and preferences.

Outline for an Essay Based on Inductive Argument

I. Introduction
- A. Lead-in to your topic
  - Startling statistic and/or
  - Interesting example
- B. Statement of the generalization you have reached through your research; the proposition or claim you are going to defend in your argument

II. Narration
- A. Statement of background information to clarify your topic and to illustrate the problem you are dealing with. You might need to include here definitions of terms relevant to your argument.
- B. Statement listing in one sentence at least three major pieces of evidence (x, y, and z) that support your generalization or claim.

III. First major piece of supporting evidence as topic sentence
- A. Subtopic #1 supporting X
  - Examples
  - Statistics
  - Authority
- B. Subtopic #2 supporting X
  - Examples
  - Statistics
  - Authority

IV. Second major piece of supporting evidence as topic sentence.
- A. Subtopic #1 supporting Y
  - Examples
  - Statistics
  - Authority
- B. Subtopic #2 supporting Y
  - Examples
  - Statistics
  - Authority

V. Third major piece of supporting evidence as topic sentence.
- A. Subtopic #1 supporting Z
  - Examples

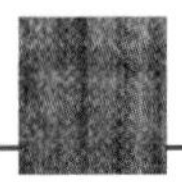

Statistics
Authority
B. Subtopic #2 supporting Z
Examples
Statistics
Authority
VI. Refutation (optional—see discussion of refutation above)
A. Statement of counterargument (alternative conclusion) #1
Evidence #1 to refute or mitigate the force of A
Evidence #2 to refute or mitigate the force of A
B. Statement of counterargument (alternative conclusion) #2
Evidence #1 to refute or mitigate the force of B
Evidence #2 to refute or mitigate the force of B
VII. Conclusion A strong appeal for acceptance of your generalization and/or a call to action

While this format is the standard method of organizing an inductive essay, it offers options to the student in the construction of the introductory paragraph (you may wish to combine paragraphs I and II in the above outline), and you may prefer to insert your refutation into each of the body paragraphs rather than have a separate section for refutation at the end of the essay. Consult your instructor for guidelines and preferences.

THESES, CLAIMS, AND FORMS OF ARGUMENT

Writing an Effective Thesis

College writing typically involves argumentative writing, and argumentative writing requires a thesis. A thesis can come in different forms (direct or indirect) and appear in different places in a paragraph or paper. However, almost all essays have a thesis in the first paragraph that is as direct as the scope of the paper allows. Although you may not be able to capture the who, the what, the when, the where, and the how all in one sentence, the arguable parts of who, what, when, where, why, and how are important to present in your thesis. The rest will be provided by the other sentences of your opening paragraph.

Also, a thesis must not just be a fact or facts. Argument is opinion, so you must get beyond a fact or description of your subject and into your opinions.

Topic/Fact: Albert Einstein discovered the theory of relativity in the early twentieth century.

Broad Thesis: Albert Einstein's theory of relativity is the greatest scientific advance in the history of humankind.

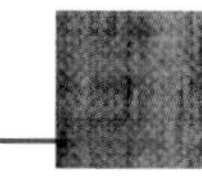

Narrower Thesis: Albert Einstein's theory of relativity, introduced in 1905, was initially rejected by the community, but not as much as some history books have claimed.

Your thesis must always be appropriate to your assignment length. Discussion of all scientific discovery before and including Einstein's would be difficult to accomplish in a college paper, whether three, five, or ten pages. Most likely a *book* containing a history of science would be required. The Narrower Thesis is researchable and narrow enough to present background information and competing claims in a longer paper of eight to ten pages.

Fact: *Star Wars*'s success at the box office is predictable and interesting.
Broad Thesis: *Star Wars*, like other science fiction, can always compete at the box office with other types of storytelling and fiction.
Narrower Thesis: *Star Wars* was destined for box office success because of the nation's ongoing interest in space exploration, as well as its epic plot, which was absent from much previous science fiction.

Avoid general terms like "interesting." The narrower *Star Wars* thesis offers reasons with sharper focus for the movie's box office success. It mentions the "type" of storytelling that the Broad Thesis does not, and it separates the movie from other science fiction instead of combining it with other science fiction, as the Broad Thesis does.

Who, What, When, Where, Why, and How (WWWWWH)

A quick check to guarantee you have all the components of a strong thesis is asking yourself, Who, What, When, Where, Why, and How? Not all of these components may fit into a single sentence definable as your thesis, but these important areas of information will almost always appear in your introductory paragraph or paragraphs. To be sure that you've included all the relevant information to your readers, you may wish to outline your subject as follows:

Who:
What:
When:
Where:
Why:
How:

If you are not solving a problem or using a methodology for your writing purpose, or writing on a topic that includes these, the "how" does not always exist. Still, you can double check your basic information and its depth, guaranteeing a stronger focus for yourself and for your readers.

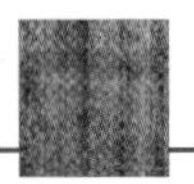

Let's revisit our Star Wars example:

> *Star Wars* was destined for box office success because of the nation's ongoing interest in space exploration, as well as its epic plot, which was absent from much previous science fiction.

Who: *Star Wars*
What: destined for box office success
When: late 1970s
Where: United States? The world?
Why: ongoing interest in space exploration, epic plot
How: ?

The Star Wars example demonstrates several interesting points. First, the *Who* may not be a person. The *Who* is the subject of your essay. It may be people, an object, an idea, or other things. However, it is the focus. Second, certain bits of information are often implied. Although the paragraph doesn't say the late 1970s, everyone knows that this is the date of *Star Wars* release and subsequent box office records. The author is trusting the audience to know the period of the movie's release. Not all subjects will be as universally known as *Star Wars*. Dates may need to be included.

Also, the *Where* is missing as well. While either "the United States" or "the world" would work, the author may want to add this information to the introduction, signaling the limits "where" that will be discussed in the essay. Also, the *how* is absent. I would suggest that here, because no problem is being solved, the *how* is absent. Or the *why* and the *how* are very similar in this case because of an interest in space exploration and because of an epic plot. Lastly, as we shall see in the Einstein example, WWWWWH can often be refocused, reshaping your thesis and filling in missing categories.

Now let's look at our Einstein example:

> Albert Einstein's theory of relativity was initially rejected by the community, but not as much as some history books have claimed.

List the information from above below, also noting what is absent:

Who:
What:
When:
Where:
Why:
How:

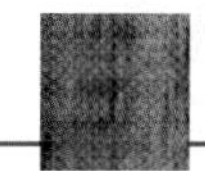

You'll notice a fair amount of key information is absent. As a writer, you would have to decide, based upon your audience and subject, whether or not these absences will be filled in by the reader's general knowledge. I would suggest the following for our thesis on Einstein:

Who: Albert's Einstein's theory of relativity
What: initially rejected
When: [early twentieth century]
Where: scientific community
Why: ?
How: ?

In the above example, *where* is not a place, but a body of people with shared knowledge. Much like *who*, the answers to these questions might not conform to your ideas of Who, What, When, Where, Why, and How. This is because much argument is theoretical, so it takes place nowhere, so to speak. If applied and practiced, then it may take on physical features. If only hypothetical, some parts of the WWWWWH grid may not conform to your expectations.

Also, we have extra information that doesn't fit well: *but not as much as some history books have claimed.* This is because of the writing style. The *What* most likely is:

> the initial rejection of the theory of relativity is overstated in history books

You may have noticed the *why* behind the rejection of Einstein's theory of relativity is absent from this sentence. The absent information could be included somewhere else in the introductory paragraph. After all, not everything can fit into one sentence. Or it may be because our subject needed to be refocused because of our new *what.*

Who: Historians
What: overstated the initial rejection of the theory of relativity in history books.
When: during the twentieth century
Where: the world? Europe?
Why: ?
How:?

You can see how the WWWWWH grid has allowed us to refocus our first paragraph, providing the absent information. You can read the Who, What, and When and get a thesis equally strong or stronger than the initial version. The *Where* doesn't seem to have changed, and everyone knows historians are found in countries everywhere. However, as a writer, you should try to define your limits in each category, such as *Historians in Europe*, or *historians before the 1960s,* or whatever

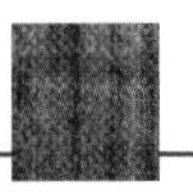

specific group or individual one is writing about. Also, the *why* and *how* behind the rejection of the theory seem easier to imagine now: common belief and trends in historical writing.

These are ideas that challenge the WWWWWH grid, but by using the method, you can see upcoming challenges in presenting complex information, you can detail general information, (such as missing actors, as with *historians*) and you can guarantee you have provided a beginning framework for your explanation or argument.

Identifying Argumentative Claims

Previously, we learned that arguments forward specific claims about the truth, legitimacy, or effectiveness of ideas. Any argument offering a workable solution or answer to a problem, whether scientific or philosophical, starts with a claim. Poor arguments also start with a claim, but poor arguments may be underspecified, may not solve the problem, and may lack enough support and evidence to be legitimate answers to questions.

Claims, good or poor, are statements that can be denied or affirmed. If your statement or thesis cannot be denied or confirmed, then you may only be explaining, not arguing. Statements such as "All individuals are born free," "Stem cell research is immoral," "Nurturance predicts behavior better than biology," and "Stan is a good guy" are all claims. In short, a person can argue *for* them or *against* them. Imagine evidence arguing both for and against each of the four claims just stated. If you can imagine arguments existing both for and against, you have an argument.

Claims will typically be written in the form of declarative sentences. This is undoubtedly the strongest form to state an argumentative claim. Some writers may try to state their claim through a question, but it is doubtful whether or not this is always an effective form to convince your audience.

For Discussion: Are the following argumentative claims? Or are they only facts? For each of the above statements that is an argumentative claim, imagine evidence to both support and refute the validity of these claims. Discuss the answers as a class or in small groups.

- Dogs are man's best friend.
- Diamonds are a girl's best friend.
- The average human head weighs eight pounds.
- Natural diamonds are compressed coal.
- The post-World War II Leavitt Town was the model for later American suburbs.
- Leave me alone.
- Germans are an efficient people.
- It is easier to do good than evil.
- We have not yet discovered all the elements that comprise our universe.
- *Peanuts* is written by Charles Schultz.

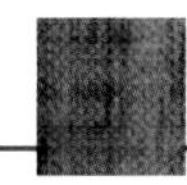

- *Peanuts* is a comic strip representing the common personality types of twentieth-century American life.
- The sun is a star.
- Not everything is a claim.
- Trying times make heroes of all women and men.
- Some people don't look good in warm colors.
- There are sixteen ounces in a pound.

Recognizing Claims in the Classroom

Sometimes instructors may give you a claim to defend, as in the following:

Argue that Ophelia's relationship to her father parallels Hamlet's relationship to his mother.

Defend the claim that science and creationism can co-exist without detriment to either science or faith.

Most often you'll receive an argumentative prompt offering you a choice:

Discuss whether current environmental laws focusing on greenhouse emissions are firm enough to reverse global warming trends.

Agree or Disagree: Freud's psychological theory is rooted not in the mysteries of the human mind, but in the anxieties of his own mind.

What role does race play in class divisions in twenty-first-century America?

The term *claim* can be viewed as simply another term for *thesis* or *proposition*. Arguments have one major thesis; however, they have many claims in their network of evidence and support. And remember, argumentative claims are not a summary of an idea. Argumentative claims suggest that you "take a side" or "make a point." Arguments don't just explain an idea, event, or item. They explain how the idea, event, or item is a valid conclusion about an open-ended topic with a variety of viewpoints.

Five Forms of Argument

After you have read widely, outlined your goals for writing, and narrowed your topic, you will begin to write. Your first draft should keep audience and purpose in mind. The first draft will have a lot of excess material that will be edited. This is OK. Keep the excess material. You cannot predict which ideas you will keep, which ideas you will erase, and which ideas will be the seed for more ideas in future drafts. Upon completing the imagination and prewriting required at the beginning of the writing process, you will need to re-examine and organize your thoughts.

Eventually, you will have to revise the language of these thoughts. In the early stages of writing, language can be revised, but language is not the only feature that needs to be revised. Thinking must also be revised.

Why does thinking need to be revised and re organized? Because no thought spills from our mind perfect, united, and organized. The following types of argument have been used for centuries upon centuries. Most arguments utilize more than one form at various points in a communication. Long arguments may utilize all. Because these categories are the basic modes of making sense of the world around us, it is often helpful to look at your thesis and basic support and ask which mode you are using. Although there are many forms of argument and exposition, here are some forms common to academic argument:

- Argument by definition
- Argument by comparison and contrast
- Argument by illustration and example
- Argument by classification and division
- Argument by cause and effect

Each form has certain predictable qualities that you use every day without realizing it. Your prewriting thesis, no matter how unformed, will contain elements of one of these forms of thought. To help you tidy up your thoughts, you may wish to ask yourself which argument your prewriting thesis most closely resembles. You are asking yourself basic questions: How am I thinking? How am I suggesting that the world works? How am I talking about a particular event or idea? What events and ideas am I surrounding the event with to give it importance?

Argument by Definition

In argument by definition, your thesis is not based upon situational solutions. Instead, you are concentrating on the qualities internal to an idea itself. You will suggest that your subject has the qualities of a certain class of things, therefore it should be treated the same as other members of this class of things. Your argument will show why it belongs in the class it does and how other opinions have wrongly classified it, providing an incorrect solution to the problem.

You won't spend a lot of time comparing how your idea is better or worse than a similar idea. Instead, you will be arguing that the qualities of the "thing" you are promoting are highly valuable. Those who argue from definition on social issues may believe their values and solutions permanent and timeless and applicable to a variety of problems, so argument by definition typically doesn't aim for a "multiple answer" mentality to solving problems. Instead, it outlines its ideals

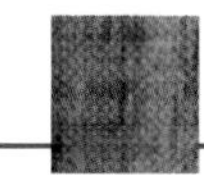

and values, defends them, and suggests that readers would be wise to adopt these ideals and values as well.

Argument by definition entails defining the limits of your subject. You must set boundaries. Your support and claims will reinforce these boundaries of the good and the less good, the fair and the not-so-fair, the useful and the less useful, and the efficient and the inefficient. You and your thesis are walling off certain parts of the world, finding that some ideas should not be as highly valued as others. If you are arguing that democracy is the most benevolent form of government, then you are walling off other forms of government such as theocracy, communism, and monarchy. You would begin by defining the qualities of a good government. They may be:

- Equality of all citizens
- Right to own property
- Right of people to create own laws and legislative bodies
- Right of people to amass wealth through hard work
- Religious freedom
- Social mobility

You can see that these are a few of the qualities of democracy not offered by other governmental schemas. If you argue that these are the most important values to humankind when building a government, you are arguing from definition. Abraham Lincoln often argued from definition. His most famous argument from definition was an argument over what the definition of a human being is. Why would this be important to Lincoln? Obviously, Lincoln was arguing for the Emancipation Proclamation, and he needed Americans to see not black and white, but only the human being. Arguing from definition allowed Lincoln to set up his qualities and values in such a way that neither race nor the need for cheap labor could be a valid proposition for continuing slavery. Many argument theorists suggest that definition is the strongest form of argument. Lincoln certainly thought so. He did not risk history to another form of argument. Many other "core values" arguments, typically derived from either religious principles or the United States constitution, are arguments by definition.

Argument by definition typically follows this formula: *X is a Y because it has features A,B,C, etc.* Or the following is possible: *X is not a Y because it does not have features A,B,C, etc.* It is easy to see that a hot-button issue can be argued from both conservative and liberal viewpoints through definition.

Conservative argument by definition:

> Stem cell research is immoral and murderous because scientific theory denies the sanctity and preservation of all life, and the stem cell research process destroys stem cell clusters.

Liberal argument by definition:

> Stem cell research is moral because science can better help those living with disabilities and illness, and the stem cell research process destroys embryos or cell clusters that will never grow into a human being.

Each of these definitions of what is moral depends upon limiting the qualities of what defines "morality." The values of each speaker are different. Thus, their definition will be different. Here are some other examples: *Video game violence is/is not equal to real violence because... Stepparents are/are not as compatible with children as biological parents because ... Stealing a library book that no one has read in fifty years is/is not a crime because ... Common-law marriage is/is not a marriage because ...*

Syllogisms

The syllogism is an ancient device that proves methodically that one thing is the same as another. You can see why this would be useful when arguing by definition. Here is the rational for syllogisms:

Claim:	X is a Y
Reason:	Because it has qualities A, B, and C
Grounds:	X has certain qualities
Warrant:	If something has A, B, and C, then it can be called an X
Backing:	Evidence that Y has A, B, and C

Not everyone may agree that Y has qualities A, B, and C. Think of the stem cell example. The qualities of A, B, and C are different for each. Those who disagree with a viewpoint can argue either the grounds or the warrant.

Exercise:
If someone has the conservative view of stem cell research, what would they say when attacking the liberal grounds?

First, figure out what the liberal grounds are. List them.

1.

2.

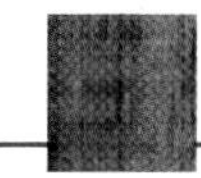

Now, discuss how these grounds are different than the conservative grounds. You may wish to list the conservative grounds.

If this same person of conservative viewpoint chose to attack the liberal warrant, what specific qualities of the liberal argument would they be attacking?

For practice, you may wish to repeat this exercise from the liberal standpoint as well.

Here are some examples of syllogisms. I will condense the entire syllogism into three parts and show only how X is a Y. This means that I am leaving out the qualities or reasons (A, B, C, etc.) that allow one to argue from definition. As you read these, imagine what the qualities or reasons are, and also imagine if there is any way to refute the qualities or reasons.

Major premise:	All men are mortal.
Minor premise:	Socrates is a man.
Conclusion:	Socrates is mortal.
Major premise:	Stainless steel will not rust.
Minor premise:	This can is made from stainless steel.
Conclusion:	This can will not rust.
Major premise:	Only politicians that are sensible are electable
Minor premise:	That politician is electable.
Conclusion:	That politician is sensible.
Major premise:	All students who graduate will get a good job.
Minor premise:	That student will graduate.
Conclusion:	That student will get a good job.

The first syllogism is the classic example of syllogisms. Are the other examples perfectly constructed and inevitable as the first? Is it possible that the syllogism can provide faulty logic as well sound logic? What is different about the fields of study covered by the last three syllogisms that does or does not guarantee their logic is flawless. Anyone who argues knows that not all claims and grounds are universal. Different people have different values. Even people with similar values will change their opinion as an idea moves from one situation to another. Stem cell research, for instance, may be murder to someone until a loved one is struck with an illness treatable through stem cell research. The situation has changed and the idea of stem cell research has a different frame—one where the good of science counts for more than it did previously. Or, even if they believe in the values behind their argument by definition, the *situation* has changed and the old values don't seem to count. Likewise, an argument to go to war may be founded upon being attacked, but what constitutes an attack may differ from situation to situation. And even then, people will either see or not see that the qualities and evidence necessitate going to war or not.

Knowing the general idea behind argument by definition can help you see if you are thinking of your topic as an idea that does not require comparison, contrast, causes, or effects to make it a

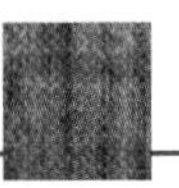

viable solution or answer to a problem. The definitional idea itself applies to any related issues or conundrums. There is no cause or effect that can alter the definition's ability to provide an answer. An answer can always be made based upon the values of the definition itself.

Argument by Comparison and Contrast

Unlike argument by definition, contrasting and comparing examines both the good and bad of two distinct ideas, texts, problems, or solutions. Your own argument and solution may draw upon the good and bad of both idea A and B, or may demonstrate how idea B encapsulates idea A and goes beyond idea A, or may discredit one in favor of the other. You can always expect that you will have both an A and a B to compare and contrast, whether they are theories, texts, solutions, organizations, or people.

Comparison points out similarities. *Contrast* points out differences. You'll need similarities to prove to your audience that A and B should be discussed together. Your thesis or introductory paragraph should suggest these similarities. Yet your reasons for comparing A and B, as well as the major differences, should also appear in your thesis.

Like other types of argument, you must think critically about your subject. Discussing similarities and differences is a good start. However, you must be sure to do more than summarize when arguing. Your paper's points of comparison and contrast should be based on the particular problem you are tackling, and theses points should become your support for your solution as well.

Building Criteria:
You may wish to develop a framework or graph to help you organize your criteria. It may look like the following example. The criteria are what each generally shares, yet the qualities of these criteria will vary, helping you make your decision:

Criteria:	**Reading Books:**	**Watching TV:**
Amount of time:	takes more time	takes less time
Amount of information:	more information	less information
Depth of information:	detailed research expected	less detail expected
Ability to validate sources:	can see sources listed	some sources cited
Specificity on a subject:	topics can be very specific	broad or specific
Availability:	must be found ahead of time	always broadcasting

While it may look like books are the winner here, your argument for what is "best" depends upon your thesis. Here are several arguments that could use the above list:

- Compare and contrast the quality and detail of information that we receive from both books and television.
- Compare and contrast two types of communication, organizing your criteria to choose a medium that gives a lot of general information quickly.
- Compare and contrast the ability to verify sources between two modes of communication.

These are not the only possibilities. You'll notice that some of these questions ask you to choose a "victor" after you've compared and contrasted. Others do not explicitly ask this. You should decide whether or not your purposes require a victor. If you are arguing, naturally you must choose a position and defend it through criteria like those listed above. Often, your criteria alone won't result in a victor; your criteria will present you with a well-planned answer to a question or solution to a problem. Yet you must find support and evidence to persuade your audience the criteria are relevant and effective.

You may also notice that a list like that one above is not highly specific. Each claim, such as books making it easier to verify sources, may or may not be true. It would depend on what type of books you are examining. Popular culture books and nonfiction can be argumentative yet written without a single source to support them. The support may simply come from the writer's own thought. This is both freeing and dangerous, argumentatively speaking. You may wish to discuss as a class both the freeing and dangerous aspects of people who argue without including the opinion of others qualified to speak on a subject. Also, you can see that the things you examine (ideas, problems, texts, people, etc.) need to be well-selected for similarities, and the criteria must be detailed enough to provide an in-depth analysis. Otherwise, the differences won't be highly relevant and won't support your position.

Your criteria can be based on the type of things you are examining. Based on the categories I've provided, you may wish to ask the following questions to get your comparison and contrast started:

Theories (Ideas, Problems):
What are these theories about? What problem to they attempt to define or solve? Are the theories applicable in the same fields? Does each theory originate in the same historical period? Does the period of origin matter when evaluating the theory? Is your problem the same as the original problem the theory was meant to solve? How have the theories been used in the past? What types of people used them for what situations? Were they successful?

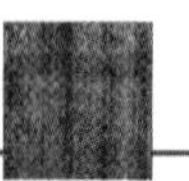

Texts and Art (print, visual, and otherwise):
What themes do these texts describe and discuss? Are these themes timeless, or are they historically bound? Does that change the way the themes are viewed by the writer compared to modern readers? By what qualities does the text wish and deserve to be judged (style, theme, characterization, plot, writer's intention, historical importance, historical representation, etc.)?

People:
What is the origin of this person? Are their formative years (education, environment, opportunities, etc.) normal or unique? Does the journey define their later accomplishments? What are this person's values? Are they groundbreaking for the "type" of person they are (gender, race, class, religion, etc.) or for their accomplishment only?

Groups:
What is this group's origins? What was its original purpose? Has that purpose changed? What effect has the group had on the area of society they wish to affect? What is their strategy? Have the purposes or strategies had any unwanted side effects? Does the group have a recognizable political persuasion?

Recognizing Argument by Comparison and Contrast

Recognizing assignments of this type is fairly easy. The key words are typically *compare*, *contrast*, *similarities*, and *differences*. Here are some examples. Notice that both similarity and difference may not be asked for in the question, but it will be expected that you provide it to some degree.

> *Compare the political events surrounding President Lincoln's assassination with the political events surrounding President Kennedy's assassination.*

> *Contrast the ways in which liberal theory and neo-conservative theory use tax revenues to support education. Argue that one provides a comprehensive educational plan.*

> *What are the differences between the comedy of Mark Twain and the comedy of modern day sitcoms? Which one qualifies as satire?*

You'll notice that the first question doesn't ask for an argument, although the second and third questions do. You may wish to ask your instructor if argument is a requirement if the assignment prompt doesn't specify this important point. The second prompt asks for an argument. The third prompt is the trickiest. It indirectly asks that you organize your differences around the criteria for satire, yet it doesn't state so directly. If you organized your criteria for any other purpose than discovering which one is satirical, you will not have answered the second question.

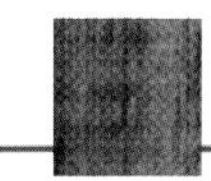

Your thesis will generally contain your major findings on the differences of A and B. Often, your thesis will contain the brief similarity as well.

Example Thesis:

> While both liberal and neo-conservative educational plans provide a comprehensive educational plan for all American schoolchildren, the neo-conservative plan to offer school vouchers and privatize education offers choice and quality in education that the liberal plan cannot provide.

Example Thesis:

> While neo-conservative educational plans provide more choice to some American families, the voluntary segregation and unequal funding of public schools that would result from privatization are not part of the democratic ideals or equal opportunity upon which America is based; only liberal theory guarantees higher learning rooted in American democracy's ideals.

You can easily spot both A and B, liberal and conservative viewpoints, in these sample theses, despite slightly different approaches to presenting the information in each.

Organizing Your Essay

Most comparison and contrast essays work from similar structures. You can present idea A first in its entirety, evaluating it point-by-point. Afterward, you present idea B point-by-point in its entirety.

The second method of organization is to evaluate idea A by one point, then evaluate idea B by the same point. This method offers an instant comparison for the reader, but it offers only parts without giving the audience a whole A or B. You will have to decide which method is best for your assignment. Here are some questions to help you decide:

1. Will people forget a point-by-point analysis too easily because of a large amount of information?
2. Depending on how familiar with the topic and ideas my audience is, how much do I need to explain A and B as separate whole entities before dissecting them into parts?
3. Which type of comparison and contrast essay allows me to illustrate and support my thesis and argument quickly?
4. Which type of organization allows me to most easily demonstrate how my immediate claim and contrast relate to my thesis?

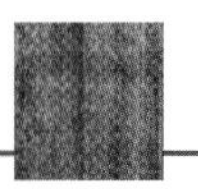

As you can see from the questions, your audience's familiarity with your subject is important to your organization, as is the ability to quickly show the relevance of important differences to your thesis. Remember that these "differences" will often rely on previous comparison and contrast— this is where organization becomes important in comparison and contrast essays. No essay is mathematically organized from beginning to end. Although discussing only idea A then idea B, or discussing each criterion point-by-point would be organizationally perfect, you may have to break out of either pattern at times to relate details to your argument.

Comparing and contrasting is a basic mode of thought. We all make choices every day based on a better/worse scale. Comparing and contrasting can help you build criteria to support for your prewriting ideas, and it can help you continue to think of related material. Even if you don't choose to argue by comparison and contrast, you'll add to your prewriting ideas by thinking with this method.

Argument by Illustration or Example

Argument by illustration is a unique form of argument that provides a "story" of sorts to argue why something works well. If you are arguing about how a professional sports team should be managed, you may use the story of a championship team to illustrate the finer points of managerial strategy. Your story, however, is not just a story of victories, great plays, and game by-game analysis. Your illustration would cover all the criteria of other forms of argument that are less story driven. For example, the managerial strategies for a sports team would probably include argument about how to choose a coach, the coach's relationship with management, how to draft players, how to construct a team identity, etc.

The story of how you were elected class president would contain a blueprint on how to self-nominate, campaign, communicate your views, and debate an opponent.

While each of these would be told as part of the story of the championship season, each part of the story would serve as an example of how a team should be run. This means you would analyze and abstract certain principles from the story that could be used as advice for any coach of a sports team. These abstractions are the argumentative structure. The story of the team is one form of support. Although it may not matter how you arrive at these abstract lessons on how to manage a sports team, it is these abstractions that make your story more than just an inspiring story.

You will also need sources for your argument. These will typically work in support of the abstractions from your argument.

Exercise: The following could be passages from the story of a championship season in the making. Write an abstract principle below each.

1. Coach Bruce Smith was a man destined for Super Bowl greatness. As a player, he won two MVP awards and back-to-back Super Bowls. As a college coach, his team ranked in the Top Ten eleven out of his fifteen years.

2. While an assistant coach in the NFL, Coach Smith worked closely with general manager Avery Shield, trading advice and recruiting strategies.

3. Coach Smith personally talked to and recruited Tom Johnson and D. D. Tavrick, his star wide receiver and quarterback.

4. During the years leading up to the championship season, Coach Smith dismissed an All-Pro tight end, Chuck Bearweather, for consistently being late for practice. He also dismissed a kick returner Jim Shackford for publicly criticizing the return coverage during the preseason.

5. Although his top three recruits did not display much promise two years ago, Coach Smith gave these players assignments on special teams. All three of these draftees started during the championship season, and one was nominated All-Pro. All three have signed contracts for another three years, despite offers from other clubs.

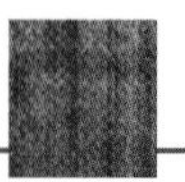

Potential Answers:

1. Players who are successful as professional players and college coaches will be good professional coaches.
2. A football team with a coach and management that cooperate and share ideas may increase their chances of a successful season.
3. Coaches who have personal contact with potential players will have a better chance of signing those players.
4. Dismissing players who are undisciplined or critical may help team cohesion.
5. Developing rather than dismissing developing players can lead to their better play and a dedication to the team rather than money and free agency.

Each of these are argumentative claims that could work in other forms of argument as well. Abstracting these from the story allows you to support them with similar opinions from secondary sources—in this case, secondary sources on management and leadership in professional sports and perhaps management in general. Many of the student essays in this book are argument by illustration. Look to these for examples of how a story provides an argumentative structure.

Because illustration represents the natural stories of life, it can be very helpful for extending your prewriting thoughts. Imagining how your topic fits into the story of your life or others' lives can help you use your life experience to discover ideas that may never enter your mind while making abstract lists.

Argument by Classification and Division

The purpose of argument by classification and division is to create categories that explain your problem and/or your solution. Classifying your problem or solution can help to explain differences to both yourself and your audience. These differences can go beyond explanation into argument in a variety of ways. After classifying the problem different ways, you can offer a solution that solves each class of problem. You would most likely engage each problem with your solution in separate paragraphs, but not necessarily so.

Classification and division allows you to solidly and predictably *order* your topic, problems, and solutions. While some essays are a mosaic or weave of claims, support, and counterargument with a unique and unpredictable order, classification often visually presents its contents with subject headings for each problem or solution.

Your problems, once classified, should not overlap. Creating clear cut categories is a hallmark of this type of argument. When categories creating a problem are fuzzy, as they often are in life, argument by classification and division may not be the right choice to communicate or persuade. However, this type of argument can potentially help you distinguish and limit fuzzy categories, making them clearer.

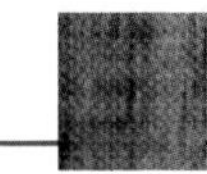

As always, your essay will need a thesis. This thesis may list all the categories and their solution, or it may discuss just the problem and solution generally.

> While the infrastructural problems of America divide neatly into bridges, interstates, water pipes, and sewer pipes, the allotting of government funds for repair cannot be divided so neatly due to the level of disrepair for each category.

An essay of this type often has headings after the introduction:

> ***BRIDGES***
> A government report suggests that all the bridges of America are in need of repair. The report found that bridges built before 1960 are architecturally less sound, yet corrosion levels and structural stress are higher than recommended on a majority of bridges built before 1980.
>
> ***INTERSTATES***
> A majority of state and federal analyses of interstates found that although the roads are in disrepair, they do not pose excessive danger to drivers. Furthermore, funding for these highly visible problems is consistent with federal estimates.

It is easy to imagine the rest of the essay. It is also easy to imagine several ways to communicate the solutions. First, you could reach conclusions on the urgency of particular classes' disrepair. Then, using the same headings as the first half of your essay, you could provide solutions. This format may work well with some essays. However, you would be separating your solution from the in-depth explanation of the problem. Thus, providing a solution immediately following each problem's description may be more appropriate and easier on your reader's memory and understanding.

Two Outline Strategies for Classification and Division

Outline One:

I. Introduction/Thesis

II. Problems

- A. Bridges
- B. Interstates
- C. Water Pipes
- D. Sewer Pipes

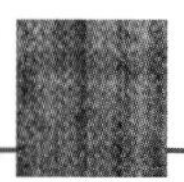

III. Solutions
- A. Bridges
- B. Interstates
- C. Water Pipes
- D. Sewer Pipes

IV. Conclusion

Outline Two:

I. Introduction/Thesis

II. Classifications
- A. Bridges
  - a) problems
  - b) solutions
- B. Interstates
  - a) problems
  - b) solutions
- C. Water Pipes
  - a) problems
  - b) solutions
- D. Sewer Pipes
  - a) problems
  - b) solutions

III. Conclusion

Arguments by classification and division can be useful when you have a wealth of information but are not sure how to organize it. Separating your material into classes can help you see which strands of information, ideas, problems, and solutions belong together. Even if you choose not to argue through definition and classification, the process of classifying your prewriting thoughts and any research will help you organize information for any type of essay.

Argument by Cause and Effect

Cause and effect arguments explain the reasons or results of an event, idea, or situation. This mode of communication will also work well for explanation. Whether or not you have an argument will depend on whether or not your causes or effects are opinions rather than facts. If your thesis is an opinion, not fact, then even if you use facts as causes or effects, they are working in service of your opinion. Contentious scientific issues such as global warming, deforestation, and stem cell research are examples of scientific fact used in the service of a values-laden argument.

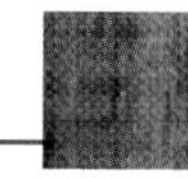

Cause and effect can also be used for cultural "values" arguments as well, where causes and effects are hypothetical.

There are three basic types of cause and effect arguments: multiple causes/one effect, one cause/multiple effects, and chain or domino effect.

The multiple causes/one effect can be organized as follows:

> Thesis:
> American children are not being protected from dangerous Chinese toys for three reasons: lack of Chinese governmental oversight, lack of US testing on Chinese imports, and lack of US trade penalties against China for lax toy safety laws.

Three Outline Strategies for Cause and Effect

This essay could easily be organized in the following manner:

I. Introduction/Thesis
II. Lack of Chinese governmental oversight
    a) reason/cause
    b) reason/cause
III. Lack of US testing
    a) reason/cause
    b) reason/cause
IV. Lack of US trade penalties against China
    a) reason/cause
    b) reason/cause
V. Conclusion

The one cause/multiple effects will be similar to the following. Fill in any gaps left in the outline:

> Obesity is one of the major problems facing Americans today. It can result in physical and mental health problems, as well as removal from an active lifestyle.

I. Introduction/Thesis
II. Physical Health Problems
    a)
    b)
    c)

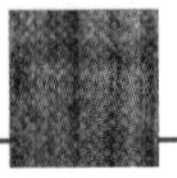

III. Mental Health Problems
  a)
  b)
IV. Removal from an active lifestyle
  a)
  b)
V. Conclusion

The third type of cause and effect argument is a chain effect, also known as a domino effect. The above argument against obesity could be easily organized as a domino effect.

Write a thesis for the simple outline below:

I.
II. Obesity has been linked to physical health problems such as
  a) high blood pressure
  b) diabetes
  c) shortness of breath
III. Physical symptoms can inhibit an active lifestyle
  a) fewer endorphins in bloodstream
  b) accelerates the body's aging process
IV. The inactive lifestyle can result in
  a) low self-esteem
  b) mild depression
  c) lack of sexual drive
V. Conclusion

The above example of the cause/domino effect demonstrates the *potential* effects of a cause. They are not guaranteed. You may wish to think about what fields deal in absolute domino effects and which fields have only the potential for various domino effects.

Exercise: Identifying Argument: Which type of argument is the following thesis and outline?

> Twenty-four hour TV news channels distort or omit important information required for a full discussion of current events and politics.

I. Reporting distorts information
  a) Hosts have political bias
  b) Station owners have political bias

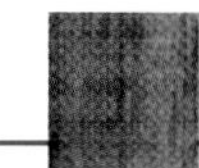

II. Medium distorts information
- a) argument, not cooperation, encouraged
- b) extremist views encouraged
- c) entertainment valued over neutral information

III. Medium omits information
- a) Two minute stories lack detail
- b) Point-counterpoint format not used

Each of the above is a cause. The effect is the misrepresentation of current events by cable news shows. This claim is argumentative. Some of the support for these claims may be data or surveys. Others may merely be opinion. Also, you may see that certain sections have more causes than others. Also, some causes may be placed under a variety of areas. This is OK. Not all causes and effects can be easily categorized.

As with other forms or argument, cause and effect may be a good organizing strategy for your prewriting. Gathering together a cause for each effect may help you see what information belongs together. If you find a cause with no effect or vice versa, you can fill in what is most likely a gap in your original prewriting.

Out of the Dark

Many times we have an abundance of information but are unsure how the information relates or how to order it in an essay. The focus of this chapter was to demonstrate not only forms of argument that many essays follow, but to demonstrate how forms of argument can shape your incomplete prewriting thoughts. Putting your early thoughts into these "containers" will help you extend your thought and fill in gaps. It may also help you choose a form that best communicates your information to your audience clearly.

CHAPTER EIGHT

Writing

WRITING RHETORICALLY

Use the Tools of a Skilled Rhetor

At the end of one semester, one student reflected on what she'd learned during the semester. She said:

> I used to sit down to write, and whatever ended up on the page was what I typed and handed in. I had no concept of the invention process and the difference it could make in the content of the essay. This became clearer when I completed our final essay. The invention work was instrumental in helping me remember vivid details, people, even my feelings, all of which were important components of the paper.

This student is on the path toward becoming a skilled rhetor. Already, she has learned how spending time on activities *before* writing can help her writing. She is learning methods that can help improve her writing, similar to how students of rhetoric in ancient Greek and Rome studied the art of composition as a way of learning to be effective orators, an essential skill for a citizen in those cultures.

The Five Parts of Rhetoric

Greek and Roman rhetoricians divided rhetoric into five parts or **faculties** that correspond to the order of activities involved in creating a speech: **invention, arrangement, style, memory,** and **delivery**. These five parts, or faculties, of rhetoric are described in many handbooks of rhetorical instruction, including the *Rhetorica ad Herennium,* which was composed by an unknown author between 86 and 82 CE:

> The speaker . . . should possess the faculties of Invention, Arrangement, Style, Memory, and Delivery. Invention is the devising of matter, true or plausible, that would make the case convincing. Arrangement is the ordering and distribution of the matter, making clear the place to which each thing is to be assigned. Style is the adaptation of suitable words and sentences to the matter devised. Memory is the firm retention in the mind of the matter, words, and arrangement. Delivery is the graceful regulation of voice, countenance, and gesture.

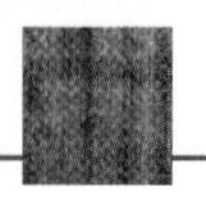

Today, classes in composition or writing studies still emphasize the necessity of **invention**, now interpreted as prewriting activities that enable writers to develop the logic and words needed for effective arguments. **Arrangement** currently involves organizing an argument into a logical format that leads the reader easily from the thesis to the conclusion. **Style** has to do with the author's voice, tone, and structure of sentences and paragraphs. **Memory** is used somewhat differently today, as students are no longer required to memorize compositions for oral presentation. Instead, memory is utilized in ways such as remembering how and where to retrieve information from the Internet, books, and other reference materials. Finally, **delivery**, which once involved gestures and tone of voice in an oral presentation, today has to do with document design, so that the final product is presented in a professional manner according to Modern Language Association (MLA) or American Psychological Association (APA) style. Delivery also involves grammatical accuracy because surface errors detract from the effective impact of a document.

The Writing Process Overview

When you are planning to write, what do you do? Do you talk to a friend about the topic you are writing about, or do you go to the library to look up what experts have said about your topic? Do you write in your head as you drive to school, or do you sit at your kitchen table with your favorite pen and create an extensive outline before you begin typing your paper into the computer? Do you only write a sentence down when you know it is perfect, or do you allow words to flow on to the page unedited, checking for spelling and grammar errors later? Do you ask people to read and respond to your writing, or are you hesitant even to show it to your instructor? Maybe you put off writing until the evening before your paper is due, then you sit down to write at midnight, hoping you will finish before breakfast.

Every writer, even the student writer, has developed habits of writing. These habits may help a writer complete thoughtful and well-written essays, or they may keep a writer from doing his or her best work. No matter what habits you have developed, examining the habits of successful writers can help you get better ideas and write more thorough and thoughtful essays. It is likely your instructor will ask you to follow a set of steps in order to write your essays for this class. The steps the instructor asks you to follow are not just random requirements. Instead, they have come from careful analysis of the activities of successful student and professional writers.

Inventing:

Writing is not only about putting the pen to paper. As did rhetors in ancient Greece and Rome, you have to think deeply and critically about the subject before you begin a composition. The invention step of the writer's process is designed to help you find a worthwhile topic and develop your ideas about that topic before you start to write a draft. It includes writing, discussion, and research, as well as informal writing to help you explore your thoughts and feelings about a sub-

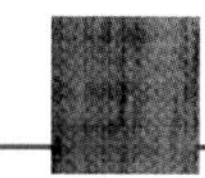

ject. Whatever method you choose, keep a record of your thoughts and the discoveries that come up as you spend this time in close examination of your subject.

Drafting:

It may seem odd that writing a draft should come in the middle of the writer's process. However, research has shown that students and professionals alike write more effective essays when they don't reach for the pen too quickly. If you have spent enough time in the invention stage, the actual drafting stage may go more quickly. You write the first draft, then in succeeding drafts you add details, observations, illustrations, examples, expert testimony, and other support that will help your essay entertain, illuminate or convince your audience.

Revising:

Today, we talk more about the revision stage of writing than did ancient rhetoricians. If your habits have included writing your class essays at the last minute, you may have missed this step entirely, yet many writers claim this is the longest and most rewarding step in the writing process. To revise, you must, in a sense, learn to let go of your writing. Some students think their first drafts should stay exactly the way they are written because they are true to their feelings and experience. Many writers find, however, that first drafts assume too much about the reader's knowledge and reactions. Sometimes readers, reading a first draft essay, are left scratching their heads and wondering what it is the writer is trying to convey. Writers who revise try to read their writing as readers would note gaps in logic, absence of clear examples, need for reordering information, etc. Then they can revise content with the reader in mind.

Editing and Polishing:

Once writers have clarified their messages and the methods by which they get their points across, one more step must be taken. Particularly because their compositions are written, rather than presented orally, they must go over their work again to check for correct spelling, grammar, and punctuation, as well as the use of Standard Written English. Some students finish with an essay, print it, and turn it in without ever examining the final copy. This is a critical mistake, because misspelled words and typographical and formatting errors can make an otherwise well-written essay lose credibility.

Using *Topoi* to Develop a Topic into an Essay

Students in ancient Greece, like modern students, generally began the composition process with a subject or topic and then explored the topic from a variety of perspectives or viewpoints—something like our contemporary prewriting process. For example, they would define terms and the meanings associated with those terms, and then consider the moral connotations of those meanings. Aristotle and other teachers of rhetoric did this by employing ***topoi***, which might be translated literally as "places" or more generally as "topics." A *topoi* is a strategy or heuristic made up of questions about a topic which allows a rhetor to construe an argument. *Topoi* applicable to any topic are sometimes called common topics or common places. Following is an outline of Aristotle's common topics which can be applied to develop research paper topics into essays. It is based upon a schema developed by Edward P. J. Corbett and Robert J. Connors for *Classical Rhetoric for the Modern Student*.

In each case, you would answer the question and then elaborate on your answer. In the process of answering the questions, you may develop an approach to discussing the topic.

QUESTIONS OF DEFINITION

Genus or classification: What larger class does your subject belong to? If, for example, you are writing about stem cell research, the larger class might be medical ethics.

Species or division: What makes your topic unique in terms of its class? For stem cell research, you might discuss embryonic stem cells as different from adult stem cells.

QUESTIONS OF COMPARISON

Similarity: What characteristics does your topic share with others? How is the stem cell research controversy similar to other medical controversies such as the use of animals to test new drugs and medical procedures?

Difference: What makes your topic unique? How is it different from others? How does research with stem cells differ from other medical research controversies?

Degree: How significant are those similarities and/or differences?

Cause and Effect: What makes your topic happen? What are the consequences of your topic and how significant are they? Embryonic stem cells were chosen for research because they have not yet differentiated into cell types such as heart cells or skin cells and, thus, offer more opportunities for modification into cells that can be used for medical treatment. A consequence of the use of embryonic stem cells, however, is that it involves the destruction of human embryos.

QUESTIONS OF RELATIONSHIPS

Antecedent and Consequence: What came before your topic? What will happen because of it? In other words, you might ask the question of your subject: "If your topic occurs, then what?" For example, if the embryos come from fertility clinics and were to be destroyed anyway, is there a problem with using them for research? Some argue that a consequence of using embryonic stem cells is that it opens the door to cloning human cells.

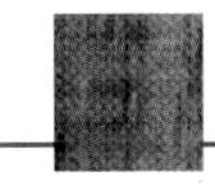

Contraries: What is the argument that proves the opposite of your argument? For example, instead of arguing that embryonic stem cells should or should not be used for research, you might argue that diseases should not be treated by alteration of genetic material. Thus, no stem cells should be used for research.

Contradictions: What other interpretations could there be of your topic? If your topic is not what you think it is, what else might it be? For example, early on, stem cell researchers feared that the public would protest "the technological power" of stem cells and question what would happen if someone put human stem cells into the brain of a rat. Would you have a human mind in a rat's brain?

QUESTIONS OF CIRCUMSTANCE

Possible and Impossible: How feasible and/or workable is your topic? What factors make your topic either possible or impossible? For example, you can question whether it is moral to leave unexplored medical research that could lead to cures for diabetes and other major illnesses.

Past Fact and Future Fact: What precedents are there for your topic? Has it happened or been tried before? Based on past experience, what can you predict for the future of your topic? Based on other medical research, how feasible is it that using embryonic stem cells could lead to cures for diseases?

QUESTIONS OF TESTIMONY

Authority: What sources of information do you have to support your topic? What makes your sources authoritative? For example, have you based your argument upon recognized medical authorities? Are there those in the medical community who might disagree? Indeed, are medical leaders the proper authorities for your argument?

Testimonial: Who has personally experienced your topic? How might their experience enhance or detract from the credibility of your position on your topic? Do you have examples of the testimony of couples who have donated embryonic cells to this research? Do you have testimony of individuals who have diabetes and other diseases that might be cured by such research?

Statistics: What documented research can you find that gives insight about your topic? How widespread or significant is your topic? Do you have statistics that result from studies using embryonic vs. adult stem cells? Do you have statistics about the diseases that may be receptive to treatment with stem cells?

Other Invention Strategies

Great myths have grown up around writers who can supposedly sit down, put pen to paper, and write a masterpiece. If these myths had developed about any other type of artist—a musician or

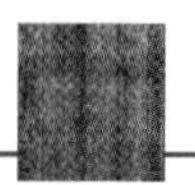

a painter—we would scoff about them and ask about the years of study and practice those artists had spent before they created their masterpieces. Since all of us can write to some degree, perhaps it seems more feasible that great authors simply appear magically amongst us. Alas, it is not so; like all talented artists, good writers must learn their craft through consistent and continuous practice. Similar to how the ancient Greeks used *topoi* to generate raw material for their compositions, many writers today use the following invention strategies as prewriting activities:

Freewriting:
One practice method developed in the 1970s and often attributed to Peter Elbow, author of *Writing Without Teachers*, is called *freewriting*. And the method is just what it sounds like—writing that is free of any content restrictions. You simply write what is on your mind. Use freeform, but there is some structure—you must set a time limit before you begin, and once you begin, you must not stop. The time period is usually ten to twenty minutes, and you must keep your pen or pencil moving on the page—no hesitations, no corrections, no rereading. Don't worry about spelling, or punctuation, or grammar—just download onto the paper whatever comes to mind. It will seem awkward at best; some have said it is downright painful. But after a few weeks practice, you will realize it is effective, and a wonderful individual method of getting at your thoughts on a subject.

Invisible Freewriting:
If you just cannot stop paying attention to your spelling and grammar, or if you find yourself always stopping to read what you have written, you can **freewrite invisibly**. To do this, you will need carbon paper and a pen that is retracted or out of ink. You sandwich the carbon paper, carbon side down, between two sheets of paper and write on the top sheet with your empty pen. You cannot see what you are writing, but you will have it recorded on the bottom sheet of paper. You can easily modify this to work on the computer by taping a blank sheet of paper over the monitor while you type.

Focused Freewriting:
When freewriting, you are writing without sticking to any particular topic. You are exploring many ideas and your sentences may roam from your day at work, the letter you just got from your sister, or a story you read in the paper about a man who tracks the nighttime migrations of songbirds. With ***focused freewriting,*** you are trying to concentrate on one particular subject.
You can write that subject at the top of the page to remind you of your topic as you write. The rules are the same, but when you are focusing, you are more aware of exploring one question or idea in depth.

One drawback of focused freewriting is that students sometimes confuse it with a different step in the writing process, drafting. Remember that freewriting is invention work, intended only to help you explore ideas on paper. Drafting takes place only after you have explored, analyzed,

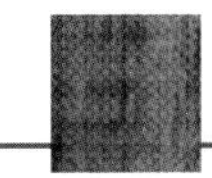

and organized those ideas. Freewriting helps you think and write critically about a topic while drafting occurs once you have done the critical thinking necessary to come up with a unified, cohesive, and organized plan for an essay.

Listing/Brainstorming:

This method of mapping is the least visual and the most straightforward. Unlike freewriting, where you write continuously, with **listing** you write down words and/or phrases that provide a shorthand for the ideas you might use in your essay, much as you would a grocery or "to-do" list. **Brainstorming** is a bit looser. Lists usually follow line after line on the page; brainstorming consists of words and phrases placed anywhere on the page you want to write them down.

Clustering:

When you think of a cluster, you think of several like things grouped together, often with something holding them together. *Peanut clusters*, a type of candy, are peanuts joined together with milk chocolate. *Star clusters* are groupings of stars, like the Pleiades or the Big Dipper connected by their relative positions to each other in space. You can create **clusters** of like ideas by grouping your ideas around a central topic on a blank sheet of paper.

Organizing or Arranging:

The invention process is intended to get our ideas out of our heads and onto a piece of paper, but rarely do these ideas arrive in the most logical or effective order. Take some time (an hour or so for a short essay) to analyze your inventions. Place all the ideas in a logical order, and join similar ideas. Next, look for your most significant point—the most important thing you want to say about your subject. This may become your tentative thesis. Then identify which of the other items on your list will help you communicate your point and delete items that are irrelevant to your thesis.

Establish an Occasion for Writing

Why do writers write? To express ideas. To persuade an audience. To respond to an event in their lives. To learn new ideas. To discover themselves. You may be able to add other motivations to the list. Combine one of these personalized motivations with a topic and an audience, and you have an occasion for writing. You may think that you do not need to be concerned about an occasion for writing because the text and perhaps your instructor provide you with assignments. Do not be misled, however. Assignments as phrased in this textbook or as given by your instructor are not in themselves occasions for writing.

Organize Your Essay

Classical rhetoricians based their teaching of arrangement, or organization of a composition, on the practices they noticed among the most outstanding orators of their day. The basic arrangement of material then is much the same as familiar organization today. An orator would begin by attracting the audience's attention in what they called the *exordium*, which we would call the opening or introduction. Next, they would provide background information in a *narratio* or narration, followed by an *explication* in which they would define terms and enumerate the issues. During the *partition* they would express the thesis or main issue to be discussed, and in the *confirmation* they would provide evidence to support the thesis. Opposition arguments would be addressed in the *refutatio*, and the composition would be wrapped up with a *peroratio* or conclusion. The order of these different elements was not rigid in ancient times, nor it is today, and sometimes one or more sections were eliminated if they were not needed, but then, as now, an effective text included most of these elements. For example, if your audience is very familiar with a particular subject, you would not need to define terms, as you would with an audience who was unfamiliar with the material.

As you begin to draft your research paper, you might want to keep the elements of an effective composition in mind, perhaps checking as you complete your first draft to be sure either that all are present or that there is a reason for eliminating one or more parts. Like the ancient Greeks, you will begin with an opening and end with a conclusion. However, in between the bookends of your essay, you will likely want to rearrange the elements somewhat, as we have done in the discussion that follows in the chapter.

Elements of Effective Organization from Ancient Rhetoric

Opening (Exordium): Attracts the audience's attention to the issue.

Background or narration (Narratio): Details the history or facts of the issue.

Definition or explication (Explicatio): Defines terms and outlines issues.

Thesis (Partitio): States the particular issue that is to be argued.

Proof (Confirmatio): Develops the thesis and provides support evidence.

Refutation or opposition (Refutatio): Addresses the arguments opposing the thesis.

Conclusion (Peroratio): Reiterates the thesis and may urge the audience to action.

Write a Thesis Statement

A **thesis** may be a sentence or a series of sentences, or in a few cases may be implied rather than stated explicitly; but a thesis is at the heart of a piece of writing. If a reader cannot identify your thesis, the meaning of your text is not clear. How do you develop a thesis? First, you determine your occasion for writing—who is your audience, what is your purpose, and what special circumstances there are, if any. Then you write a working thesis that makes an assertion or claim about your topic—something that will be affected by your audience and purpose. For example, if you are writing a research paper about the advantages and disadvantages of biodiesel fuel, your claim may be stated differently if your audience is an English class than if it is a chemistry

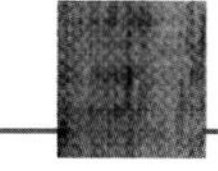

class. In the latter, you might need to use technical language that would be unfamiliar to your English professor.

Working theses are statements that develop and change as essays are written; they are basic frameworks which provide a connection for the ideas you have decided to convey to your reader. Later, after you have completed a draft of your text, examine your working thesis. If needed, rewrite your thesis so that it clearly states the main idea of your essay in a clear and engaging fashion.

EXAMPLES OF A THESIS STATEMENT

The United States should implement a guest worker program as a way of reforming the illegal immigration problem.

Nuclear power should be considered as part of a program to reduce the United States' dependence on foreign oil.

Compose an Introduction

Experienced writers have different methods of creating a good introduction. One who tends to discover his paper as he goes along swears the best way to write an introduction is write the entire paper, then move the conclusion to the beginning of the essay and rewrite it as the introduction. Another writer lets the paper sit around for a few days before she writes her introduction. A third always writes two or three different introductions and tries them out on friends before deciding which to use. However you choose to write the introduction, make sure it is interesting enough to make your reader want to read on.

The introduction to your essay is an invitation to your reader. If you invite readers to come along with you on a boring journey, they won't want to follow. In magazine and newspaper writing, the introduction is sometimes called a hook because it hooks the reader into reading the text. If a magazine writer does not capture the reader's attention right away, the reader is not likely to continue. After all, there are other and possibly more interesting articles in the magazine. Why should readers suffer through a boring introduction? Depending on the topic and pattern of your essay, you might employ one of the following techniques to hook your readers and make them keep reading:

- An intriguing or provocative quotation
- A narrative or anecdote
- A question or series of questions
- A vivid sensory description
- A strongly stated opinion

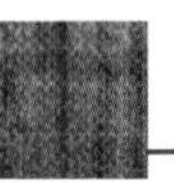

Your introductory paragraph makes a commitment to your readers. This is where you identify the topic, state your thesis (implicitly or explicitly), and give your readers clues about the journey that will follow in the succeeding paragraphs. Be careful not to mislead the reader. Do not ask questions you will not answer in your paper (unless they are rhetorical questions). Do not switch topics from your introduction to your paper.

Although the introduction is the first paragraph or so of the paper, it may not be the first paragraph the writer composes. If you have problems beginning your essay because you cannot immediately think of a good introduction, begin with the first point in your essay and come back to the introduction later.

Combine Your Ideas with Support from Source Materials

A research paper, by definition, makes use of source materials to make an argument. It is important to remember, however, that it is *your* paper, *not* what some professors may call a "research dump," meaning that it is constructed by stringing together research information with a few transitions. Rather, you, as the author of the paper, carry the argument in your own words and use quotes and paraphrases from source materials to support your argument. How do you do that? Here are some suggestions:

- After you think you have completed enough research to construct a working thesis and begin writing your paper, collect all your materials in front of you (photocopies of articles, printouts of electronic sources, and books) and spend a few hours reading through the materials and making notes. Then, put all the notes and materials to the side and freewrite for a few minutes about what you can remember from your research that is important. Take this freewriting and make a rough outline of main points you want to cover in your essay. Then you can go back to your notes and source materials to flesh out your outline.
- Use quotes for three reasons: 1.) You want to "borrow" the ethos or credibility of the source. For example, if you are writing about stem cell research, you may want to quote from an authority such as Dr. James A. Thomson, whose ground-breaking research led to the first use of stem cells for research. Alternatively, if you are quoting from the *New England Journal of Medicine* or another prestigious publication, it may be worth crediting a quote to that source. 2.) The material is so beautifully or succinctly written that it would lose its effectiveness if you reworded the material in your own words. 3.) You want to create a point of emphasis by quoting rather than paraphrasing. Otherwise, you probably want to paraphrase material from your sources, as quotes should be used sparingly. Often, writers quote source material in a first draft and then rewrite some of the quotes into paraphrases during the revision process.
- Introduce quotes. You should never have a sentence or sentences in quotation marks just sitting in the middle of a paragraph, as it would puzzle a reader. If you quote, you should al-

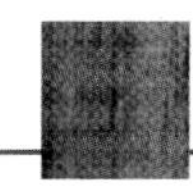

ways introduce the quote by saying something like this: According to Dr. James A. Thomson, "Stem cell research......"

- Avoid plagiarism by clearly indicating material that is quoted or paraphrased.

Support Your Thesis

After you have attracted the interest of your audience, established your thesis and given any background information and definitions, you will next begin to give reasons for your position, which further develops your argument. These reasons are, in turn, supported by statistics, analogies, anecdotes, and quotes from authorities which you have discovered in your research or know from personal knowledge. Ideally, arrange your reasons so that the strongest ones come either at the beginning or the end of this portion of the paper and the weaker ones fall in the middle which are not points of emphasis.

Answer Opposing Arguments

If you are aware of a contradicting statistic or other possible objection to your argument, it may be tempting to ignore that complication, hoping your audience will not notice. However, that is exactly the worst thing you can do. It is much better to anticipate your audience's possible questions or objections and address them in your discussion. Doing so prevents you from losing credibility by appearing to deceive your audience or from the perception that you are not aware of all the facts. Also, acknowledging possible refutations of your position actually strengthens your position by making you seem knowledgeable and fair-minded.

Vary Your Strategies or Patterns of Development

When composing your essay, you have many different strategies or **patterns of development** available to you. You may write entire essays where the strategy is argumentation or comparison and contrast, but more often, you will combine many of these different modes while writing a single essay.

- Analysis entails a close examination of an issue, a book, a film, or other object, separating it into elements and examining each of the elements separately through other writing modes, such as classification or comparison and contrast.
- Argumentation involves taking a strong stand on an issue supported by logical reasons and evidence intended to change a reader's mind on an issue or open a reader's eyes to a problem.
- Cause and effect is an explanation of the cause and subsequent effects or consequences of a specific action.
- Classification entails dividing and grouping things into logical categories.

- Comparison and contrast examines the similarities and differences between two or more things.
- Definition employs an explanation of the specific meaning of a word, phrase, or idea.
- Description uses vivid sensory details to present a picture or an image to the reader.
- Exemplification makes use of specific examples to explain, define, or analyze something.
- Narration uses a story or vignette to illustrate a specific point or examine an issue.

Write a Conclusion

After they have read the last paragraph of your essay, your readers should feel satisfied that you have covered everything you needed to and you have shared an insight. You may have heard the basic rules: A conclusion cannot address any new issues, and it should summarize the main points of the essay. Although these are valid and reliable rules, a summary is not always the best way to end an essay. The prohibition against new ideas in the final paragraph also might limit certain effective closures like a call to action or a question for the reader to ponder.

One effective technique for writing a conclusion is to refer back to your introduction. If you began with a narrative anecdote, a sensory description, or a question, you can tie a mention of it to your ending point. Or, if you are composing an argumentative essay, you might choose to summarize by using an expert quote to restate your thesis, giving the reader a final firm sense of ethos or credibility. You might also end with a single-sentence summary followed by a suggestion or a call to action for the reader. Another effective way to end an argument can be a paragraph that suggests further research.

A conclusion doesn't have to be long. As a matter of fact, it does not even need to be a separate paragraph, especially if your essay is short. If your closing comments are related to the final paragraph of the essay, one or two sentences can easily be added to the final body paragraph of the essay.

REVISING RHETORICALLY

Role of Revision

In ancient times, the focus of the rhetor was upon presentation of oral arguments in the form of speeches, and students trained to perform in pressured situations before a law court or assembly. Though a speaker might spend time in preparation, most speeches were one-time opportunities. If the words were not well-chosen and well-spoken the first time, there was no second chance to influence an audience.

With modern written documents, a composition does not have to be perfect when the words first appear on the page. A document is not truly finished until it is transmitted to an audience,

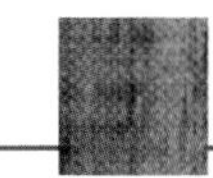

and, even then, important documents are often circulated in draft stages to colleagues for comments before the process is complete, and it is presented to an audience.

Many writers claim that revising is the most rewarding step in writing, the time when they have words on a page to work with and can manipulate them to create a composition which communicates effectively. Yet, many students feel that their first drafts should stay exactly the way they've written them because these writings are truest to their feelings and experience.

They are sure they have made their point clearly, but the reader may be left scratching his or her head and wondering what it was the writer meant to say. To communicate effectively, a writer must learn to interact with his reader to ensure he has communicated his message clearly.

Begin Revision by Rereading

The first step of revising is rereading. This step can be simple, if you are reading something written by someone else, but when it is your own writing it becomes infinitely more difficult. After all, you know what you meant to say—you know the research behind the writing and why you chose certain words or phrases. You even know how every sentence is supposed to read—even though you left out a word or two or three—and your mind can trick you into seeing the missing words right where they belong. Unfortunately, the reader does not have your understanding, and communication can break down. You need to learn to read your own work critically, as if it were written by a stranger. One of the first aids in this process is to read your work aloud. You can often hear stumbling blocks quicker than you can see them.

You can also learn to read your own work more objectively by reading and commenting on other writers' work. Look at the structure of essays, at the way the writers use transitions and topic sentences, and at the sentence structure and choice of words. As you learn to see how good writers put ideas and words together, you will begin to think about the readings in a more thorough manner—thinking of alternative, perhaps even better, ways to express the message of each essay. You will also learn to read your own work with a more critical eye.

Qualities of Effective Writing

After reading the work of some professional writers, you may have developed the idea that the best writing is writing that is difficult to understand, writing that sends the reader to the dictionary with every sentence, or writing that uses many technical or specialized terms. Often, we think something difficult to read must be well written. Although it is sometimes difficult to read about topics that are new to us because we're learning new vocabulary and struggling with complex ideas, it simply is not true that the best writing is hard to read. Indeed, the most effective writing, the kind of writing you want to produce in your classes, is simple, concise, and direct.

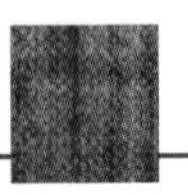

Keep It Simple

Simple means "unadorned" or "not ornate." *Writing simply* means saying something in common, concrete language without too much complication in the sentence structure. Writing simply doesn't mean you have to use only short or easy words. It doesn't mean that all your sentences will be simple sentences. It doesn't mean that you can't use figures of speech or intricate details. Simple writing means that you try to get your point across in a direct and interesting way. You aren't trying to hide your ideas. Instead, you are trying to amplify those ideas and begin an intelligible conversation with your reader.

Rely on Everyday Words

When writing about computers or other technical subjects, it's tempting to use *jargon* or specialized words you might use when talking to others with the same knowledge, interest, and background. When writing for a limited audience whose members are familiar with technical terms, a bit of jargon might be acceptable. However, most of the writing you will do in college and later in the workplace will address a larger audience. You will want to avoid the use of highly technical terms, acronyms, and abbreviations.

If it seems that the writers in this text use many big words or technical terms, stop for a minute to consider the original audience for each of the essays. Consider how your vocabulary grows each year as you read, discuss, and consider new ideas. The everyday words of a tenth-grade student will probably be fewer in number than the everyday words of a junior in college. Similarly, the everyday words of a college freshman will be different from the everyday words of a computer professional with three years of work experience. Use words that are comfortable and familiar to you and your readers when you write, and you will write clear, effective essays.

Use Precise Words

We sometimes assume that our reader will know what we mean when we use adjectives like *beautiful, quiet,* or *slow.* However, the reader has only his or her own ideas of those adjectives. You can make your writing more interesting and effective by adding the concrete details that will give the reader an image using at least two of the senses.

You can use details from all of the senses to make your writing more concrete, more precise. What are some of the sensual qualities of the experience or thing? Can you compare it to another thing that your readers may be familiar with to help them understand it better? Can you compare it to something totally unlike it? Can you compare it to a different sense to surprise the readers and help them understand the image you are trying to create?

A good way to practice your ability to write original concrete images is to expand on a cliché. A cliché is an overused saying or expression. Often, clichés begin as similes that help make images more concrete. They become clichéd or overused because they lose their originality or they don't contain enough detail to give us the entire picture. Choose a cliché and write a sentence that

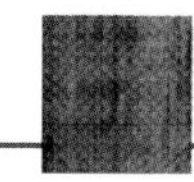

expands the cliché and uses the senses to create a clear picture of the thing described. You might try some of the following clichés:

She is as pretty as a picture.
It smelled heavenly.
It was as soft as a baby's bottom.
His heart is as hard as stone.
It tastes as sour as a pickle.
We stared at the roaring campfire.
We listened to the babbling brook.

Precise details allow us to experience the world of the writer. We leave our own views and perceptions and learn how someone else sees the world. What *quiet* is like for one writer. What *beautiful* means to another. Fill in the gaps between your words and ideas with vivid images and your writing becomes more interesting and more effective.

Be Concise

Rid your writing of excess words and leave only that which makes your meaning clear and concrete. Becoming aware of several common problems can help you make your writing more concise. When you begin a sentence with either *it is* or *there is,* you transfer all the meaning of the sentence to the end of the sentence. This is known as a *delayed construction.* You have delayed the meaning. The reader must read on to find out what *it* or *there* refer to. They don't get anything important from the beginning of the sentence.

Examine the following sentences:

It is important to change the oil in older gasoline engines.
There is an apple on the table.
There isn't anything we need to fear except our own fear.

We can rewrite these sentences, making them more concise, by deleting the *there is* or the *it is* and restructuring the sentence.

Changing the oil in older gasoline engines is important.
An apple is on the table.
We have nothing to fear but fear itself.

Notice that the second group of sentences is shorter and the important information is no longer buried in the middle. Revising this type of sentence can make your writing more concise and get information to the reader more effectively.

If you're afraid you use *it is* and *there is* (or *it's* and *there's*) too often, you can use most word processing programs to seek these constructions out. Use the *Search* or *Find and replace* tool that's found in the Edit portion of your pull-down menu. Type *it is* and ask your computer to find every place you use this construction in your document. When you find a sentence that begins with *it is,* revise the sentence to make it more concise. Do the same with *there is, it's,* and *there's.* After you become more aware of these errors by correcting them, you'll find that you notice the errors before or as you make them. You will begin to write more concisely, and you'll have fewer delayed constructions to revise.

You can also make your writing more concise by avoiding common wordy expressions. Sometimes when we're nervous about writing or insecure about our knowledge of a topic, we try to hide that insecurity behind a wall of meaningless words, such as does the following sentence:

> At this point in time, you may not have the ability to create a web page due to the fact that you've avoided using computers for anything other than playing Solitaire.

This sentence is full of deadwood phrases that add no meaning to the sentence. If we take out the unneeded words, we have this sentence:

> You may not be able to create a web page because you've only used your computer to play Solitaire.

Your computer may have a grammar-checker that will identify some commonly used wordy expressions. If your computer doesn't have a grammar-checker, or if your instructor has asked you not to use the grammar-checker in your computer, you can still learn to revise the wordiness out of your paragraphs. Use the computer to separate a paragraph of your writing into sentences. As you scroll through the paragraph, hit the "hard return" or "enter" key on your keyboard twice every time you find a period. Once you have separated the sentences, look at each sentence. What is the important idea in the sentence? What words are used to convey that idea? What words don't add any meaning to the sentence? Delete words that don't convey meaning, and revise the sentence to make it more concise.

Use Action Verbs

Action verbs are words that convey the action of a sentence. They carry much of our language's nuance and meaning. Many inexperienced writers use only "to be" verbs: *am, is, are, was, were, be, been,* and *being.* If you use too many of these verbs, you risk losing much of the

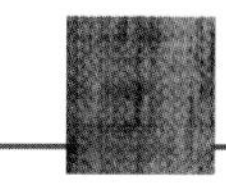

power of language. If I say someone is coming through the door, I've created a picture of a body and a doorway. If I say someone marches or slinks through the door, I've added not only the information about movement but also about the qualities of that movement. I've given my subject the attitude of a soldier or a cat. For example, consider this sentence written by Howard Rheingold:

> Thirty thousand years ago, outside a deceptively small hole in a limestone formation in the area now known as southern France, several adolescents shivered in the dark, awaiting initiation into the cult of toolmakers.

By using the verb *shivered,* especially when accompanied by the words *in the dark,* Rheingold paints a word picture much more vivid than he would have conveyed with the use of a "to be" verb. Using interesting verbs can enliven your writing.

If you want to focus on using more action verbs, skim through your essay and circle all the "to be" verbs. Read the sentences with circled "to be" verbs more closely, and choose several to rewrite using active verbs in place of the "to be" verbs. You won't be able to do this for every sentence, but replace them where you can and your writing will become more lively, more concise, and more effective.

Fill in the Gaps

When we write, we sometimes forget that we are writing to an audience other than ourselves. We expect that our readers are people just like us, with our experiences, memories, and tastes. Because they're so much like us, we think we sometimes expect readers to be able to read more than what we've written on the page. We expect them to read our minds. We may leave large gaps in our essays, hoping the reader will fill in with exactly the information we would have included.

If I'm writing an essay about my childhood in the South and I say it was always so hot in the summer that I hated to go outside, I might think my reader knows what I mean by hot. However, there are many different ways to be "hot." In east Texas where I grew up, the hot was a sticky hot. Eighty degrees made me long for a big glass of sweetened iced tea with lots of ice. The heat made my clothes cling. Sweating didn't help because the sweat didn't dry. I spent the day feeling as if I'd never dried after my morning shower. In New Mexico, I never really felt hot unless the temperature got above 110 degrees. At that point, the heat would rush at me, making it difficult to breathe. I would open the door to leave the house, and it felt as if I had opened the oven door to check on a cake. If I say I was hot in the summer without describing how the heat felt to me, my reader may not get the message I'm trying to convey. Don't expect your reader to know what you mean by "hot" or by any other general description. Instead, take a minute to add details that will fill in the gaps for the reader.

Speak Directly

To *speak directly* is to say, up front, who is doing what. Sometimes we don't tell the reader who is completing the action or we tell them too late. Let's look at the following sentences:

> The steak was stolen from the grill.
> The decisive battle was fought between the Confederate and the Union armies in Vicksburg, Mississippi.
> The red truck has been driven into the side of the green car.

Although we might be able to guess who the actors are in each of the sentences, the first and last sentences don't tell us directly. Even if the reader can guess that it was a dog who stole the steak from the grill or my neighbor who drove the red truck into the side of the green car, the reader has to stop and figure out who is doing what before he or she can read on. This slows the reader down and diminishes the effectiveness of your writing.

Language professionals call this passive voice. The action comes before the actor. Note that sometimes, as in the first and last sentences above, the writer doesn't mention the actor at all. These are tests for passive verbs:

- Look for verbs coupled with another action word that ends in *-ed* or *-en* such as *was stolen* or *was forgotten.*
- Find the action and the actor in the sentence to make sure that they are in the most effective order. The most effective sentence order is actor first, then action. If the sentence does not specify the actor but leaves it implied, chances are that it is a passive sentence. For example, read this sentence: The red truck was driven into the green car. It does not say who the driver was, and, thus is a passive sentence.

Rewriting some of your sentences that have passive voice will make your writing stronger and more interesting.

Remember to Proofread

It is understandably difficult to find the errors in an essay you have been working on for days. A few tricks used by professional writers might help you see errors in your essay more clearly.

1. With pencil in hand, read the essay aloud, slowly, preferably to an audience. When you are reading aloud, it is more difficult to add or change words, so you tend to catch errors you would not see reading silently to yourself. Plus, the reactions of your audience may point out areas where future readers may become confused or lose interest.
2. Another trick is to read the essay backwards, sentence by sentence. This forces you to look at sentence structure and not at the overall content of the essay. If you are working

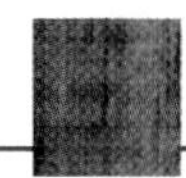

on a computer, another way to accomplish this is to create a final edit file in which you hit the hard return twice at the end of every question or statement. You might even go so far as to number the sentences so they look more like grammar exercises. Then look at each sentence individually.

Gain Feedback by Peer Editing

Your instructor may schedule class periods for peer workshops. These workshops are opportunities for you to get responses from your readers. Often, you will be divided into groups of three or four students and you will be given a list of questions to answer about your peers' essays. Your peers will get copies of your essay, and they will give you comments as well. The first peer workshop can be a difficult experience. It is never easy to take criticism, constructive or not. Taking criticism in a small group is even more difficult. There are several things you can do to make your peer groups more productive.

When your essay is being reviewed:

1. Write down everything the reviewers say. You think you will remember it later, but often you will forget just that piece of advice you need. More importantly, writing while the reviewers speak is an effective way to keep the channels of communication open. It is hard to come up with a defense for your paper if you are busy writing.
2. Save your comments until all the reviewers are done. If you have specific questions, write them in the margins of your notes. If they ask you questions, make a note to answer them when everyone is done. If you allow yourself to speak, you will be tempted to start defending your essay. Once you start defending your essay, two things happen. First, you stop listening to the comments. Second, you offend your reviewers, making it less likely that they will give you honest criticism in the future.
3. The first comment you should make to your reviewers is "Thank You." The second comment can be anything but a defense. Your readers are only telling you how they interpret your essay. They are giving you their opinions; you do not have to make the changes they suggest.
4. Save all the comments you get on your essay. Set them aside for a day or so. Then make the changes that you think will make your essay better.

When you are the reviewer:

1. Read an essay through, at least one time, just to browse the content of the essay. Appreciate the essay for what it does well. Try to ignore any problems for now. You will get back to them the second time you read and begin your comments in the margins. Every essay will have at least one thing good about it.
2. Always begin your comments with a sincere discussion of what you like about the essay.

3. Be specific in your comments. Your peers will probably understand you better if you say, "The topic sentence in paragraph four really sets the reader up for what the essay accomplishes in paragraph four. But I can't really find a topic sentence for paragraph six, and the topic sentences in paragraphs two and three could be improved." Note how this statement gives a positive response and then identifies specific places where the author can improve the essay. This works much better than a generalized statement like, "Topic sentences need work."
4. Be descriptive in your comments. It is often helpful for students to hear how you are reading their essays. "Paragraph five seems to be telling me . . ." or "I got the feeling the essay's overall message is . . ." are good ways to start descriptive sentences.
5. Realize that you are analyzing a paper and not a person. Directing your comments toward the essay, "Paragraph nine doesn't really have anything new to add, does the paper need it?" sounds better to the listener than "You repeat yourself in paragraph nine. Do you really need it?"

Independent Reviewing

If your instructor does not require peer editing, you can ask someone to review your essay. Choose someone you trust to give you an honest opinion. It might not be effective to ask a parent, spouse, or girlfriend/boyfriend to give you a critique if you know they are going to like anything you write, just because you wrote it. It might be better to ask another student who has recently had an English class, or is enrolled in yours currently. In exchange, you might offer to look over their work. Remember, you learn to read your own essays better by reading other peoples' essays more critically. Have your reviewer answer the following questions about your essay.

Sample Questions for Peer Review

When you have revised your paper several times, have someone answer these questions for overall content, paragraph development, word choice, and sentence structure.

Overall Content

1. What is the thesis or main point of the essay? Where does the writer state this main point? If the main point is implied rather than stated, express it in a sentence. Does the main point give a subject and an opinion about the subject? How might the writer improve his/her thesis?
2. What is the purpose of this essay? What are the characteristics of the audience the writer seems to be addressing? (formal, fun-loving, serious, cynical, laid-back, etc.)

Paragraph Development

1. Do each of the paragraphs in the essay work to support the main point of the essay? Which paragraphs seem to wander from that main point? What other information needs to be added to develop the main point?
2. List two places in the essay where the writer uses vivid sensory details. How effective are those details? Are they used to support the thesis of the essay? Identify two places in the essay where the writer needs more details that are effective. What kind of details might he or she include?
3. What grade would you give the introduction? How does it draw the reader into the essay? What specific things can the writer do to make the introduction more inviting?
4. Which paragraph do you like the best? Why? Which paragraph in the essay do you like the least? Why? What can the writer do to improve his/her paragraphs?
5. What grade would you give the conclusion? How does it provide closure for the essay? What specific things can the writer do to make the conclusion more effective?

Word Choice and Sentence Structure

1. Are adequate transitions used between the paragraphs? Find an effective paragraph transition and identify it. Why does it work? Find two places between paragraphs that need more or better transitions. What can the writer do to improve these transitions?
2. Is a variety of sentences used? Where might the writer vary the sentence structure for better effect? What two sentences in the essay did you find most effective? Why?
3. Are there any words that seem misused or out of place? What positive or negative trigger words are used? Do they enhance the message of the essay or detract from it?

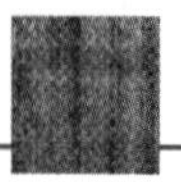

EDITING AND PROOFREADING

Editing is the final step of the writing process. As you learned in the last section, many students make the mistake of focusing on error correction and proofreading *before* taking the time to develop, clarify, and organize ideas fully through drafting and revision. Although the parts of the writing process are not finite and sometimes do overlap, editing is a separate activity designed to address what writing specialists call **local issues**, such as:

- grammar
- sentence variety
- mechanics
- spelling
- formatting

When Should You Edit?

Editing should come *after* you feel confident about the choices you have made in content, organization, and style. You might compare editing and proofreading to washing, waxing, and polishing your car. It would be absurd to take the time to do these things to a vehicle that does not run! Drafting and revising ensure that your writing is first fine-tuned; then, you edit to make it shine on the surface.

The Different Levels of Editing

Paragraph-Level Editing

The first step in editing is to check your paragraphing. Think of paragraphs as larger forms of punctuation that broaden the connections shown by traditional punctuation marks, such as commas, semicolons, and periods. Punctuation marks indicate pauses, relationships, and connections within and between sentences. Likewise, paragraph indentations and lengths provide readers with visual guidance to relationships and connections between major ideas.

When you begin editing at the paragraph level, ask yourself:

1. What does each paragraph say (main idea) and do (introduce, provide proof or support, give an example, illustrate, connect, conclude)?
    - Begin a new paragraph for each new idea.
    - The order of the paragraphs should be logical.
    - Look at what the paragraphs do, and question the usefulness of each.
2. Are sentences within paragraphs unified and consistent? Check for:
    - Unrelated ideas
    - Illogical sequences and series
    - Mixed metaphors and/or confusing comparisons

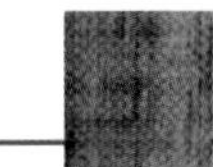

- Mismatched subjects and verbs—e.g., *butter reads* or *books believe*
- Transitional words or phrases

Sentence-Level Editing

When you begin editing on the sentence level, ask yourself:

1. Are the connections between ideas effectively communicated through subordination and coordination? Check for:
    - Short, choppy sentences
    - Excessively long, hard-to-follow sentences
    - Unclear emphasis due to faulty or excessive subordination
2. Are individual sentence structures clear and easy to follow? Check for:
    - Misplaced parts
    - Modifiers that have no referent in the sentence
    - Modifiers that are too far from the words they modify
3. Are ideas balanced through the use of parallel elements?
4. Are there any sudden shifts in grammatical structures, tone, or style? Check for:
    - Consistent use of verb tense
    - Consistency in person and number
    - A unified tone/style
5. Do sentences vary in length and construction?
6. Are sentences concise free of dead weight or unnecessary words? Check for:
    - Placeholders like *there, it, this,* and *these*
    - Excessive use of forms of the verb to be. Replace be with strong, specific verbs.
    - Are sentences direct? Check for use of active voice, where the subject performs the action of the sentence—e.g., *The registrar misplaced your transcripts.*
    - Purposeful use of passive voice to avoid assigning blame or for emphasis—e.g., *Your transcripts were misplaced.*
7. Are there any fragments, comma splices, or fused sentences?
8. Do all subjects and verbs agree? Do all pronouns agree with their antecedents? Are all verb forms correct?

Word-Level Editing

When you edit for word choice, ask yourself:

1. Are any words vague? Check for:
    - General nouns—replace with specific or concrete nouns—e.g., replace *school* with *NSU* or *vehicle* with *Jeep Wrangler.*
    - General verbs—replace with specific, active verbs—e.g., replace *says* with *argues* or replace *ran* with *sprinted.*

- Have you avoided sweeping generalizations that cannot possibly be supported? If not, replace with statements that acknowledge exceptions or qualifications.

2. Are any words or phrases overused? Check for:
   - Repeated words at beginnings of sentences
   - Use of clichés
3. Have unnecessary words been cut out?
4. Does the vocabulary reflect sensitivity to audience, purpose, and context? Check for:
   - Stereotypes
   - Biased language based on gender, race, ethnicity, sexuality, religious affiliations, age, or social class
   - Connotations associated with words. When using a thesaurus, make sure you understand how the word is used and the nuances of meaning associated with the word in various contexts or cultures
   - Jargon. Technical words should be defined or explained.
5. Does your tone (attitude towards the subject) engage your readers? Check for:
   - A hostile tone
   - Assumptions about the readers or their beliefs
   - The use of *you*

When Should You Proofread?

Once you have revised and edited your essay, you should proofread and format it. The proofreading stage of the writing process is just as important as the other stages; be sure that you proofread carefully. Because you have written the essay, you expect to see what you thought you wrote, so you might miss errors—especially minor ones such as a missing comma or apostrophe. To proofread well, read the essay aloud very slowly or read it backwards. Place a ruler under each line as you read to stop yourself from reading faster than you should be reading. Read the essay more than once while paying attention to every sentence, word, and punctuation mark. Care should be taken to keep the content of the essay from distracting you while you proofread.

Punctuation

When you edit for punctuation, ask yourself:

1. Do sentences have the correct closing punctuation?
2. Are commas, semicolons, dashes, apostrophes, and other internal punctuation marks used correctly?
3. Are quotations correctly introduced, punctuated, and carefully cited? Are quotation marks turned the right way—towards the quoted material?
4. Are in-text citations correctly punctuated?

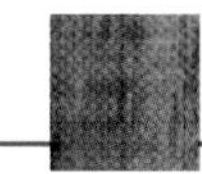

Spelling

When you edit for spelling, ask yourself:

1. Are all words spelled correctly? Remember that spell-checkers are **not** always foolproof! Check for commonly confused words.
2. Have you used the correct forms? Double-check any abbreviations, contractions, or possessive nouns.
3. Have you used hyphens correctly? Double-check any hyphenated words

Capitalization and Italics

When you edit for capitalization and italics, ask yourself:

1. Are words capitalized appropriately?
2. Are quotations capitalized correctly?
3. Are proper names and titles distinguished with appropriate capitalization and punctuation?
4. Are titles punctuated correctly with italics or quotation marks? (See "Using MLA" for a list of rules.)

Formatting

Formatting correctly shows that you care about the presentation of all your hard work. However, looks can be deceiving; a paper that looks good can still contain serious errors. Computers have made it much easier to produce a professional-looking document, but editing is still essential.

When you edit for formatting, ask yourself the following questions.

1. Have you followed all of your instructor's directions about formatting?
2. Are the margins correct?
3. Is the spacing correct between words, sentences, and paragraphs?
4. Is the assignment block present and correct? Does it contain all of the required information in the correct order and form?
5. Do you have a title that is centered and spaced correctly and not underlined, italicized, boldface, in quotation marks, or in a different font?
6. Do you have a header with your name and page numbers?
7. If needed, do you have a works cited page that follows MLA guidelines? (See "Using MLA.")

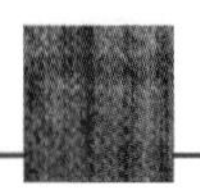

Sentence Guide[1]

This list describes some common sentence-level problems.

Agreement: The subject should agree in number with the verbs and pronouns that go with it; that is, plural nouns require plural verbs and pronouns, and so on. Example: "Each of these weasels are enormous." (Problem: The verb *are* is plural, but the subject *each* is singular.) Solution: "Each of these weasels is enormous."

Comma Splice: Avoid connecting two sentences with a comma. Don't say, "George is always late to the office, I think he loses his keys every day." Say instead, "George is always late to the office; I think he loses his keys every day." Or, if you prefer, separate the two sentences by adding a period.

Dead Weight: Eliminate dead weight from your sentences. Don't say, "The thing that bothers me about Peterson's article is that he says the moon is made of mozzarella cheese." (nineteen words) Notice the dead weight here: "~~The thing that~~ bothers me ~~about~~ Peterson's article is ~~that~~ he says the moon is made of mozzarella ~~cheese~~." This rewritten version is stronger, more precise: "I find Peterson's proposition about the moon being made of mozzarella silly." (twelve words)

Sentence Fragment: Don't write in sentence fragments; instead, write in complete sentences.

Fragment: "Dressing in women's clothing." (No verb) Complete sentence: "Dressing in women's clothing, the comedian poked fun at conventional gender distinctions." (verb underlined)

Fused Sentence: Don't fuse two sentences without any punctuation. Don't say, "Phyllis drove to Chicago today in fact I think she's not coming back." Say, "Phyllis drove to Chicago today. In fact, I think she's not coming back." Or, if you prefer, separate the two with a semicolon.

Lacks Transition: Provide transitions, or bridges, between sentences and paragraphs. Consider these sentences: "Dennis wrecked his car. The cost of his insurance increased." No transition links these sentences, but the ideas *should* be connected. State this connection: "Dennis wrecked his car. As a result, the cost of his insurance increased." Here, "as a result" indicates the proper relationship between ideas. Always link your ideas (and your sentences and paragraphs) whenever you can.

[1]Source: McDowell, Sean. "To Grammar, or Not to Grammar?: The Question and an Answer." In Our Own Voice: Graduate Students Teach Writing. Ed. Tina Lavonne Good and Leanne B. Warshauer. Needham Heights, MA: Allyn and Bacon, 2000. 251-261.

Dangling Modifier: Modifiers are parts of a sentence that describe or modify other parts. Do not misplace modifiers within a sentence and create unintended, incorrect meanings: "Plagiarizing a famous poem, the dean suspended the student indefinitely." The modifier ("Plagiarizing a famous poem") is supposed to describe the student. But because it has been placed immediately beside "the dean," the sentence suggests the dean is plagiarizing, not the student. A corrected version of this sentence reads: "The dean suspended the student for plagiarizing a famous poem." Notice how much clearer this version is.

Overgeneralization: Do not make sweeping generalizations that ignore possible exceptions. Example: "All people who live in Florida have dark tans." The troublesome word here is *all*; not all people in Florida are tan. Think carefully before making sweeping statements such as this one.

Reference: Be sure that your reader knows exactly who or what each of your pronouns refers to. If you don't, the reader will become frustrated. Example: "Cheryl washed her car, bought groceries, folded her laundry, and ordered a pizza. This helped her prepare for the weekend." *Which of* these actions prepared Cheryl for the weekend? A better lead for the second sentence is "these activities helped prepare. . ."

Weak Repetition: Avoid repeating the same words or phrases unnecessarily. For instance, if five sentences in a row begin with the same word or words, your repetition is most likely weak because you are ignoring variety.

Vague: Always prefer a precise word (i.e., *Guatemalans*) to a general word (*people*). If you write vaguely, you will confuse your reader or give the impression that you don't know what you are talking about.

Voice: Prefer active voice to passive voice whenever possible. Try not to say, "The suspect was given a sentence of twenty years in prison by the judge." Instead, say, "The judge sentenced the suspect to twenty years in prison." Notice how the second example uses a stronger verb (*sentenced* vs. *was given*) and presents the information more concisely and forcefully.

Weak Lead: Eliminate passive or weak subject-verb combinations (e.g., "There is," "It is . . . that") whenever you can. Be suspicious if you discover you are using forms of the verb "to be" *(is, are, am, be, being, been, was, were)* or "to have" *(have, has, had, having)* excessively. Example: "There is a reason why jack drove to the store." Solution: "~~There is a reason why~~ Jack drove to the store." If you want to, add the reason: "Jack drove to the store because he wanted a candy bar."

Weak Verb: Substitute strong verbs for weak verbs. Don't say, "The author gets the point across that we should treat people equally." Instead, say, "The author suggests that we should treat people equally."

You (Addressing reader): Avoid addressing the reader in your writing, especially as "you." Example: "Stephanie would teach you everything you needed to know to make a pillow." Do not make assumptions about what the reader does, learns, and so on. Instead, say, "Stephanie taught me everything I needed to know to make a pillow."

CHAPTER NINE

Using Sources

QUOTE, PARAPHRASE, SUMMARY

You have engaged in a *dialogue with the text.* You have *analyzed texts.* You have *written essays* about texts. Now, when you want to *convey* part or all of the information from a text to someone else, you have a few options for how to do that.

- Quote
- Paraphrase
- Summary

You will want to use each of these options for a different purpose.

Let's take the beginning of an article that *The New Yorker* magazine published on September 5, 2005. Then we'll look at how the author, John Seabrook, uses **quote, paraphrase,** and **summary** to prove his THESIS.

> *Renaissance Pears*
> The Fiorentina[1] is a squat and hippy pear, its dark-green skin blemished with black freckles. It is to supermarket fruit as real people are to supermodels. Until recently, the pear was thought to have disappeared from central Italy, where it once flourished. But Isabella Dalla Ragione, a forty-seven year old agronomist[2] in Perugia,[3] continued to look for it.
>
> Dalla Ragione[4] has straight brown hair and crooked teeth; she can look twenty years younger than her age or ten years older, depending on the angle of her head. She is a fast driver and an even faster talker, with a gift for making archeologia arborea,[5] as she calls her vocation—the pursuit and recovery of old varieties of fruit—sound

---

[1]The Fiorentina is a type of pear that has almost become extinct.

[2]An agronomist studies soils and plants.

[3]A major city in central Italy, the capital of the province of Umbria.

[4]This is the family name of the woman, Isabella Dalla Ragione.

[5]Archeologia arborea is the study of the archeology, or the history, of trees

thrilling. She finds clues in many places: Renaissance paintings,[6] obscure books, and the records that were kept by former estate owners in Umbria and Tuscany,[7] where the climate is peculiarly advantageous for many kinds of fruit. Last year, while studying the catalogue of a large estate that once belonged to the Bufalini family,[8] on the northern tip of Umbria, she came across a reference to the Fiorentina. The Bufalini maintained villas[9] with extensive gardens and orchards, from the fifteenth century on up to the nineteen-eighties, when the final landlord left the property to the state.

Pear trees can live for more than two hundred and fifty years—among fruit trees, only olives live longer—and so Isabella thought a Fiorentina[10] might remain on the former Bufalini lands. She knew what the pear looked like, thanks to a memoir left by an itinerant[11] early-twentieth-century musician, Archimede Montanelli, whose travels had taken him all over Umbria. She also happened to have an uncle, Alvaro, who hunted in that part of Umbria and was acquainted with some of the farmers who lived there. Eventually, one of them told Alvaro that a Fiorentina remained on his farm.

Earlier this summer, I accompanied Isabella on a trip to visit the old pear tree. We drove into a mountainous region above the town of Pietralunga, a land of thick woods with small farms in the valleys. Stone houses where the landowners had once lived, many of them now abandoned, sit on the tops of hills. The old orchards are gone, but the landscape is dotted with a few rugged arboreal[12] survivors: almonds, olives, and pears.

The Fiorentina was growing in the Valdescura, the Valley of Darkness. When we arrived, relatives of several families, spanning four generations, were sitting under the big shade trees outside the farmhouse. The matriarch[13] was an eighty-four-year-old woman named Sergia. She wore a ragged shift and filthy slippers, and carried a long walking stick. Hearing my accent, she recalled the Americans who had escaped from a nearby Fascist[14] prison and turned up one night in 1943; she had given them shelter and something to eat.

---

[6]The Renaissance is a period of time that took place in Italy from about 1420–1600.

[7]Tuscany is another Province of Italy, just to the west of Umbria.

[8]The Bufalini were a wealthy Renaissance Italian family, like the Medici family, that owned huge estates.

[9]A villa is a huge home on an Italian estate.

[10]The Fiorentin is the tree that bears the Fiorentina pear.

[11]An itinerant musician is someone who travels around to perform his or her art in different places.

[12]Arboreal is the adjective meaning "trees."

[13]A matriarch is the oldest living female in a family, usually the grandmother or great-grandmother.

[14]The Fascists were the party that governed Italy in the early twentieth Century and took Italy into World War II.

There was a cherry tree beside the house, and Isabella walked with Sergia to gather some cherries. Or, rather, Isabella gathered them; Sergia ate them, the pits tumbling down her whiskery chin as more cherries went into her mouth.

Then the farmer, a nephew of Sergia's, led us through a potato field to the Fiorentina, which was growing next to a rutted[15] old road. Its black bark had deep crevices, and the trunk and lower branches were covered with scabrous[16] white lichen.[17] Isabella fought through the high weeds around the tree and patted its trunk. "Sometimes when I find one of these old trees I feel like weeping," she said. "If only they could talk—what a story they could tell." Then she frowned, and said, "But I think, maybe it is better they cannot talk. They would probably curse us."

For thousands of years, peasants in Umbria and Tuscany cultivated fruit trees. Most tended small pomari, or family orchards, with no more than ten trees. A fruit tree provided food, shade in summer, fuel in winter, furniture, and children's shoes, which were made from the wood of fig trees. Fruit was also a staple of the cooking of the region, in dishes like salt cod with roasted pears, and pork with plums; whole cherries in agrodolce—pickled in vinegar and sugar—were served as a chutney[18] with roasted meat. The farmers planted as many varieties as possible because the different trees would bear fruit at different times over the growing season. The mountainous topography[19] of Umbria, and its lack of roads, insured that varieties common to one valley were unknown in the next. When a woman married, she often carried seeds from her family's farm with her in order to prepare her mother's recipes, which were based on the particular varieties of fruit in her home valley.

This feudal[20] way of life endured, more or less unbroken, for two thousand years, until it abruptly ended in the two decades following the Second World War.[21] Nine million Italians, about a sixth of the population at that time, left their rural homes and went to the cities. They acquired Fiats,[22] Vespas,[23] televisions, and fashionable clothes—all the trappings of modern Italian identity. The old fruit trees were among the things they left behind.

---

[15]A rutted road is a bumpy, uneven, potholed road.

[16]Scabrous means something with a rough surface.

[17]Lichen are organisms that grow over rocks and trees.

[18]Chutney is a relish served with food.

[19]Topography means a way of describing a landscape.

[20]A feudal system was a country way of life, where landowners dominated the peasants living on their land.

[21]World War II took place from 1939–1945.

[22]A Fiat is a European brand of car.

[23]A Vespa is a popular brand of motor scooter.

> The varieties eaten in Umbria and Tuscany were replaced, first, by generic[24] fruit grown in the Emilia-Romagna[25] region, where much of Italy's agricultural industry is concentrated, and, more recently, by fruit from other countries—peaches and cherries from Spain, pears from Argentina, and apples from China. In most markets in Italy you can find only three kinds of apple (Golden Delicious, Stark Delicious, Rome Beauty), and lately the Fuji apple, from China, has begun to replace those. It's not hard to imagine a day when there will be only one kind of apple for sale in the whole industrial world.
>
> The Dalla Ragiones' orchard is an open-air museum of Old World fruit. It was begun by Isabella's father, Livio, forty years ago, on his land in northwestern Umbria, and is now maintained by Isabella. The trees grow on a hilltop in San Lorenzo di Lerchi, a hamlet[26] about seventy miles southeast of Florence[27] and thirty miles northwest of Perugia; Livio lives in a stone farmhouse that overlooks the orchard. There are about four hundred trees in the collection: pears, apples, plums, cherries, peaches, quinces,[28] and medlars.[29] Most were common in Umbria as recently as sixty years ago; now they have all but disappeared. Some of the Dalla Ragiones' specimens are believed to be the last examples of that variety.

Seabrook has written about saving varieties of fruit trees threatened by extinction. In doing that, he also writes about history, art, food, culture, and how the people he encounters form their identities by interacting with the landscape they live in. Notice how Seabrook handles all these different subjects, how he organizes his essay to include all this interesting material, while, at the same time, he never loses touch with his **thesis**.

You can read the rest of this essay in the September 5, 2005 issue of *The New Yorker,* to find out what happened to Isabella Dalla Ragione and her adventures in saving the ancient fruit trees of Italy.

---

[24]Generic refers to something general, in this case, something not from a local family farm, but from a large corporate farm.

[25]Emilia-Romagna is another Province of Italy, south of Umbria and Tuscany.

[26]A hamlet is a small village.

[27]Florence is the capital city of the Province of Tuscany.

[28]A quince is a pear-shaped fruit.

[29]A medlar is an apple-shaped fruit.

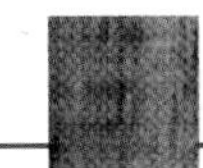

Quote

We use a **quote** to support and prove our thesis. To quote, we copy the exact words from a text, be it a written text or an oral text (someone speaking). John Seabrook quotes Isabella Dalla Ragione in his essay. (All quotes are in bold.)

> "**Sometimes when I find one of these old trees I feel like weeping,**" she said. "**If only they could talk—what a story they could tell.**" Then she frowned, and said, "**But I think, maybe it is better they cannot talk. They would probably curse us.**"

Paraphrase

We may not always want to use the exact language of a text by quoting it. When we paraphrase language from a text, we restate that language in our own terms. A paraphrase is often about the same length, nearly the same number of words, as the original, but rewritten in our own words.

You may want to use paraphrase to vary the style of your essay. You might want to use paraphrase if a quote is too long for your essay. You might want to use paraphrase to give your reader the flavor of your own language or to make your reader feel that you are talking directly to him or her.

She's a fast driver and an even faster talker, with a gift for making archeologia arborea, as she calls her vocation—the pursuit and recovery of old varieties of fruit—sound thrilling.

Summary

When you **summarize**, you give the main points of the material from the text. A summary should be much shorter than the original.

You might want to use a summary:

- if you give a summary of the text you're analyzing, your reader will better understand what you're talking about;
- to give your reader a lot of information with a few words;
- if you have a lot of information to convey to your reader, but you don't have a lot of space to do that in;
- if the original contains important information, but it does not read well or is boring;
- if you have a lot of information to convey from the original, but you want your reader to hear your voice speaking in the essay.

Here, John Seabrook summarizes Isabella Dalla Ragione's research:

She finds clues in many places: Renaissance paintings, obscure books, and the records that were kept by former estate owners in Umbria and Tuscany, where the climate is peculiarly

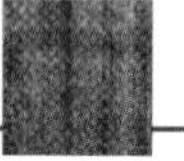

advantageous for many kinds of fruit. Seabrook doesn't want to go into all the detail of Isabella's work. He wants to give the sense of what she does and how she does it. He uses **summary** to do that. Seabrook uses all these methods—**quote, paraphrase,** and **summary**—to convey information to us, information that, as evidence, supports his thesis. We use quote, paraphrase, and summary to give our reader information from the material are writing about.

- A quote repeats the original source language.
- A paraphrase restates the original source language in your own words.
- A summary conveys the main ideas of the original source.

MLA

When you do research to find supporting evidence for your ideas or arguments, you need to credit your outside sources. Depending on what type of essay you are writing or which type of course you are writing for, you will need to choose a documentation style and continue with that style for the entire essay. Two of the most common styles, especially for freshman and sophomore students, are MLA (Modern Language Association) and APA (American Psychological Association).

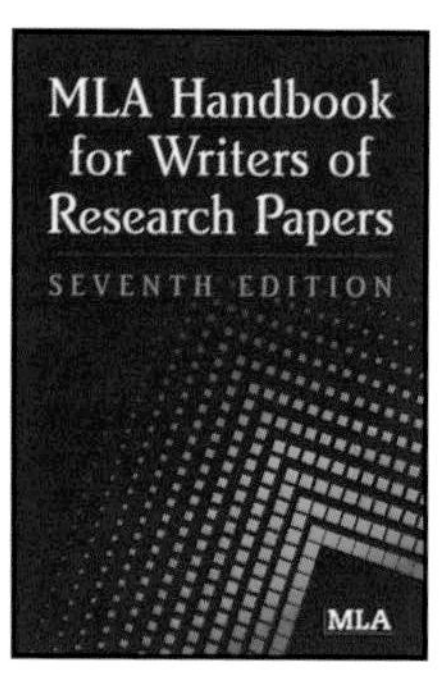

If you write in composition, language, linguistics, and literature courses, you will often be asked to use documentation guidelines created by the Modern Language Association. The *MLA Handbook for Writers of Research Papers*, in its seventh edition, provides a full description of the conventions used by this particular community of writers; updates to the *MLA Handbook* can be found at <www.mla.org>.

MLA guidelines require that you give both an in-text citation and a works cited entry for any and all sources you use. Using accurate in-text citations helps guide your reader to the appropriate entry in the works cited section. For example, the in-text citation given below in parentheses directs the reader to the correct page of the book given in the works cited.

In-text citation➔When a teenager sleeps more than 10 hours per night, it is time to question whether she is having significant problems (Jones 63).

Entry in Works Cited➔
Jones, Stephanie. *The Signs of Trouble*. Boston: Dilemma Publishing, 2010. Print.

This chapter provides a general overview of MLA documentation style and an explanation of the most commonly used MLA documentation formats, including a few significant revisions since the previous edition.

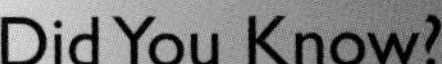

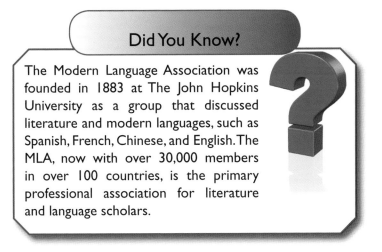

The Modern Language Association was founded in 1883 at The John Hopkins University as a group that discussed literature and modern languages, such as Spanish, French, Chinese, and English. The MLA, now with over 30,000 members in over 100 countries, is the primary professional association for literature and language scholars.

Using MLA In-text Citations

In-text citations (also called *parenthetical citations*) point readers to where they can find more information about your researched supporting materials. When you use MLA documentation style, you need to indicate the author's last name and the location of the source material (page or paragraph number). Where this in-text information is placed depends on how you want to phrase the sentence that is summarized, paraphrased, or quoted. Be sure that the in-text citation guides the reader clearly to the source in the list of works cited, where complete information about the source is given.

The following are some of the most common examples of parenthetical citations.

1. Author's name in text

When using a parenthetical reference to a single source that is already named in the sentence, use this form: (Page number). Note that the period goes after the parentheses.

➔ Stephanie Jones, author of *The Signs of Trouble*, describes "excessive sleeping, refraining from eating, and lying about simple things" as signs to look for when parents are concerned about their children (63).

2. Author's name in reference

When the author's name is not included in the preceding sentence, use this form for the parenthetical information at the end of the sentence: (Author's Last Name Page number). Note that there is no comma between the name and page in an MLA parenthetical reference, and also note that the period comes at the end of the sentence after the parentheses.

- ➔ When a teenager sleeps more than 10 hours per night, it is time to question whether she is having significant problems (Jones 63).

3. No author given

When a work has no credited author, use a clipped version of the work's title.

- ➔ In a recent *Time* article, a list of 30 common signs of teenage trouble cites lack of sleep as the most common sign ("Thirty" 3).

4. Two or three authors given

When you use a source that was written by two or three authors, use all the names in the text of the sentence or in the citation.

- ➔ The idea that "complexity is a constant in biology" is not an innovative one (Sole and Goodwin 2).
- ➔ Most signs in English that the authors encountered on the road had "grammar mistakes, misspellings, or just odd pictures" (Smith, Jones, and Best 55).

5. Four or more authors given

MLA documentation style allows a choice when there are four authors or more of an item to be cited. You can either name all the authors or include only the first author's name followed by *et al.* (Latin for "and others").

- ➔ In Hong Kong, most signs are in Chinese and English; however, once you are in mainland China, English is rarely found on signs, except in tourist areas (Li, Smith, Jones, and Franz 49).
- ➔ In Hong Kong, most signs are in Chinese and English; however, once you are in mainland China, English is rarely found on signs, except in tourist areas (Li, et al. 49).

6. Authors with the same last names

If your source material includes items by authors who happen to have the same last name, be sure to use each author's first name or initial in the parentheses.

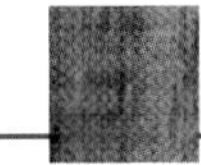

➔ When a teenager sleeps more than 10 hours per night, it is time to question whether she is having significant problems (S. Jones 63).

➔ Another sign of trouble can be when you do not see your child for meals (B. Jones 114).

7. Encyclopedia or dictionary unsigned entry

When you use an encyclopedia or dictionary to look up a word or entry, be sure to include the word or entry title in the parenthetical entry.

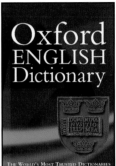

➔ The word *thing* has more definitions than any other entry in the *Oxford English Dictionary* ("thing").

8. Lines of verse (plays, poetry or song lyrics)

For plays, give the act, scene, and line numbers that are located in any edition of the play. Separate the act, scene, and line numbers with periods. For example, the quotation below comes from *Romeo and Juliet*, Act II, Scene 2, lines 43 and 44. The MLA also advises using this method with biblical chapters and verses. Be sure, though, that the sequence goes from largest unit to smallest unit.

➔ Juliet grapples with how names can influence feelings as she questions, "What's in a name? That which we call a rose / By any other name would smell as sweet" (2.2.43-44).

Use a slash (/) to signify line breaks when you quote poetry or song lyrics, and put line numbers in the in-text citation instead of page numbers.

➔ An early song by Will Smith shows the frustration of children as he sings, "You know parents are the same / No matter time nor place / They don't understand that us kids /Are going to make some mistakes" (1-4).

9. Indirect quotation

When you use a quotation of a quotation—that is, a quotation that quotes from another source—use *qtd. in* to designate the source.

➔ Smith has said, "My parents really didn't understand me" (qtd. in Jones, par. 8).

Using Long or Block Quotations

Long or block quotations have special formatting requirements of their own.

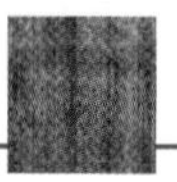

1. Block quote of prose

If you quote a chunk of prose that is longer than four typed lines, you are using what is called a *block quotation*. Follow these MLA guidelines for block quotations:

1. If introducing the block quotation with a sentence, use a colon at the end of the sentence.
2. Begin the quotation on a new line.
3. Do not use quotation marks to enclose the block quote.
4. Indent the quote one inch from the left margin, and extend the right margin to the end of the line.
5. Double space the entire quotation.
6. Put a period at the end of the quotation, and then add the parenthetical citation.

➔ However, Lansky states:

> Despite the statement on <www.signspotting.com> that we don't accept signs with the intention of being funny, people like sending them in. I've opted not to use these as it could encourage people to start making them, sticking them up in their driveway, and snapping a picture. Plus, funny signs are so much more amusing when the humor is accidental. (72)

2. Block quote of poetry, drama, or song lyrics

For songs and poems, be sure to give line numbers rather than page numbers and to use the original line breaks.

➔ The Fresh Prince, an early Will Smith character, sings about parents not understanding:

> You know parents are the same
> No matter time or place
> They don't understand that us kids
> Are going to make some mistakes
> So to you other kids all across the land
> There's no need to argue
> Parents just don't understand. (4-7)

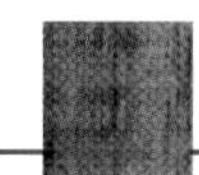

Adding or Omitting Words in a Quotation

1. Adding words to a quotation

Use square brackets ([ ]) to point out words or phrases that are not part of the original text.

➔ Original quotation: "When we entered the People's Republic of China, we noticed that the signage began dropping English translations."

➔ Quotation with added word: She said, "When we entered the People's Republic of China, [Dunkirk and I] noticed that the signage began dropping English translations" (Donelson 141).

You can also add your own comments inside a quotation by using square brackets. For example, you can add the word *sic* to a quotation when you know that there is an error.

➔ Original quotation: "When we entered the People's Repulic of China, we noticed that the signage began dropping English translations."

➔ Quotation with added comment: She said, "When we entered the People's Repulic (sic) of China, we noticed that the signage began dropping English translations" (Donelson 141).

2. Omitting words in a quotation

Use an ellipsis (. . .) to represent words that you delete from a quotation. The ellipsis begins with a space, then has three periods with spaces between them, and then ends with a space.

Original quotation➔ "The Great Wall is something that can be seen from space. When we reach a time when advertisements can be seen from space, we have probably gone too far."

Quotation with words omitted in middle of sentence➔ Frank Donelson, author of *Signs in Space,* remarks, "The Great Wall . . . can be seen from space. When we reach a time when advertisements can be seen from space, we have probably gone too far" (178).

If you omit words at the end of a quotation, and that is also the end of your sentence, use an ellipsis plus a period with no space before the ellipsis or after the period.

Original quotation➔ "The Great Wall is something that can be seen from space. When we reach a time when advertisements can be seen from space, we have probably gone too far with our advertising and signage."

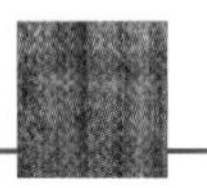

Quotation with words omitted at end of sentence➔ Frank Donelson, author of *Signs in Space*, remarks, "The Great Wall is something that can be seen from space. When we reach a time when advertisements can be seen from space, we have probably gone too far. . ." (178).

MLA guidelines can change with a new edition. Sometimes, class textbooks can use an older MLA documentation style. Always check with your instructor if rules seem to be in conflict.

Citing Online Sources

In the MLA documentation style, online or electronic sources have their own formatting guidelines since these types of sources rarely give specific page numbers.

The MLA recommends that you include in the text, rather than in an in-text citation, the name(s) of the person (e.g., author, editor, director, performer) that begins the matching works cited entry. For instance, the following is the recommended way to begin an in-text citation for an online source:

➔ Roger Ebert says that Shyamalan "plays the audience like a piano" in the film *Signs* (par. 8).

If the author or creator of the Web site uses paragraph or page numbers, use these numbers in the parenthetical citation. If no numbering is used, do not use or add numbers to the paragraphs, pages, or parenthetical citation.

When Web site does not number paragraphs➔ In his review of the film *Signs*, Roger Ebert says that Shyamalan "does what Hitchcock said he wanted to do, and plays the audience like a piano."

When Web site numbers paragraphs➔ In his review of the film *Signs*, Roger Ebert says that Shyamalan "does what Hitchcock said he wanted to do, and plays the audience like a piano" (par. 8).

General Formatting Guidelines for the MLA Works Cited

If you cite any sources within a paper, be sure to include a list of works cited at the end of the paper. Here are some general formatting guidelines to follow when setting up a works cited list.

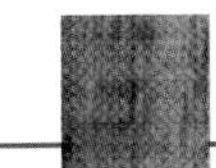

1. Put the works cited list at the end of your paper as a separate page.
2. Use one-inch margins on all sides.
3. Include any header used for the paper on the list of works cited.
4. Center the title *Works Cited* at the top of the page, using no underlining, quotation marks, or italics.
5. Place the first line of each entry flush left with the margin. Indent any additional lines of the entry one-half inch (or one tab).
6. Double space the entries in the works cited list, not adding any extra spaces between entries.
7. Alphabetize the list of works cited. Use the first major word in each entry, not including articles such as *a, an,* or *the*, to determine the alphabetical order. If the cited source does not have an author, alphabetize by using the first word of the title of the source.
8. Put author's last name first (e.g., Ebert, Roger). Only reverse the first author's name. If more than one author, follow the first author's name with a comma, and add the other author names in the order of first then last names (e.g., Ebert, Roger, and Gene Siskel).
9. Use hyphens when you use more than one source from the same author. Alphabetize the titles, the author's full name for the first entry, and then use three hyphens to replace the author's name in all entries after the first (see 37f3).
10. Capitalize all words in titles except for articles, conjunctions, and short prepositions. Always capitalize the first word of a subtitle.
11. Use quotation marks for titles of shorter works, including articles, book chapters, episodes on television or radio, poems, and short stories.
12. Italicize the titles of longer works, including album or CD titles, art pieces, books, films, journals, magazines, newspapers, and television shows.
13. Give the edition number for works with more than one edition (e.g., *MLA Handbook for Writers of Research Papers*, 7th edition).
14. Use the word *Print* after print sources and *Web* for Internet or Web sources.

Formats for Print Sources

1. Books (includes brochures, pamphlets, and graphic novels)

Author's Name. *Title of Book*. Place of publication: Publisher, date of publication. Print.

➔Lansky, Doug. *Signspotting*. Oakland, CA: Lonely Planet, 2005. Print.

Helpful hint

Only use the state after the city if the city is not a place that would be commonly known or if there may be more than one commonly known city by that name.

2. Books with two or more authors

A comma is used between the author names, even if there are only two authors.

First Author's Name, and second Author's Name. *Title of Book.* Place of publication: Publisher, date of publication. Print.

➔**Maasik, Sonia, and Jack Soloman.** ***Signs of Life in the USA: Readings on Popular Culture for Writers.*** **6th edition. Boston: Bedford/St. Martin's, 2008. Print.**

3. Two books by the same author

Use three hyphens and a period in place of the author name(s) in the consecutive entries. Be sure the entries are in alphabetical order.

➔**Maasik, Sonia, and Jack Soloman.** ***California Dreams and Realities: Readings for Critical Thinkers and Writers.*** **3rd edition. Boston: Bedford/St. Martin's, 2004. Print.**

➔**---.** ***Signs of Life in the USA: Readings on Popular Culture for Writers.*** **6th edition. Boston: Bedford/St. Martin's, 2008. Print.**

4. Anthology or collection

Editor's Name(s), ed. *Title of Book.* Place of publication: Publisher, date. Print.

➔**Smith, Allison D., Trixie G. Smith, and Karen Wright, eds.** ***COMPbiblio: Leaders and Influences in Composition Theory and Practice.*** **Southlake, TX: Fountainhead Press, 2007. Print.**

5. Work within an anthology

Author's Name. "Title of Work." *Title of Anthology*. Ed. Editor's Name(s). Place of publication: Publisher, date. Pages. Print.

➔**Tan, Amy. "Mother Tongue."** ***The Norton Field Guide to Writing*****. Ed. Richard Bullock, et al. New York: Norton, 2010. 564-70. Print.**

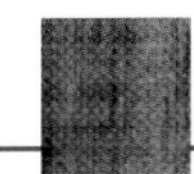

6. Article in a scholarly journal

Author's Name. "Title of the Article." *Journal Title* vol. number (date of publication): pages. Print.

➔**Holbrook, Teri. "An Ability Traitor at Work: A Treasonous Call to Subvert Writing from Within."** ***Qualitative Inquiry*** **16.3 (2010): 171-83. Print.**

7. Article in a scholarly journal that uses only issue numbers

Author's Name. "Title of the Article." *Journal Title* issue number (date of publication): pages. Print.

➔**Franks, Lola. "The Play in Language."** ***Child Signs*** **73 (2006): 3-17. Print.**

8. Article in a newspaper

Author's Name. "Title of Article." *Newspaper Title* Day Month Year: pages. Print.

➔**Genzlinger, Neil. "Autism is Another Thing that Families Share."** ***New York Times*** **6 Apr. 2010: A4. Print.**

Note: when citing English language newspapers, use the name on the masthead but be sure to omit any introductory article (*New York Times*, not *The New York Times*).

9. Article in a magazine

Author's Name. "Title of Article." *Magazine Title* Day Month Year: pages. Print.

Note: only use day if magazine is published on a weekly or bi-weekly basis.

➔**Musico, Christopher. "Sign 'Em Up!"** ***CRM Magazine*** **Nov. 2009: 49. Print.**

10. Review

Reviewer's Name. "Title of Review." Rev. of *Title of Work*, by name of author (editor, director, etc.). *Journal or Newspaper Title* Day Month Year: pages. Print.

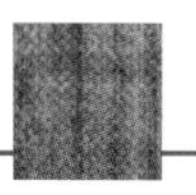

➔Ebert, Roger. "A Monosyllabic Superhero Who Wouldn't Pass the Turing Test." Rev. of *X-Men Origins: Wolverine*, by Dir. Gavin Hood. *Chicago Sun-Times* 29 Apr. 2009: E4. Print.

11. Article in a reference book

Author's Name. "Title of Article." *Title of Reference Book.* Ed. Editor's Name. Location: Publisher, date. Pages. Print.

➔Jones, Amber. "Semiotics." *Encyclopedia of Signs.* Ed. Jeffrey Haines and Maria Smith. Boston: Brown, 2003. 199-202. Print.

12. Religious works

Title of Work. Ed. Editor's Name. Place of publication: Publisher, date. Print.

➔*Zondervan NIV Study Bible.* Fully rev. ed. Ed. Kenneth L. Barker. Grand Rapids, MI: Zondervan, 2002. Print.

Formats for Online Sources

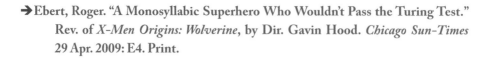

Including the URL is optional under the 7th edition of the *MLA Handbook for Writers of Research Papers*, so only include it after the "Date of Access" **in angle brackets** (<, >) if your source cannot be easily found by typing the author and title into a search engine or if your professor requires it.

Author's Name (if author given). *Name of Page.* Name of institution or organization associated with the Web site. Date of posting/revision. Web. Date of access.

➔*Services Locator.* United States Post Office. 2010. Web. 9 Feb. 2010.

2. Article on a Web site (including blogs and wikis)

Author's Name. "Article Title." *Name of Web site.* Name of institution or organization associated with the Web site. Date of posting/revision. Web. Date of access.

Note: If there is no author given, begin the citation with the article title.

➔"China's Traditional Dress: Qipao." *China Today*. Oct. 2001. Web. 9 Feb. 2010.

➔Ebert, Roger. "Signs." *rogerebert.com Movie Reviews. Chicago Sun-Times*. 2 Aug. 2002. Web. 9 Feb. 2010.

3. Online newspaper or magazine

Author's Name. "Title of Article." *Newspaper Title* Day Month Year: pages. Web. Date of access.

➔Bailey, Holly. "The Sign of the Red Truck." *Newsweek* 2007: 1. Web. 9 Feb. 2010.

4. Online journal article

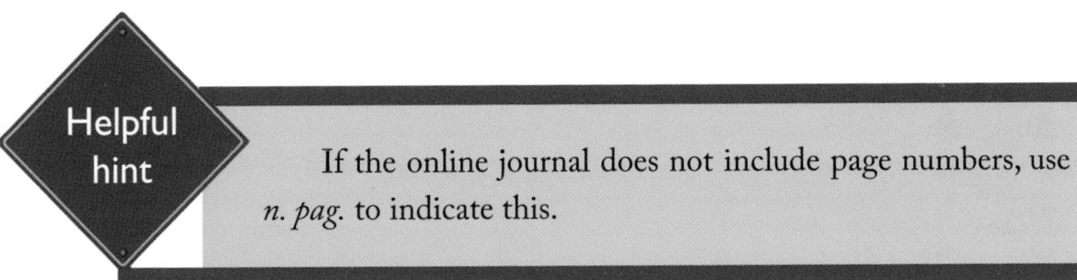

If the online journal does not include page numbers, use *n. pag.* to indicate this.

Author's Name. "Title of Article." *Title of Journal* Vol. Issue (Year): pages. Web. Date of access.

➔Austen, Veronica. "Writing Spaces: Performances of the Word." *Kairos* 8.1 (2003): n. pag. Web. 9 Feb. 2010.

5. Article from an online service, such as General OneFile or LexisNexis

Author's Name. "Title of the Article." *Journal Title* vol. issue (Date of publication): pages. Name of database or other relevant information. Access Provider. Web. Date of access.

Franks, Elizabeth. "Signing Up for Trouble." *Semiotics and Signs* 13.4 (2009): 112-7. *InfoTrac OneFile*. Thomson Gale. Middle Tennessee State University. Web. 9 Feb. 2010.

6. Article from an online reference work

Author's (or editor's) Name. "Title of Article." *Title of Reference Work*. Location, Date of publication (Day Month Year). Web. Date of access (Day Month Year).

Jones, Amber. "Semiotics." *Encyclopedia of Signs*. U of AK, 20 Mar. 2009. Web. 21 Sept. 2010.

Formats for Other Commonly Used Sources

1. Television or radio program

"Title of Episode or Segment." *Title of Program or Series.* Name of network. Call letters and city of the local station (if applicable). Broadcast date. Medium of reception (e.g., Radio, Television). Supplemental information (e.g., Transcript).

➔**"Signs and Wonders." *The X Files.* FOX. 23 Jan. 2000. Television.**

2. Sound recording

Artist/Band. "Song Title." *Title of Album.* Manufacturer, year of issue. Medium (e.g., Audiocassette, CD, Audiotape, LP, Digital download).

➔**Five Man Electrical Band. "Signs." *Good-byes and Butterflies.* Lionel Records, 1970. LP.**

➔**Tesla. "Signs." *Five Man Acoustical Jam.* Geffen, 1990. CD.**

3. Film

Title. Dir. Director's Name. Perf. Actor's Name(s) (if relevant). Distributor, year of release. Medium.

➔***Signs.* Dir. M. Night Shyamalan. Perf. Mel Gibson. Touchstone, 2002. Film.**

You may also include other information about the film, such as the names of the writers, performers, and producers, after the director's name.

➔***Signs.* Dir. M. Night Shyamalan. Perf. Mel Gibson. Ex. Prod. Kathleen Kennedy. Touchstone, 2002. Film.**

If you would like to highlight the specific contribution of one actor, director, or writer, you may begin the entry with that person's name, as you do with an author for a book.

➔**Phoenix, Joaquin, perf. *Signs.* Dir. M. Night Shyamalan. Touchstone, 2002. Film.**

4. Advertisement

Name of product, company, or institution. Advertisement. Publisher date of publication. Medium of publication.

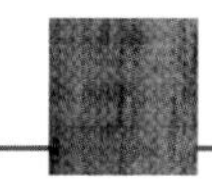

➔SunChips. Advertisement. *Newsweek* 15 Jan. 2010: 33. Print.
➔SunChips. Advertisement. NBC. 15 Jan. 2010. Television.

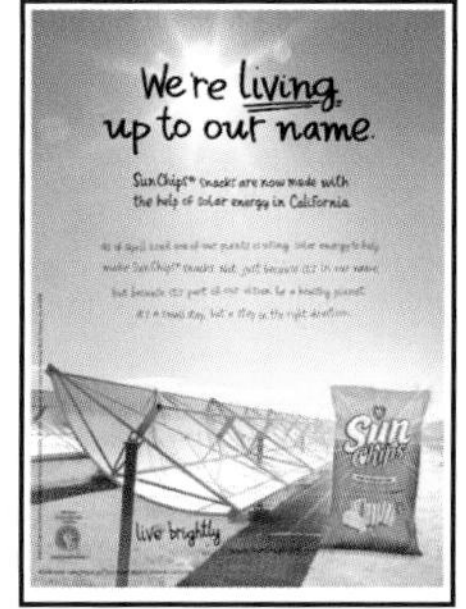

Note the difference in how the citations for print and television advertisements are formatted.

5. Painting, sculpture, or photograph

Artist's Name. *Title*. Creation date (if known). Medium of Composition. Name of institution that houses the work or the individual who owns the work, City.

➔da Vinci, Leonardo. *Mona Lisa*. c. 1503-6. Oil on Poplar. Louvre, Paris.

6. Interview

Interviewee's Name. Descriptive Title of Interview (e.g., Personal, Telephone, Webcam). Date of interview.

➔Elbow, Peter. Personal Interview. 1 Jan. 2009.

7. Lecture, speech, address, or reading

Author's Name. "Title of Speech." Relevant information of where speech was given. Date of presentation. Descriptive label (e.g., Lecture, Speech, Address, Reading).

➔Stephens, Liberty. "The Signs of the Times." MLA Annual Convention. Hilton Downtown, New York. 28 Dec. 2009. Address.

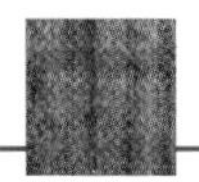

Sample Works Cited Using MLA

Following is an example of how a completed list of works cited would look at the end of your paper.

Your Last name 14

Works Cited

Ebert, Roger. "Signs." *rogerebert.com Movie Reviews. Chicago Sun-Times*. 2 Aug. 2002. Web. 9 Feb. 2010.

Five Man Electrical Band. "Signs." *Good-byes and Butterflies.* Lionel Records, 1970. LP.

Signs. Dir. M. Night Shyamalan. Perf. Mel Gibson. Touchstone, 2002. Film.

Stephens, Liberty. "The Signs of the Times." MLA Annual Convention. Hilton Downtown, New York. 28 Dec. 2009. Address.

APA DOCUMENTATION

When you do research to find supporting evidence for your ideas or arguments, you need to credit your outside sources. Depending on what type of essay you are writing or which type of course you are writing for, you will need to choose a type of documentation style and continue with that style for the entire essay. Two of the most common styles, especially for freshman and sophomore students, are MLA (Modern Language Association) and APA (American Psychological Association).

If you write an essay in the social sciences, you will usually be asked to use documentation guidelines created by the American Psychological Association. The *Publication Manual of the American Psychological Association*, in its sixth edi-

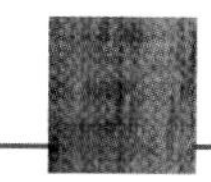

Did You Know?

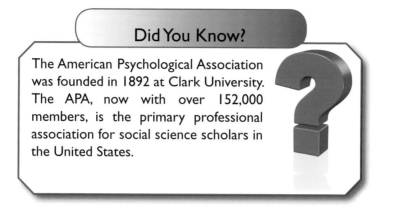

The American Psychological Association was founded in 1892 at Clark University. The APA, now with over 152,000 members, is the primary professional association for social science scholars in the United States.

tion, provides a full description of the conventions used by this particular community of writers; updates to the APA manual can be found at <www.apastyle.org>.

This chapter provides a general overview of APA documentation style and an explanation of the most commonly used APA documentation formats.

Using APA In-text Citations

In-text citations (also called *parenthetical citations*) point readers to where they can find more information about your researched supporting materials. In APA documentation style, the author's last name (or the title of the work, if no author is listed) and the date of publication must appear in the body text of your paper. The author's name can appear either in the sentence itself or in parentheses following the quotation or paraphrase. The date of publication can appear either in the sentence itself, surrounded by parentheses, or in the parentheses that follow the quotation or paraphrase. The page number(s) always appears in the parentheses following a quotation or close paraphrase.

Your parenthetical citation should give enough information to identify the source that was used for the research material as the same source that is listed in your references list. Where this in-text information is placed depends on how you want to phrase the sentence that is summarized, paraphrased, or quoted. Be sure that the in-text citation guides the reader clearly to the source in the references list, where complete information about the source is given.

The following are some of the most common examples of in-text citations.

1. Author's name and date in reference

When using a parenthetical reference to a single source by a single author, use this form: (Author's Last name, Year of publication). Note that the period is placed after the parenthetical element ends.

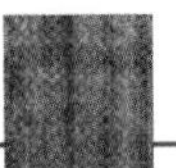

➔ When a teenager sleeps more than 10 hours per night, it is time to question whether she is having significant problems (Jones, 1999).

2. Author's name and date in text

In APA, you can also give the author's name and date within the sentence, using this form: Author's Full Name (Year of publication)

➔ Stephanie Jones (1999) describes the signs to look for and when to be concerned.

3. Using a partial quotation in text

When you cite a specific part of a source, give the page number, using *p.* (for one page) and *pp.* (for two or more pages).

➔ Stephanie Jones (1999) describes the signs parents should look for when concerned about their children: "excessive sleeping, refraining from eating, and lying about simple things" (p. 63).

4. No author given

When a work has no credited author, use the first two or three words of the work's title or the name that begins the entry in the references list. The title of an article or chapter should be in quotation marks, and the title of a book or periodical should be in italics. Inside the parenthetical citation, place a comma between the title and year.

➔ In a recent *Time* article, a list of 30 common signs of teenage trouble cites lack of sleep as the most common sign ("Thirty," 2010).

5. Two to five authors given

When you use a source that was written by two to five authors, you must use all the names in the citation. For the in-text citation, when a work has two authors, use both names each time the reference occurs in the text. When a work has three to five authors, give all authors the first time the reference occurs in the text, and then, in subsequent citations, use only the surname of the first author followed by *et al.* (Latin for "and others") and the year for the first citation of the reference in a paragraph.

➔ The idea that "complexity is a constant in biology" is not an innovative one (Sole & Goodwin, 1997, p. 63).

The last two authors' names in a string of three to five authors are separated by a comma and an ampersand (e.g., Jones, Smith, Black, & White).

➔ Most signs in English that the authors encountered on the road had "grammar mistakes, misspellings, or just odd pictures" (Smith, Jones, & Best, 1999, p. 55). The most common mistake was an "incorrect or misplaced apostrophe" (Smith, et al., p. 56).

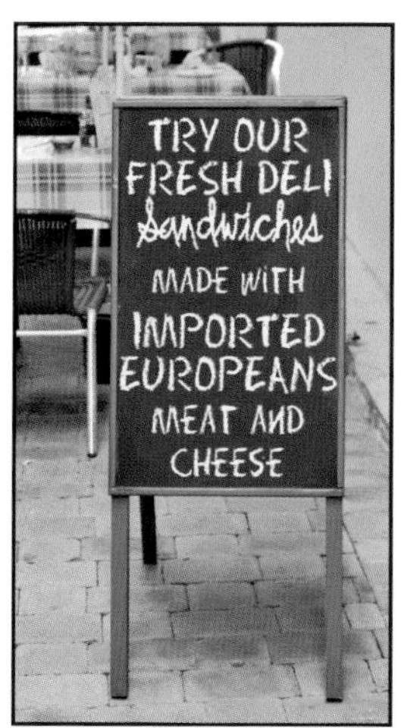

6. Six or more authors given

When there are six authors or more of an item to be cited, include only the first author's name followed by *et al.* (Latin for "and others"). Use this form for the first reference of this text and all references of this text after that. Note: Be sure, though, to list all six or more of the authors in your references list.

➔ In Hong Kong, most signs are in Chinese and English; however, once you are in mainland China, English is rarely found on signs, except in tourist areas (Li, et al., 2007).

7. Authors with the same last names

If your source material includes items by authors who happen to have the same last name, be sure to use each author's initials in all text citations.

➔ When a teenager sleeps more than 10 hours per night, it is time to question whether she is having significant problems (S. Jones, 1999, p. 63).

➔ Another sign of trouble can be when you do not see your child for meals (B. Jones, 2003, p. 114).

8. Encyclopedia or dictionary unsigned entry

When you use an encyclopedia or dictionary to look up a word or entry, be sure to include the word or entry title in the parenthetical entry.

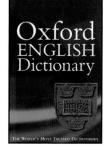

➔ The word *thing* has more definitions than any other entry in the *Oxford English Dictionary* ("thing," 2001).

9. Indirect quotation

When you use a quotation of a quotation—that is, a quotation that quotes from another source—use "as cited in" to designate the secondary source.

➔ Smith has said, "My parents really didn't understand me" (as cited in Jones, 1990, p. 64).

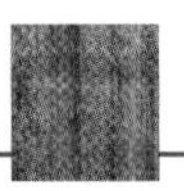

10. Personal communication

Personal communications—private letters, memos, non-archived e-mails, interviews—are usually considered unrecoverable information and, as such, are not included in the references list. However, you do include them in parenthetical form in the text, giving the initials and surname of the communicator and providing as exact a date as possible.

➔ A. D. Smith (personal communication, February 2, 2010)

➔ J. Elbow (personal interview, January 6, 2009)

Using Long or Block Quotations

Long or block quotations have special formatting requirements of their own. If your quotation is prose and longer than 40 words, this is called a *block quotation.* Follow these APA guidelines for block quotations.

1. If introducing the block quotation with a sentence, use a colon at the end of the sentence.
2. Begin the quotation on a new line.
3. Do not use quotation marks to enclose the block quote.
4. Indent the quote five spaces from the left margin, and extend the right margin to the end of the line.
5. Double space the entire quotation.
6. Indent the first line of any additional paragraph.
7. Put a period at the end of the quotation, and then add the parenthetical citation.

➔ However, Lansky (1999) states:

> Despite the statement on <www.signspotting.com> that we don't accept signs with the intention of being funny, people like sending them in. I've opted not to use these as it could encourage people to start making them, sticking them up in their driveway, and snapping a picture. Plus, funny signs are so much more amusing when the humor is accidental. (p. 72)

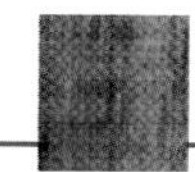

Adding or Omitting Words in a Quotation

1. Adding words in a quotation

Use square brackets ([ ]) to point out words or phrases that are not part of the original text.

- ➔ Original quotation: "When we entered the People's Republic of China, we noticed that the signage began dropping English translations" (Donelson, 2001, p. 141).
- ➔ Quotation with added word: She said, "When we entered the People's Republic of China, [Dunkirk and I] noticed that the signage began dropping English translations" (Donelson, 2001, p. 141).

You can also add your own comments inside a quotation by using square brackets. For example, you can add the word *sic* to a quotation when you know that there is an error.

- ➔ Original quotation: "When we entered the People's Repulic of China, we noticed that the signage began dropping English translations" (Donelson, 2001, p. 141).
- ➔ Quotation with added comment: She said, "When we entered the People's Repulic [sic] of China, we noticed that the signage began dropping English translations" (Donelson, 2001, p. 141).

2. Omitting words in a quotation

Use an ellipsis (. . .) to represent words that you delete from a quotation. The ellipsis begins with a space, then has three periods with spaces between them, and then ends with a space.

Original quotation➔ "The Great Wall is something that can be seen from space. When we reach a time when advertisements can be seen from space, we have probably gone too far" (Jones, 1993, p. 101).

Quotation with words omitted in middle of sentence➔ Frank Jones, author of *Signs in Space,* remarks, "The Great Wall . . . can be seen from space. When we reach a time when advertisements can be seen from space, we have probably gone too far" (1993, p. 101).

If you omit words at the end of a quotation, and that is also the end of your sentence, you should use an ellipsis plus a period with no space before the ellipsis or after the period. Only use an ellipsis if words have been omitted.

Original quotation➔ "The Great Wall is something that can be seen from space. When we reach a time when advertisements can be seen from space, we have probably gone too far with our advertising and signage" (Jones, 1993, p. 45).

Quotation with words omitted at end of sentence➔ Frank Jones, author of *Signs in Space,* remarks, "The Great Wall is something that can be seen from space. When we reach a time when advertisements can be seen from space, we have probably gone too far . . ." (1993, p. 45).

APA guidelines can change with a new edition. Sometimes, class textbooks can use an older APA documentation style. Always check with your instructor if rules seem to be in conflict.

Citing Online Sources

In the APA documentation style, online or electronic sources have their own formatting guidelines since these types of sources rarely give specific page numbers.

The APA recommends that you include in the text, rather than in an in-text citation, the name(s) of the person that begins the matching references list entry. If the author or creator of the Web site uses paragraph or page numbers, use these numbers in the parenthetical citation. If no numbering is used, do not use or add numbers to the paragraphs, pages, or parenthetical citation.

When Web site does not number paragraphs➔ In his review of the film *Signs*, Roger Ebert says that Shyamalan "does what Hitchcock said he wanted to do, and plays the audience like a piano."

When Web site numbers paragraphs➔ In his review of the file *Signs*, Roger Ebert says that Shyamalan "does what Hitchcock said he wanted to do, and plays the audience like a piano" (para. 8).

General Formatting Guidelines for the APA References List

If you cite any sources within a paper, be sure to include a references list at the end of the paper. Here are some general formatting guidelines to follow when setting up a references list.

1. Put the references list at the end of your paper as a separate page.
2. Use one-inch margins on all sides.
3. Include any header used for the paper on the references page.
4. Center the title **References** at the top of the page, using no underlining, quotation marks, or italics.

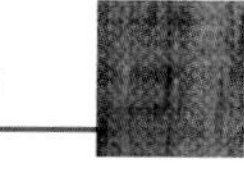

5. Place the first line of each entry flush left with the margin. Indent any additional lines of the entry one-half inch (or one tab) to form a hanging indent.
6. Double space the entries in the references list, not adding any extra spaces between entries.
7. Alphabetize the references list. Use the first major word in each entry, not including articles such as *a, an,* or *the*, to determine the alphabetical order. If the cited source does not have an author, alphabetize by using the first word of the title of the source.
8. Put author's last name first and then the initial representing the author's first name and the initial for the author's middle name, if given (e.g., Ebert, R.). If a work has more than one author, invert all the authors' names, follow each with a comma, and then continue listing all the authors, putting a comma and ampersand (, &) before the final name (e.g., Ebert, R., & Siskel, G.).
9. Arrange two or more works by the same author(s) in the same name order by year of publication.
10. Capitalize only the first word in a title and a subtitle unless the title or subtitle includes a proper noun, which would also be capitalized.
11. Do not use quotation marks for titles of shorter works, including articles, book chapters, episodes on television or radio, poems, and short stories.
12. Italicize the titles of longer works, including album or CD titles, art pieces, books, films, journals, magazines, newspapers, and television shows.
13. Give the edition number for works with more than one edition [e.g., *Publication manual of the American Psychological Association* (6th ed.)].
14. Include the DOI (digital object identifier), a unique alpha-numeric string assigned by a registration agency that helps identify content and provides a link to the source online. All DOI numbers begin with a *10* and contain a prefix and suffix separated by a slash (for example, 10.11037/0278-6133.27.3.379). The DOI is usually found in the citation detail or on the first page of an electronic journal article near the copyright notice.

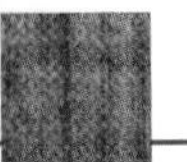

stet Detail

Title:

An Ability Traitor at Work: A Treasonous Call to Subvert ***Writing*** From Within.

Authors:

Holbrook, Teri[1] *tholbrook@gsu.edu*

Source:

Qualitative Inquiry; Mar2010, Vol. 16 Issue 3, p171-183, 13p

Document Type:

Article

Subject Terms:

*DISABILITIES
*QUALITATIVE research
*MANAGEMENT science
*SIGN language
*WRITING

Author-Supplied Keywords:

assemblage
disability
multigenre
multimodal writing

NAICS/Industry Codes:

541930 Translation and Interpretation Services

Abstract:

In questioning conventional qualitative research methods, St. Pierre asked, "What else might ***writing*** do except mean?" The author answers, it oppresses. Co-opting the race traitor figurative, she calls on qualitative researchers to become "ability traitors" who interrogate how a valuable coinage of their trade—the written word—is used to rank and categorize individuals with troubling effects. In this article, she commits three betrayals: (a) multigenre ***writing*** that undermines the authoritative text; (b) assemblage as a method of analysis that deprivileges the written word; and (c) a gesture toward a dis/comfort text intended to take up Lather's example of challenging the "usual ways of making sense." In committing these betrayals, the author articulates her "traitorous agenda" designed to interrogate assumptions about inquiry, power, equity, and ***writing*** as practice-as-usual. [ABSTRACT FROM AUTHOR]

Copyright of Qualitative Inquiry is the property of Sage Publications Inc. and its content may not be copied or e-mailed to multiple sites or posted to a listserv without the copyright holder's express written permission. However, users may print, download, or e-mail articles for individual use. This abstract may be abridged. No warranty is given about the accuracy of the copy. Users should refer to the original published version of the material for the full abstract. (Copyright applies to all Abstracts.)

Author Affiliations:
[1]Georgia State University
ISSN:
10778004
DOI:
10.1177/1077800409351973
Accession Number:
47934623
Database:
Academic Search Premier
View Links:
Find Fulltext

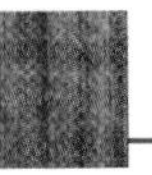

Formats for Print Sources

1. Books (includes brochures, pamphlets, and graphic novels)

Author's Last name, Author's Initial of first name. (Year of publication). *Title of book*. Place of publication: Publisher.

➔Lansky, D. (2005). *Signspotting*. Oakland, CA: Lonely Planet.

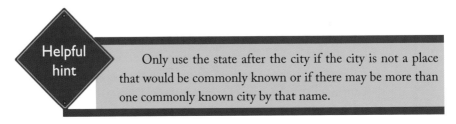

Only use the state after the city if the city is not a place that would be commonly known or if there may be more than one commonly known city by that name.

2. Books with two or more authors

A comma is used between the author names, even if there are only two authors.

First Author's Last name, First author's Initial of first name, & Second author's Last name, Second author's Initial of first name. (year of publication). *Title of book*. Place of publication: Publisher.

➔Maasik, S., & Soloman, J. (2008). *Signs of life in the USA: Readings on popular culture for writers*. Boston, MA: Bedford/St. Martin's.

3. Two books by the same author

Be sure the entries are in sequential time order with earliest date first.

➔Maasik, S., & Soloman, J. (2004). *California dreams and realities: Readings for critical thinkers and writers* (3rd ed.). Boston, MA: Bedford/St. Martin's.

➔Maasik, S., & Soloman, J. (2008). *Signs of life in the USA: Readings on popular culture for writers*. Boston, MA: Bedford/St. Martin's.

4. Anthology or collection

Editor's Last name, Editor's Initial of first name. (Ed). (Year of publication). *Title of book*. Place of publication: Publisher.

➔Smith, A. D., Smith, T. G., & Wright, K. (Eds.). (2007). *COMPbiblio: Leaders and influences in composition theory and practice*. Southlake, TX: Fountainhead.

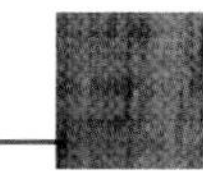

5. Work within an anthology or collection

Author's Last name, Author's Initial of first name. (Year of publication). Title of work. In Editor's Name(s) (Ed.) *Title of anthology* (page numbers). Place of publication: Publisher.

➔**Tan, A. (2010). Mother tongue. In R. Bullock, M. D. Goggin, & F. Weinberg (Eds.). *The Norton field guide to writing* (pp. 564-70). New York, NY: Norton.**

6. Article in a scholarly journal without DOI (digital object identifier)

Include the issue number if the journal is paginated by issue. If there is not a DOI available and the article was found online, give the URL of the journal home page.

Author's Last name, Author's Initial of first name. (Year of publication). Title of the article. *Journal Title, volume number* (issue number), pages. URL (if retrieved online).

➔**Holbrook, T. (2010). An ability traitor at work: A treasonous call to subvert writing from within. *Qualitative Inquiry, 16*(3), 171-183. Retrieved from E-Journals database.**

7. Article in a scholarly journal with DOI (digital object identifier)

Author's Last name, Author's Initial of first name. (Year of publication). Title of the article. *Journal Title, volume number* (issue number), pages. doi:

➔**Franks, L. (2006). The play in language. *Child Signs, 73*(1), 3-17. doi:10.1770/69873629**

8. Article in a newspaper

Use *p.* or *pp.* before the page numbers in references of newspapers.

Note: if the newspaper article appears on discontinuous pages, be sure to give all the page numbers, separating them with a comma (e.g., pp. A4, A10, A13-14).

Author's Last name, Author's Initial of first name. (Year of publication, Month and Date of publication). Title of article. *Newspaper Title*, pp. page numbers.

→**Genzlinger, N. (2010, April 6). Autism is another thing that families share. *The New York Times*, p. A4.**

9. Article in a magazine

Author's Last name, Author's Initial of first name. (Year of publication, Month of publication). Title of article. *Magazine Title, volume number* (issue number), pages.

Note: only use day if magazine is published on a weekly or bi-weekly basis.

→**Musico, C. (2009, November). Sign 'em up! *CRM Magazine, 13*(11), 49.**

10. Review

Be sure to identify the type of work being reviewed by noting if it is a book, film, television program, painting, song, or other creative work. If the work is a book, include the author name(s) after the book title, separated by a comma. If the work is a film, song, or other media, be sure to include the year of release after the title of the work, separated by a comma.

Reviewer's Last name, Reviewer's Initial of first name. (Year of publication, Month and Date of Publication). Title of review [Review of the work *Title of work*, by Author's Name]. *Magazine or Journal Title, volume number* (issue number), pp. page numbers. doi number (if available).

→**Turken, R. (2008, May 5). Life outside of the box. [Review of the film *Signs*, 2002]. *Leisure Times*, pp. A12.**

11. Article in a reference book

Author's Last name, Author's Initial of first name. (Year of publication). Title of chapter or entry. In A. Editor (Ed). *Title of book* (pp. xx-xx). Location: Publisher.

→**Jones, A. (2003). Semiotics. In B. Smith, R. Lore, and T. Rex (Eds.). *Encyclopedia of signs* (pp. 199-202). Boston, MA: Rutledge.**

12. Religious and classical works

In APA, classical religious works, such as the Bible and the Qur'an, and major classical works that originated in Latin or Greek, are not required to have entries in the references list but should include reference to the text within the sentence in the essay. Note: it is always a good idea to check with your instructor on this type of entry since there can be some variety across instructors and schools.

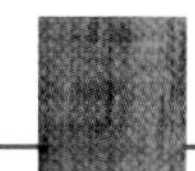

Formats for Online Sources

1. Web site

The documentation form for a Web site can also be used for online message, blog, or video posts.

Author's Last name, Author's Initial of first name (if author given). (Year, Month Day). *Title of page* [Description of form]. Retrieved from http://www.xxxx

→**United States Post Office (2010). *United States Post Office Services Locator* [search engine]. Retrieved from http://usps.whitepages.com/post_office**

2. Article from a Web site, online newspaper, blog, or wiki (with author given)

Author's Last name, Author's Initial of first name. (Year, Month Day of publication). Title of article. *Name of Webpage/Journal/Newspaper*. Retrieved from http://www.xxxxxxx

→**Ebert, R. (2002, August 2). Signs. *Chicago Sun-Times*. Retrieved from http://rogerebert.suntimes.com/**

3. Article from a Web site, online newspaper, blog, or wiki (with no author given)

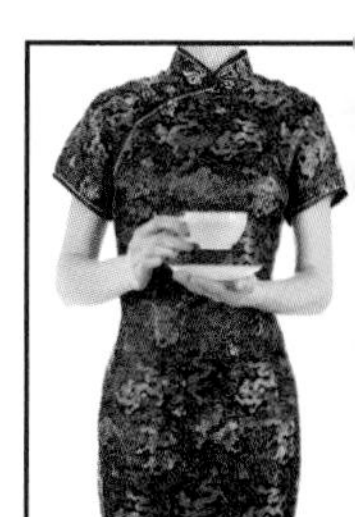

Title of article. (Year, Month Day of publication). *Name of Webpage/Journal/Newspaper*. Retrieved from http://www.xxxxxxx

→**China's traditional dress: Qipao. (2001, October). *China Today*. Retrieved from http://chinatoday.com**

4. Online journal article

The reference for an online journal article is set up the same way as for a print one, including the DOI.

Author's Last name, Author's Initial of first name. (Year of publication). Title of the article. *Journal Title*, *volume number* (issue number), pages. doi:xxxxxxxxxxx

→**Franks, L. (2006). The play in language. *Child Signs*, *73*(1), 3-17. doi:10.1770/69873629**

If a DOI is not assigned to content you have retrieved online, use the home page URL for the journal or magazine in the reference (e.g., Retrieved from http://www.xxxxxx).

→**Austen, V. (2003). Writing spaces: Performance of the word. *Kairos*. Retrieved from http://kairos.com**

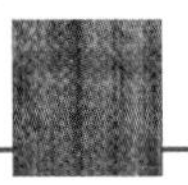

5. Article from an online service, such as General OneFile, Lexis-Nexis, JSTOR, ERIC

When using APA, it is not necessary to include database information as long as you can include the publishing information required in a normal citation. Note: this is quite different from using MLA documentation, which requires full information about the database.

6. Article in an online reference work

Author's Last name, Author's Initial of first name. (Year of publication). Title of chapter or entry. In A. Editor (Ed). *Title of book.* Retrieved from http://xxxxxxxxxx

➔Jones, A. (2003). Semiotics. In B. Smith, R. Lore, and T. Rex (Eds.). *Encyclopedia of signs*. Retrieved from http://brown.edu/signs

Formats for Other Commonly Used Sources

1. Television or radio program (single episode)

Writer' Last name, Writer's Initial of first name. (Writer), & Director's Last name, Director's Initial of first name. (Director). (Year). Title of episode [Television/Radio series episode]. In Executive Producer's name (Executive Producer), *Title of show*. Place: Network.

➔Bell, J. (Writer), Carter, C. (Creator), & Manners, K. (Director). (2000). Signs and wonders [Television series episode]. In C. Carter (Executive Producer), *The X files*. New York, NY: FOX.

2. Sound recording

Writer's Last name, Writer's Initial of first name. (Copyright year). Title of song. [Recorded by Artist's name if different from writer]. On *Title of album* [Medium of recording]. Location: Label. (Date of recording if different from song copyright date).

➔Emmerson, L. (1970). Signs. [Recorded by Five Man Electrical Band]. On *Good-byes and butterflies* [LP]. New York, NY: Lionel Records.

➔Emmerson, L. (1970). Signs. [Recorded byTesla]. On *Five man acoustical jam* [CD]. New York, NY: Geffen. 1990.

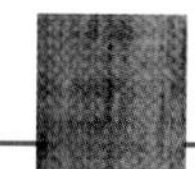

3. Film

Producer's Last name, Producer's Initial of first name. (Producer), & Director's Last name, Director's Initial of first name. (Director). (Year). *Title of film* [Motion picture]. Country of Origin: Studio.

➔**Kennedy, K. (Producer), & Shyamalan, M. N. (Director). (2002). *Signs* [film]. USA: Touchstone.**

4. Painting, sculpture, or photograph

Artist's Last name, Artist's Initial of first name. (Year, Month Day). *Title of material.* [Description of material]. Name of collection (if available). Name of Repository, Location.

➔**Gainsborough, T. (1745). *Conversation in a park.* [Oil painting on canvas]. Louvre, Paris, France.**

5. Personal interview

Unlike MLA documentation, personal interviews and other types of personal communication are not included in APA references lists. Be sure to cite personal communications in the text only.

6. Lecture, speech, address, or reading

Speaker's Last name, Speaker's Initial of first name. (Year, Month). Title of speech. *Event name.* Lecture conducted from Sponsor, Location.

➔**Stephens, L. (2009, December). The signs of the times. *MLA annual convention.* Lecture conducted from Hilton Hotel Downtown, New York, NY.**

Sample References List Using APA

Following is an example of how a completed references list would look at the end of your paper.

Your Last name 14

References

Emmerson, L. (1970). Signs. [Recorded by Five Man Electrical Band]. On *Good-byes and butterflies* [LP]. New York, NY: Lionel Records.

Franks, L. (2006). The play in language. *Child Signs*, 73(1), 3-17. doi:10.1770/69873629

Kennedy, K. (Producer), & Shyamalan, M. N. (Director). (2002). *Signs* [film]. USA: Touchstone.

Jones, A. (2003). Semiotics. In B. Smith, R. Lore, and T. Rex (Eds.). *Encyclopedia of signs*. Retrieved from http://brown.edu/signs

Lansky, D. (2005). *Signspotting*. Oakland, CA: Lonely Planet.

Stephens, L. (2009, December). The signs of the times. *MLA annual convention*. Lecture conducted from Hilton Hotel Downtown, New York, NY.

Tan, A. (2010). Mother tongue. In R. Bullock, M. D. Goggin, & F. Weinberg (Eds.). *The Norton field guide to writing* (pp. 564-70). New York, NY: Norton.

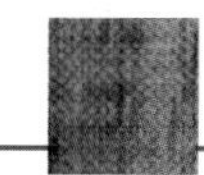

TYPES OF PLAGIARISM

1. **Direct Plagiarism:** This is copying a source word for word without indicating that it is a quotation and crediting the author.

2. **Borrowing Work from Other Students:** There is nothing wrong with students helping each other or sharing information, but you must write your own essays. This includes having another student dictate to you as you write his or her words down. Turning in a paper that someone else has written is an especially severe case of direct plagiarism.

3. **Vague or Incorrect Citation:** A writer should clearly indicate where borrowing begins and ends because not doing so, though it seems innocent, is plagiarism. *This is why it is so important to learn a citation style such as MLA style.* (See MLA Style section for more information.) Sometimes, a writer cites a source once, and the reader assumes that the previous sentence or paragraph has been paraphrased, when most of the essay is a paraphrase of this one source. The writer has failed to indicate his borrowings clearly. Paraphrases and summaries should be indicated as such by surrounding them with citation—at the beginning with the author's name, at the end with a parenthetical reference. The writer must always clearly indicate when a paraphrase, summary, or quotation begins, ends, or is interrupted.

4. **Auto-plagiarism:** This happens when an author plagiarizes his or her own writing. Students' best work usually occurs through revisions of previous drafts. But auto-plagiarism takes place when a student presents any prior writing, usually from another course or school, as entirely fresh work for course credit. A previous assignment, whether in whole or part, may not be offered as if it were a fresh submission to a course instructor.

5. **Mosaic Plagiarism:** This is the most common type of plagiarism. The writer does not copy the source directly, but changes a few words in each sentence or slightly reworks a paragraph, without giving credit to the original author. Those sentences or paragraphs are not quotations, but they are so close to quotations that they should be quoted directly or, if they have been changed enough to qualify as a paraphrase, the source should be cited.

A Case of Plagiarism

Richard Marius, in his statement on plagiarism for Harvard University, cites a case of mosaic plagiarism. G. R. V Barratt, in the introduction to *The Decembrist Memoirs,* plagiarized from several works, including *The Decembrists* by Marc Raeff. In one passage, Raeff had written:

> December 14, 1825, was the day set for taking the oath of allegiance to the new Emperor, Nicholas I. Only a few days earlier, on November 27, when news of the death of Alexander I had reached the capital, an oath of allegiance had been taken to Nicholas's older brother, Grand Duke Constantine, Viceroy of Poland. But in accordance with the act of renunciation he had made in 1819, Constantine had refused the crown. The virtual interregnum stirred society and produced uneasiness among the troops, and the government was apprehensive of disorders and disturbances. Police agents reported the existence of secret societies and rumors of a coup to be staged by regiments of the Guards. The new Emperor was anxious to have the oath taken as quickly and quietly as possible. The members of the central government institutions—Council of State, Senate, Ministries—took the oath without incident, early in the morning. In most regiments of the garrison the oath was also taken peaceably.

Barratt presented the same paragraph with only a few words and details changed:

> December 14, 1825, was the day on which the Guards' regiments in Petersburg were to swear solemn allegiance to Nicholas I, the new Emperor. Less than three weeks before, when news of the death of Alexander I had reached the capital from Taganrog on the sea of Azov, an oath, no less solemn and binding, had been taken to Nicholas's elder brother, the Grand Duke Constantine, viceroy of Poland. Constantine, however, had declined to be emperor, in accordance with two separate acts of renunciation made in 1819 and, secretly, in 1822. The effective interregnum caused uneasiness both in society and in the army. The government feared undefined disorders—with some reason, since police agents reported the existence of various clandestine groups and rumours of a coup to be effected by guardsmen. Nicholas was anxious that the oath be sworn to him promptly and quietly. At first it would seem that he would have his way; senators, ministers, and members of the Council of State took the oath by 9 A.M. In most regiments of the garrison the oath was also taken peaceably.

To see why this is mosaic plagiarism, compare these two versions line by line. What changes has Barratt made? Place brackets around the text that was not changed. Why do you think he made these changes? Why is this a case of plagiarism even though Barratt has made changes?

Guidelines for Proper Use of Sources

1. Enclose direct quotations in quotation marks. If the quotation is longer than four lines, indent it in block format. In both cases, cite the source by using MLA in-text parenthetical style and by entering the source in the works cited page.

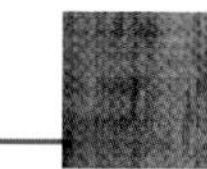

2. Use in-text parenthetical citation to cite paraphrases or summaries. Any key phrases that you borrow word for word should go in quotation marks.

3. Cite opinions, interpretations, and results of original research.

4. In general, do not cite statements of widely accepted fact, but when following a source closely, cite it even if the material is a widely accepted fact. If you are unsure if something is a widely accepted fact, then you should probably cite it. See your instructor if you have any questions about facts.

Ways to Avoid Plagiarism

1. When in doubt, CITE! It can never hurt to over-cite or cite when you do not need to.

2. Give yourself plenty of time to research and write your essay, so that you do not feel pressured because a topic proves unworkable at the last minute. When writing a paper that uses sources, give yourself time to digest the research and synthesize your findings.

3. Take careful research notes that include full bibliographic citations. If you forget to write down the bibliographic data, you may be tempted not to bother with the citation.

4. Make it a habit to put parenthetical citations for all the sources you borrow from in each draft you write.

5. Keep a good documentation guide handy (i.e., *your* handbook) when you are doing your research and writing your paper.

6. Have confidence in yourself. Even the best writers are often unaware of their good ideas and think they have nothing to say when their writing says a lot. Original ideas come from working closely with the ideas of others, not from flashes of inspiration.

7. Know where to get help. Start with your instructor and ask questions about citations about which you are not sure. Besides your instructor, you can consult a tutor in the Writing Center for help with your writing. The reference librarians can help you with your research.

Why Students Plagiarize

Some students are tempted to plagiarize because they find writing college-level essays difficult or intimidating. Such students sometimes become frustrated when an essay on which they have worked long and hard is returned with many corrections and a low grade. Frustrated and afraid of failure, they may resort to copying an essay word for word or making only a few slight changes in the wording.

Rather than plagiarizing, these students should seek assistance from their instructor, from the Writing Center, from a special tutor, or from the Counseling Center, which can provide assistance in dealing not only with a learning disability, but also with frustration, fear, and stress. The Writing Center offers intensive tutorial courses in writing.

Other students write well enough but find plagiarism tempting because they fear earning a grade lower than they or their parents expect, have fallen behind in their coursework and feel that they lack the time to write a competent essay, or feel that they cannot handle the assigned task or generate good ideas on the subject.

Start writing, even if the writing begins as a summary of some other piece of writing, and you will usually discover that you have something to say. If you fall behind, talk with your instructor. He or she may penalize you for submitting work late, but late work is preferable to plagiarized work. If you feel overwhelmed by your coursework and unable to keep up, arrange to visit a counselor at the Counseling Center. He or she can help you learn to manage your time and the stress of university life better.

Plagiarizing an essay is never an acceptable solution.

Conclusion

Learning how to use sources is one of the most important things you will learn in college. By using sources well and by clearly indicating your debts to these sources, your writing gains authority, clarity, and precision. Writers who plagiarize lose the advantages of belonging to an intellectual discourse community. If plagiarizers are professionals, they may be barred from practicing their profession, or their work may not be taken seriously. If they are students, they will carry the stigma of having plagiarized. Instructors will be suspicious of their work and will be unwilling to support any of their future efforts, write recommendations for them, or even work with them at all. Plagiarism is one of the worst mistakes anyone can make. The best way to avoid it is to be scrupulous about indicating quotation, paraphrase, and summary.

GAINESVILLE STATE COLLEGE

Plagiarism Contract

I have read and understand GSC's plagiarism information statement. I know that intentional plagiarism is a punishable offense with penalties ranging from a zero on the assignment to expulsion from the College. I also know that unintended plagiarism can occur through improper citation and/or borrowing but is still punishable. To avoid unintentional plagiarism, I will consult with my professor when I have questions.

Student's Name: (Print) ____

Course: __________ Section: _________ Instructor: ____________________

Semester and Year: ___________________________

Student's Signature: ____

Date: _______________________________________

Notes

Notes